Psychic Connection and the Twentieth-Century British Novel

Psychic Connection and the Twentieth-Century British Novel

From Telepathy to the Network Novel

Mark Taylor

EDINBURGH
University Press

Edinburgh University Press is one of the leading university presses in the UK. We publish academic books and journals in our selected subject areas across the humanities and social sciences, combining cutting-edge scholarship with high editorial and production values to produce academic works of lasting importance. For more information visit our website: edinburghuniversitypress.com

© Mark Taylor 2024, 2025

Edinburgh University Press Ltd
13 Infirmary Street
Edinburgh, EH1 1LT

First published in hardback by Edinburgh University Press 2024

Typeset in 10.5/13 Adobe Sabon by
by Manila Typesetting Company

Y
A CIP record for this book is available from the British Library

ISBN 978 1 3995 2448 3 (hardback)
ISBN 978 1 3995 2449 0 (paperback)
ISBN 978 1 3995 2450 6 (webready PDF)
ISBN 978 1 3995 2451 3 (epub)

The right of Mark Taylor to be identified as the author of this work has been asserted in accordance with the Copyright, Designs and Patents Act 1988, and the Copyright and Related Rights Regulations 2003 (SI No. 2498).

Contents

Acknowledgements	vi
Introduction: Psychic Speculations and the Porous Self	1
1. D. H. Lawrence and the Novel of Connected Individuals	17
2. Olaf Stapledon and the Scope of Interpersonal Connection	57
3. Aldous Huxley, Telepathy and the Decentring of Personality in the Novel of Ideas	89
4. Doris Lessing, Deindividuated Characters and Hybrid Identity	120
Conclusion: The Network Novel, Inclusion and Infusion	157
Notes	168
Works Cited	171
Index	183

Acknowledgements

Among the arguments of this book is that literature invested in discrete individuals distorts when it presents inspiration as a solitary thing. Attempting to trace the genesis of this project, I realise how uncountable are the conversations, email exchanges and other interactions which helped form the ideas which led to this book.

I am deeply indebted to former colleagues from HSE University, Moscow, for enabling and supporting this project, in particular Elena Ostrovskaya and Elena Zemskova. I am also thankful to a number of students of the university, particularly those on my Master's Literature and Science course, with whom I enjoyed many productive discussions on topics which feed into this book's arguments.

Thanks also to editors at Edinburgh University Press and anonymous peer reviewers whose feedback helped me to sharpen my arguments and to articulate their significance more precisely. I am also grateful to friends and family who were there to help me keep momentum on this project during periods of lockdown and during the upheaval of migrating at haste from Russia following its abhorrent invasion of Ukraine.

My deepest thanks are reserved for Maria Taylor, whose support and suggestions have shaped this project in innumerable ways.

Chapter 2 of this book incorporates material originally published in *Science Fiction Studies*, volume 47, number 2, 2020, under the title 'Olaf Stapledon and Telepathy in Literature of Cosmic Exploration'.

Introduction: Psychic Speculations and the Porous Self

In his 1999 debut novel, *Ghostwritten,* David Mitchell has writer Louisa Rey telephone a late-night radio talk show, where she offers her opinion on the relationship between author and their work. What she says encapsulates a sense which guides Mitchell and many other writers who strive to redefine the novel across the twentieth century. For Rey, 'the human world is made of stories, not people' and 'the people the stories use to tell themselves are not to be blamed' (386). Where the traditional novel of the eighteenth and nineteenth centuries is built of individuated characters shaped by innate attributes and internal desires, for Mitchell and many before him, this model is fundamentally flawed. The circumstances which lead a given person to have an idea, to have a story to tell, are multifarious and circumstantial as well as imperfectly recollected and perceived. Insight, as a feeling, is often the product of oversight, of a failure to appreciate the external triggers of an apparently personal breakthrough. Across the twentieth century, this book argues, a succession of writers have rejected the individuated character and the narratives of personal development which stem from it. Critical paradigms bound to the novel as fundamentally individualistic have failed to perceive these challenges to the novel's assumed basic unit and have thus struggled to address a major trajectory in its development across the twentieth century and into the twenty-first.

The writers this study focuses upon approach character as porous in its boundaries, changing with the often unbidden inflow and outflow of ideas. For most, the porous self is informed by theories of psychic connection: telepathy and other models of psychic connection are an explicit presence both in their novels and in their wider writings about the nature of self. Many writers in the early and mid-twentieth century were among the large numbers who believed that telepathy and other psychic faculties had been experimentally proven, either by the tests conducted by the Society for Psychical Research around the turn of the century, or the many laboratory trials of J. B. Rhine at Duke University in the 1930s. Such convictions are the function of a climate in which reputable publications were ready to cast the evidence in favour of telepathy as compelling. In the entry on telepathy in the 1911 edition of the *Encyclopædia Britannica*, it is described as being 'backed by carefully collected evidence' thanks to work of the Society for Psychical Research (Thomas 546), while, following the Duke experiments, *Harper's Magazine* is ready publish a piece by Ernest Hunter Wright in which he contends that 'the fact of extra-sensory perception, by telepathy and clairvoyance both, has now come to be indubitable' in 'the minds of the men of science who have made all these tests' (576). Criticism of the methodological flaws of research into telepathy was also published prominently – Chester E. Kellogg, for one, addresses the failings of the experiments at Duke in a 1937 piece in *The Scientific Monthly*, as well as in a letter to *The New York Times* the same year – but it is understandable why a follower of the discussion might form the picture of a new scientific paradigm dealing with doubters clinging to an established perspective.

For other writers, investigations into telepathy, clairvoyance and the like are suggestive in spite of their flaws. Later in the twentieth century, many writers who do not subscribe to telepathy as a science do value the first waves of literature which respond to it, finding in their treatment of connected, porous selfhood a means speaking to the unpredictable emergence and development of ostensibly personal thoughts. Many of these writers, like Mitchell, continue explicitly to invoke telepathy, often with its status within their work left ambiguous. Experimentally rejected as they might be, psychic occurrences let literature point to holes in science's ever-provisional understanding of the universe.

As it stands, literary criticism is routinely hesitant to engage with telepathy and related concepts (except narrowly as a trope in science fiction), even when writers are explicit that belief in psychic faculties informs their understanding of the world. A writer's belief in telepathy is often treated as an inconvenience, possibly an embarrassment, to be minimised when speaking to their acuity and that of their work. When, introducing his collection of Aldous Huxley's essays from 1939 to 1956, for instance, Robert S. Baker describes Huxley's engagement with telepathy as 'merely a superficial symptom' of his interest in religious mysticism (xv), it is even as Huxley's 'A Case for ESP, PK and Psi', included in that collection, asserts that laboratory research 'has established the case for psi on a basis too solid to be explained away' (98). By the time of this article, 1954, Huxley had been publicly extolling the credibility and significance of parapsychological research for twenty years, forming friendships with the likes of J. B. and Louisa Rhine, the most prominent academic researchers in the field. To render this aspect of Huxley's life 'superficial' considerably understates how deep and sustained his engagement with parapsychological research was and downplays the risks to his status as a public intellectual Huxley took in championing a widely mocked field. To an extent, it is understandable that as critics we might avoid address to psychic phenomena for fear of being seen as promoters of scientifically unsound theories, or for fear that we are seen as coming to bury idols by emphasising flaws in their thinking. Neither is necessary if we are generous in our appreciation of the contexts in which psychic speculations are advanced and accepted and if we appreciate that the worth of their novelistic deployment is not directly proportionate to their scientific plausibility.

As critics, we may not accept mesmerism, telepathy, clairvoyance, or any other supposedly scientific model of psychic connection. We can recognise that, without any credible evidence for its existence across more than a century of investigation, telepathy cannot be described as a scientifically accurate representation of the world. However, scientific representation is bound to strive for accuracy in a way literary representation is not. With respect to fiction, there is necessarily invention; if lifelike, the emphasis must be on the 'like'. Fiction generates the experience of unlived lives. Even in the case of the realist novel, praise for a work's artistry tends to correlate with its ability to make believable an unusual life trajectory: characters who live unusual lives and think unusual thoughts tend to be those who earn the most readerly and critical attention, for the very reason that their atypicality gives occasion to question the possibilities of human nature. Similarly, unusual and contestable representational strategies may do more to speak to life than established mimetic approaches, insomuch as they compel the reader to give more consideration to the nature of the relationship between the representation and the represented. This book contends that when writers who deploy telepathy or other models of psychic connection challenge the individual as a necessary or valuable unit of character, that challenge has value whatever the scientific status of the underpinnings. Writers invested in psychic connection have perceived and rejected the novel's individualistic bent and have demonstrated that the novel may offer coherent characters without individuation. That challenge cannot be properly assessed if we treat a writer's professed belief in telepathy and other psychic abilities as an inconvenience to be apologised for or disregarded entirely. Collectively, those challenges to the notion of the discrete novelistic subject drastically change the understanding of the limits of the novel as a form, of the kind of stories it can tell and how it tells them.

Contesting the Individualistic Paradigm

For the novel to engage with psychic connection, fundamental reformulation is impelled, insomuch as it is the discrete individual which the European novel has traditionally treated as a character. In *The Rise of the Novel*, Ian Watt offers the individuated character as an essential element of the novel, claiming that 'we can say that the novel requires a world view which is centred on the social relationships between individual persons' (83). As Watt traces, 'from the mediaeval belief in the reality of universals', by the time the novel emerges in Europe '"realism" had come to denote a belief in the individual apprehension of reality through the senses' (14). Character is formed as the product of that individual apprehension: as Nancy Armstrong argues, the 'novelistic proposition [is] that feelings well up from within the subject in response to sensations and acquire the form of ideas that enrich the subject's personal storehouse of knowledge' (16). The character, by this understanding, is forged by individual experience; feeling and thinking individually, the character develops ideas individually, containing those ideas within an individuated self. The individuated subject of the novel comes to be taken as natural and as inevitable, informing all spheres of intellectual activity. For Armstrong, the individuated subject, once established in the novel, reproduced itself 'not only in authors but also in readers, in other novels, and across British culture in law, medicine, moral and political philosophy, biography, history, and other forms of writing that took the individual as their most basic unit' (3). When, in 1855's *The Principles of Psychology*, Herbert Spencer asserts that 'individual experiences [. . .] finish what is but rudely sketched out at birth' (193), the vision of character formation his psychology is built upon is the one Armstrong associates with the nineteenth-century novel. The making of character happens alone, informed by private sensory experience and private reflection.

This understanding of character precipitates a lineage of novels concerned not so much with the construction of character, as with its constriction. Interested in the business of fitting in with society, the nineteenth-century novel often focuses on refinement, with characters denying expression to thoughts and feelings society deems undesirable. With communication suppressed, the already closed character is further estranged from others. This is encapsulated by Helen in Anne Brontë's *The Tenant of Wildfell Hall* (1848) when she complains (to herself, in a diary):

> How little real sympathy there exists between us; how many of my thoughts and feelings are gloomily cloistered within my own mind; how

much of my higher and better self is indeed unmarried – doomed either to harden and sour in the sunless shade of solitude, or to quite degenerate and fall away for lack of nutriment in this unwholesome soil! (143)

While the spur for these thoughts is her lack of a bond with her husband, Arthur, the idea of the cloistered self speaks to a more universal disconnection: considerable parts of her self are obscured from all other people – parts which, if nourished, she feels might engender connection. There is the hint that an alternative to individualism is possible, denied to the detriment of a truer and fuller self-realisation.

In the nineteenth-century British intellectual climate, with character formation seen to consist in individual experience, conformity is fundamental to society. Ideas being formed in the individual mind, group-belonging is associated with common values formed through equivalent (but not shared) experiences. Upbringing is homogenised for those in the same class and assigned the same gender: too different an upbringing threatens the formation of an unfitting character. The individuals the novel invests in, characters sufficiently interesting to read about, stand out and often risk being cast out. It is a sensibility which generates the intricacies of Jane Austen's courtship novels, wherein a person must attract notice to be considered as a partner, but should simultaneously show themselves unremarkable, able to maintain social standing through conventional conduct. When, in *Pride and Prejudice* (1813), Elizabeth Bennet unexpectedly meets Mr Darcy at Pemberley, having previously felt him affected and aloof, it is the fact he 'seemed, on this accidental meeting, most eager to preserve the acquaintance, and without any indelicate display of regard, or any peculiarity of manner' which begins to move him into her favour (238). His apparent haughtiness and disregard for society's admonition attracted attention, the fact it was misunderstood prevents his being cast aside. The individualistic novel almost inevitably flirts with the failure of its society, the character who is sufficiently distinct as to be an engaging subject being inimical to the integrity of conformist society.

For Armstrong, so bound to individualism is the pre-twentieth-century novel's approach to character that 'any way of thinking that opposes individualism' challenges it on a foundational level (16). Psychic phenomena, whether intentional telepathic transmission of information, or more nebulous forms of collective consciousness, represent literal ways of thinking contrary to the individualistic mode. In a novel which depicts psychic connection, the character, the personality, is no longer treatable as a closed system. Thought becomes more readable and with it character becomes less readable: the relationship between upbringing and personality becomes less deterministic – a thought might reach a person and resonate with them (more or less literally) irrespective of that person's direct experience. As such, chance becomes significantly more important in the development of personality, meaning that the novel coherently plotted around individual development is less tenable.

One response in the novel of psychic connection is to centre the incompatibility between a porous, responsive mode of being and societal norms formed on reading people as individuated and fundamentally predictable. This is the case in many of D. H. Lawrence's novels. For Lawrence, the literary character should not be conceived as self-contained and bounded: in order to speak to life as it is lived, the novel should render characters as open to external, unpredictable forces. As he argues in the 1925 essay 'The Novel', characters should be constructed such that 'in their words and gestures there is a flicker of the presence' of an 'unnamed and nameless flame behind them all' (182). When, in *Women in Love* (1920), Birkin speaks to the existence of 'a final me which is stark and impersonal and beyond responsibility' (146), he recognises that animating flame, though he, like many other of Lawrence's characters, experiences tension between what would feed this fire and what society demands. While Birkin insists that 'one can only follow the impulse, taking that which lies in front, and responsible for nothing', suggesting that the impersonal flame should be fed heedless of societal expectations, in practice, he finds himself restrained by social bonds. Discussing with Gerald Crich how possible it would be to 'reform the whole order of society' (54), Birkin suggests that, without fundamental change to society, he will 'shrivel inside it, as in a tight skin' (54). The identification of social pressure with the boundary of the physical body speaks to the individualistic exclusion from the self of anything which does not originate internally and which does not remain a constituent of a single bodily being. In Doris Lessing's *Briefing for a Descent into Hell* (1971), the social identification of the self solely with the bodily self is similarly experienced as engendering physical discomfort. Its protagonist, a mental patient who experiences apparent delusions of living other lives in other parts of the world, comes to feel that his 'whole body, and the level of life in it, was suffering', on account of the fact that his 'whole being had suffered a wrenching away from its proper level' (69). For the novel of psychic connection, taking the self as coextensive with the body makes the limits of the body a site of friction, thus making it apt to suffer from a narrow understanding of self.

Alternatively, the novel of psychic connection may imagine forms of society in which psychic connection between bodily individuals is accepted as a reality. Olaf Stapledon presents many such societies in his cosmic fiction, be they far future human societies, or non-human collectivities distant in the universe. *Last Men in London* (1932), for instance, details a society two billion years into the future in which telepathy is a recognised human faculty, its use associated not only with greater understanding and greater sympathy, but with the realisation of what human existence has been striving towards. The far-future narrator finds in that psychic interfusion the 'most excellently fulfilled Spirit of Man, within which my mind is organic' (596). Novels which imagine societies built around psychic connection are innately more speculative than novels in which bodily individuals apprehend their mental openness in individualistic social conditions, but they may imagine more local groupings than Stapledon does. Aldous Huxley's *Island* (1962), for instance, imagines a fictional South-East Asian nation, Pala, which embraces psychic openness in largely real-world, present-day conditions. It uses meditation, drugs and other tools to encourage in its population an awareness of 'Mind with a large "M"' (138), doing so to engender 'wider sympathies and deeper understandings' (91). Antagonism between residents of Pala is minimal; as a novel, *Island* provides tension by setting Pala's local success against the forces of an unreformed world covetous of the island's unexploited oil reserves. The more completely a novel rejects individualism, the more conflict within it will be between collectivities and large impersonal forces.

The novel of psychic connection may also centre the development of ideas instead of the development of people. In her afterword to *The Making of the Representative for Planet 8* (1982), Lessing reflects on how readerly attention might be refocused towards ideas, suggesting that 'there must be definite lifespans for ideas or sets of related ideas' and that we should 'make the attempt to treat the mechanisms of ideas as something we may study' (129). Planet 8 itself, a world wracked by catastrophic cooling, undergoes just such a project of reflection on the ideas it lives by, narrator Doeg explaining that 'the ideas that had inhabited our minds without being questioned were each one tested and – so far as everything changed for us – for the most part set aside' (9). Rendering ideas as residents of the mind, rather than possessions, reflects Lessing's sense of them as living; thriving, declining or, indeed, dying, they enact progressions suiting a novelistic subject. Huxley's novels of ideas, like *Point Counter Point* (1928) and *Eyeless in Gaza* (1936), similarly find their protagonists anxious that the unbidden inflow of ideas makes identifying a true self impossible. Philip Quarles, the protagonist of *Point Counter Point*, looking at selfhood from the perspective of the bodily individual, is reduced to asserting that 'the essential character of the self' is constituted by the 'capacity to espouse all contours and yet remain unfixed in any form, to take, and with an equal facility efface, impressions' (254). The sense among readers and critics that there is limited development in Huxley's novels of ideas comes from investing in a coherent growth of individuated characters which does not occur. By contrast, ideas do expand in his work, taking residence in more minds, evolving as they interact with other ideas.

Asking the reader to focus on the vitality of communities or ideas rather than individuals has significant repercussions for the reader's investment in a novel. For Eric Bulson, the demand of the typical novel for identification with its characters feeds into the reader's experience of selfhood at large. Introducing *The Cambridge Companion to the Novel*, he proposes that 'the identification with fictional selves is itself part of the invention of modern subjectivity' (10). When a novel asks its reader to invest in the fate of individuals, it reinforces the conceptual validity of the individuated self, whatever it presents as a desirable relationship between the individual and society. The novel which challenges the legitimacy of individuality also challenges the validity of identification with the individual character. As the stable, readable individual character dissolves, the reader is pushed to question their own formation. Porous understandings of self impel a fundamental reconsideration of the way the novel is processed.

From Mesmerism to Telepathy

The twentieth-century novel of psychic connection reacts to developments in psychic speculation: the monolithic impersonal forces of Lawrence's work are partly a function of the psychic speculation he encountered, in which psychic projection is conceived as force, while Huxley's mid-century 'mind with a large '"M"' responds to contemporary suggestions of a pervasive mindedness. Tracing a chronological path though the twentieth century, this book illustrates how changing psychic speculation feeds into literary innovation.

Until the late nineteenth century, psychic power tended to be conceived of according to an individualist paradigm. This feeds into stories in which one individual seizes control of the mind of another. In George du Maurier's 1894 novel *Trilby*, the mesmerist manipulator Svengali makes of the titular character 'an unconscious Trilby of marble, who could produce wonderful sounds – just the sounds he wanted, and nothing else – and think his thoughts and wish his wishes' (299). Under Svengali's influence, the tone-deaf Trilby performs as 'the greatest contralto, the greatest soprano the world has ever known' (297) – she is literally an instrument through whom Svengali can profit and gain status. *Trilby*, written at a time when stage performances by mesmerists and hypnotists were an established draw for audiences, imagines the wholesale command of one mind over another, rather than a subtle admixture of minds. Trilby, remembering nothing of her performances, is colonised completely by Svengali. In this much, *Trilby* invests great power in the individual mind, at the same time as suggesting that a mind can be penetrated – a fact which holds for mesmerism more widely. While mesmerists hypothesised the existence of a pervasive, mysterious magnetic fluid, through which the human will may be transmitted, the phenomenon of being mesmerised tended to be conceived of monolithically. As William Lang writes in his 1844 history of mesmerism, the magnetic fluid 'may be capable of being directed outwards, by the volition of one individual, with such energy as to produce a peculiar effect upon the organization of another' (32). Thoughts are seen as being formed and fixed in the individual mind. Svengali's thoughts and wishes are thought and wished by Trilby in the form they existed in Svengali's mind prior to transmission. Arthur Conan Doyle's *The Parasite*, also published in 1894, conceives of comparably complete mental control. Its protagonist, the student Austin Gilroy, finds himself subject to mind control by Miss Penclosa, an acquaintance of one of his professors. For the periods Miss Penclosa uses her power, Gilroy becomes 'her slave, body and soul' (88). So assumed is the reality of the individual subject that psychic interface is conceptualised without scope for fusion.

At the end of the nineteenth century, however, a shift occurred in the conceptualisation of psychic phenomena which would come to feed into literature in the twentieth century. Among psychical researchers in Britain, telepathy was superseding mesmerism and hypnosis as the primary way to approach psychic interactions, allowing for more nuanced and more diverse forms of connection to be imagined.[1] Conceived as a form of communication, rather the manifestation of physical, magnetic attraction, telepathy allowed psychic connection to be dialogic and therefore productive. Frederic W. H. Myers, who coined the term 'telepathy' in 1882, defines it as 'the communication of impressions of any kind from one mind to another, independently of the recognized channels of sense' (xxii). In this climate, mesmerism and hypnosis's dominion of one mind over another was merely an extreme in a continuum of mental connection. Unlike mesmerism, telepathy as a concept had the benefit of being centrally void: where mesmerism hypothesised a magnetic fluid generating attraction, with the viability of the concept undermined by the failure to discover this fluid, telepathy proffered only that mental items can pass between people. Specific mechanisms would be suggested by given psychical researchers, but none came to define what telepathy is. Being more open to debate, telepathy had the conceptual durability to survive experimental failures and debunked hypotheses.

While its mechanisms remained an open question, telepathy invited concrete, quantitative experimentation. After decades of small-scale, anecdotal experiments by members of the Society for Psychical Research and similar organisations (reports of which, directly or indirectly, attract the notice of Lawrence and modernist peers), J. B. Rhine's experiments at Duke University in the 1930s brought the force of numbers to bear: *Extra-Sensory Perception* (1934) alone drew upon the results of over 90,000 trials (35), each of which entailed guessing the symbol depicted on all twenty-five cards in a special deck. This repetition, for Rhine, meant that the results of the best performers were far beyond what chance could explain – he asserts, for example, that the results of one participant, A. J. Linzmayer, in a series of clairvoyance trials had over a trillion to one chance of being achieved by luck (61). Methodological flaws in Rhine's work explain what chance does not,[2] but for the many who were persuaded by their findings, the use of statistics underscored their significance. Mathematics was seen to affirm patterns as significant in a way subjective interpreters could not, with the impression for many being that an emergent or latent faculty beyond ordinary comprehension was being detected.

Rhine, as a figurehead, energised literature's engagement with psychic connection. Literary figures in the United States, Britain and elsewhere effusively celebrated his work. John W. Campbell, editor of American magazine *Astounding Science Fiction*, who volunteered for Rhine's experiments when a student at Duke (Luckhurst, *Science Fiction* 260), tells Rhine in a 1953 letter that he is 'trying to use fiction to induce competent thinkers to attack just such problems as the psi effects' (qtd in *Science Fiction* 260). This includes his own output – his 1938 story 'Who Goes There?' has the physician, Copper, assert that 'Doctor Rhine of Duke University has shown that [telepathy] exists' (324). More significantly, it also informed his work as the editor of science fiction's then pre-eminent magazine. Campbell's lasting interest in extrasensory perception makes it a core part of *Astounding Science Fiction*'s offering and, by extension, of the wider golden age of science fiction. Isaac Asimov, whose *Foundation* series was first published in *Astounding Science Fiction*, recalls, for instance, that 'a number of writers wrote pseudoscientific stuff to ensure sales to Campbell', and that he had to change the ending of his psionic story 'Belief' (1953) to please Campbell (75).

Both Stapledon and Huxley were among the British writers who celebrated Rhine's research as scientifically and philosophically significant.

In 1934 Huxley asserts that 'Professor Rhine has established a number of important facts' through his experiments ('Mind Reading' 165) and suggests that 'intensive research into the supernormal may be expected to throw light on some of the most obscure and the most important of our unsolved problems – on the nature of mind and its limitations; on the relations between individual minds and their bodies, the material world and other minds, on the nature of time and of our knowledge of it' ('Supernatural' 177). Likely alluding to Rhine's work, Stapledon claims that psychical research has 'found hints of very strange powers, such as telepathy and clairvoyance and even pre-cognition' (*Youth* 111). While he suggests that 'these hints may in the end turn out to be sheer illusions', he similarly sees significant implications for understanding human and posthuman potential, suggesting that what researchers including Rhine have found may be 'fragmentary traces of ways of experience which can reach full development only on planes beyond the reach of man'. So significant were the potential implications of telepathy, in Stapledon's view, that even with doubts concerning the evidence for it, he made exploration of those repercussions central to his literary project: telepathy or other psychic phenomena feature in every one of his novels. Psychic transmission now conceived as dialogic, Stapledon's expansive novels seek the limits of that transmission and, with it, of connection. His furthest-reaching novel, *Star Maker* (1937), imagines telepathic conversation with beings not only across this universe, but even between beings in this and other universes.

Psychotronics and Panpsychism

Novels in which psychic connection exists, especially those like Stapledon's or Lessing's where it encompasses large groups, challenge established narratological tools addressing the depiction of groups. Narratology tends to assume collectivities to be narrative fictions. Collective consciousness is not, for instance, easily read in terms of the 'intermental mind' that Alan Palmer finds to be a feature of the novel. Palmer's intermental mind is effectively a shorthand for reading a like-minded group as if it were an individual, his express interest being in the question of how 'readers, narrators, and individual characters attribute mental functioning to groups' (20). When he suggests, for example, that 'the town of Middlemarch is well defined enough to be thought of as a group mind' and as a singular 'major character' in the novel (172), the interest is in how readers – and, indeed, characters – interpret the group with (for Palmer) the same tools as they interpret an individual mind, as opposed to the ontological status of any collective consciousness. Comparably, when narratologists consider the validity of collective subjects – for example, when a 'we' narrates a text – the possibility of porousness destabilises baseline claims. Monika Fludernik's suggestion that 'a communal voice is *per se* a fiction' assumes the individual voice to be the only real possibility (188). Similarly, if individuality is not absolute, Brian Richardson's claim that the we-narrator's 'access to the contents of other minds is potentially problematic' in respect of a 'mimetic framework for the text' fails (*Unnatural* 56). When Stapledon and Lessing use we-narration, as they do extensively in *Star Maker* and *The Making of the Representative* respectively, they do so in speculative novels, but to give voice to what they each see as a real possibility for subjectivity. The porous subject disrupts the most foundational aspects of storytelling. Those writers who have sought to reflect this porousness across the length of a novel have encountered a need for new approaches to narration, characterisation and structure.

The possibility of transmitting thought probes at the foundations of thought itself and, as such, challenges core assumptions about the nature of being. For Luckhurst, 'it would be possible to multiply instances of the entanglement of the apparently marginal belief in telepathy with some of the central aspects of twentieth-century science, philosophy, literature, and culture' (*Invention* 276). Just as the concept of the individuated self spans nineteenth-century thought, coming to be taken as self-evident, the porous self shapes thought in the twentieth century. Progenitor, rather than product, of certain modern anxieties, telepathy spurs the most intense self-doubts; not only that all one's most secret desires might be known, but also that those desires were never truly one's own in the first place. When, in Huxley's *Eyeless in Gaza*, protagonist Anthony Beavis feels 'possessed, as though he were being forced to lead someone else's life and think with another person's mind' (428), there is no specific figure in mind – no identifiable Svengali or Miss Penclosa. The anxiety about self-possession has become more generalised. The very possibility of possessing thoughts as an individual is in doubt.

In science fiction, the peak for novelistic engagement with willed, intentional telepathy was in the 1950s and 1960s. Across that period, numerous writers explored the personal and social implications of telepathic abilities manifesting in a subset of the population. John Wyndham's *The Chrysalids* (1955) imagines the emergence of telepathic abilities in children in a post-apocalyptic society, Arthur C. Clarke's *Childhood's End* (1953) has a similar generational divide as alien overlords nurture telepathy in the youth of humanity, while John Brunner's *Telepathist*

(1964) considers how authorities might seek to control and utilise telepathic abilities. In each, there is a split focus: as well as questioning what it would mean to be telepathic, these novels also address society's approach to difference. The subjugation or exploitation of telepaths speaks to all-too-real social ills, with the suggestion being that society is too suspicious of difference to do anything other than feel threatened by an attribute possessed by a minority (even when that difference might be provably beneficial). The greater value of each novel, effectively, comes with reading telepathy as metaphor; to get through to that greater value it is necessary to recognise telepathy as a fiction. The deployment of telepathy in this way, as largely a red herring, is reflective of telepathy's mid-century status. By this time, parapsychological research was losing momentum in laboratories, with multiple experimenters having found Rhine's proclaimed successes impossible to replicate.[3] When, in 1972, American writer Robert Silverberg's *Dying Inside* offered a middle-aged telepath coming to terms with his waning power, it also spoke to the declining imaginative (and commercial) potency of telepathy itself.

However, the Cold War spurred new governmental support for research into the use of technology to facilitate the transmission and detection of thoughts. In the late 1960s and early 1970s, the Soviet Union invested considerable resources in exploring what it termed 'psychotronics'. It is reported to have constructed devices known as Sergeyev detectors in multiple laboratories, designed to 'detect fields associated with electroencephalographic activity at distances of the order of five meters' (Van Dyke and Juncosa 14), while the Czechoslovakian-designed Pavlita generator was claimed to be able to 'focus and direct the psychokinetic energies of human subjects' (15). In response, the United States funded research at Stanford which aimed to use a form of clairvoyance, termed 'remote viewing', to gain military intelligence (Luckhurst, 'Omega' 46). Rumours flowed regarding successes on either side, including in the public sphere. Literature responded sceptically, however. That parapsychological research turns to technology to spark new interest from governments and other sources of funding is a step which undermines the human potential it seeks to save, as Lessing realises in *The Four-Gated City* of 1969. In it, inventor Jimmy is on the verge of selling a device 'for stimulating, artificially, the capacities of telepathy, "second sight," etc' to the British government (504). However, Jimmy suggests that 'brains stimulated in such ways [. . .] might very well be destroyed' (504). So fundamentally would telepathy alter the nature of being, that its artificial inducement risks overwriting the original underlying subject. If mechanically induced telepathy is only temporary, then telepathy becomes little more than telephony channelled through the human mind.

The turn to technology only temporarily revived scientific interest in telepathy and clairvoyance; verifiable results again failed to materialise and the power of misinformation in the sphere waned. Telepathy needs both an empowered individual mind and an impersonal mindedness to function, neither of which it has been able to evidence. Psychotronics in turn inspires only a limited resurgence of thought-projection in popular fiction, as in Craig Thomas's *Firefox* (1977), which sees the CIA and MI6 acquire intelligence of a new Soviet fighter aircraft with a thought-controlled weapons system. However, as in the likes of American writer Joe Haldeman's *Tool of the Trade* (1987), in which a Soviet sleeper agent working as a professor of psychology at MIT secretly develops a mind-control device, the object of literary interest tends not to be human minds empowered by machines, but rather controlled by them. The rapidly development of information technology sees the machine, rather than the human mind, be the site of unknowable depths of potential power. At the same time, however, as science fiction imagines a human mind impotent in the face of technology, literary fiction begins to accept telepathy as an overt presence, as in Salman Rushdie's *Midnight's Children* (1981), which has all the children born in India within the hour of its independence be psychically linked to one another. Once telepathy is effectively moribund as an object of scientific speculation, it is freed to operate as a literary device speaking to need for sympathy and harmony, writers more able to deploy it without facing the assumption that they subscribe to its existence.

However, other conceptions of mental connection which exclude individually willed transmission retain advocates after telepathy has effectively become moribund as a model. Panpsychism, a position which enjoyed minor currency in the Victorian conversation around the nature of mind and the possibility of psychical connection,[4] gained renewed philosophical attention in the last years of the twentieth century. Its suggestion that there is a baseline mindedness everywhere has the appeal of explanatory economy, as well as hints of support from the physical sciences. Panpsychism removes the need to explain how mind is limited in space and how individual minds can come into being. As David Skrbina offers, 'it is arguably more logical and more natural to assume broad or even universal applicability of mind, unless one is able to convincingly argue to the contrary' (4). For Godehard Brüntrup and Ludwig Jaskolla, 'the attraction of panpsychism for philosophers of mind is that it seems to offer a world view which is capable of remaining within a broadly conceived naturalist framework whilst accounting for the emergence of a nonreductively conceived mental reality' whereby 'the mind is neither explained by divine intervention nor by inexplicable strong emergence' (3). The theory converses with the physical sciences, where there is ongoing speculation regarding the physical status of information, as in the work of Melvin M. Vopson, who suggests 'information as the fifth state of matter in the universe' ('Experimental'). The idea that brains are not unique in holding informational content opens, for advocates of panpsychism, the prospect that there is a continuity between the mindedness associated with a brain and a pervasive physical possibility to hold information. The all-pervasive psyche, as Skrbina cautions, is not equivalent to an all-pervasive consciousness (9), but nevertheless offers fuel for writers invested in kinship between humankind and nature at large and those invested in anti-individualist conceptions of self. As Jonathan Kramnick expresses, 'the exciting thing about panpsychism is that it puts experience into the building blocks of the universe' (159). It is a philosophy which begets an entity like the *noncorpum* of *Ghostwritten*, a being who consists of mind without body, able to transfer itself between bodily individuals. That figure, the narrator of one of the chapters, reveals that selves are to be seen as fluid and overlapping, with the individual body not an absolute boundary of selfhood. It also helps the reader recognise that, while protagonists may change from chapter to chapter in *Ghostwritten*, there may be a substantive continuity of being between them. More directly, panpsychism informs Lessing's *Briefing for a Descent into Hell*, in which the narrator attributes 'subtle moving thoughts' to the moon (57) and offers that all entities on and near Earth – plant, animal and mineral – manifest consciousness. Depicting the dissolute identity of its mental patient (whose vivid hallucinations are experienced as real), *Descent* is exemplar of an increasing sense across Lessing's work that the boundaries between selves are artifices socially imposed upon the 'healthy' individual.

The innovations which these writers bring to the novel as a medium feeds into their approach to genre. Writing the porous, connected self is innately a speculative project, as the boundaries of the self are uncertain – if they indeed exist. In certain cases, the writer's understanding of the reality of self precipitates textual constructions which are sufficiently unorthodox as to only be accepted by readers in the generic frame of speculative fiction; narrating the self as 'we', rather than 'I', for example. The novel being an innately speculative project for these writers, they tend not to accept a clear distinction between 'literary' and speculative or science fiction, with most of the writers this study addresses producing work fitting both categories. Interviewed in 1987, after the completion of the *Canopus in Argos* series, Lessing offers that 'it never crossed my mind with these later books that I was writing science fiction or anything of the kind' (Frick 158). Similarly, Mitchell, on being told that he helped Kazuo Ishiguro to feel confident in including science fiction and fantasy elements in his work, responds that 'the book doesn't care if it's science fiction. The book doesn't give a damn about genre, it just is what it is. And that's what I want to do' (Barr Kirtley). This book suggests, then, repercussions of the porous self in 'literary' and speculative fiction are intimately related. It does not deny the specificities of genre, but finds a history best narrated as intertwined.

In spite of its rejection of supposedly fundamental aspects of the novel, the novel of the porous, connected self has spread, examples becoming, with time, increasingly upheld as supreme accomplishments in the form. Nevertheless, criticism lags, clinging to the individuated character as the novel's core unit. When, in *Consciousness and the Novel*, David Lodge asserts that, 'if the self is a fiction, it may perhaps be the supreme fiction, the greatest achievement of human consciousness, the one that makes us human' (16), the claim makes of humanity a constrictive concept, a lie to be lived like those endured by many nineteenth-century protagonists striving to fit in. Lodge quotes neuroscientist Antonio Damasio, who, while recognising that 'there are limits to the unified, continuous, single self', suggests that 'the tendency toward one single self and its advantage to the healthy mind are undeniable' (qtd in Lodge 15). That supposedly undeniable advantage has been repeatedly questioned, if not outright refuted across twentieth- and twenty-first-century fiction. The novel is more healthy and more resilient for being accommodating of multiple understandings of selfhood and the broader humanity which emerges is a more humane one. The novelistic engagements with psychic connection which occur across the twentieth century deserve central positions in our accounts of the novel's development, given how numerous they are, and how demonstrably they inform what the novel becomes. To avoid critical consideration of the novel's engagements with parapsychology because of its failure as a science is to insist on a subservient relationship between literature and science, whereby the limits of literary analysis are determined by the limits of scientific credibility, irrespective of the ability of readers and writers to draw meaning from provisional or contestable theory. Science can only ever offer a provisional account of the universe, and a function of literature can be to expose that provisionality by showing the limits of imagination to be more expansive than the limits of science.

Chapter 1

D. H. Lawrence and the Novel of Connected Individuals

Psychic Interfusion and the Health of the Novel

According to D. H. Lawrence, the novel was in poor health in the 1920s, its sickness attributable to what he sees as its failure to recognise and value the psychic connections between people. In his view, the novel is complicit in entrenching a misapprehension that human experience is necessarily individuated. Offering the work of James Joyce, Marcel Proust and Dorothy Richardson as exemplars of an overly narrow self-consciousness ('Future' 151), Lawrence contends that many novels of his time provide 'something awfully lifelike', but 'as lifeless as most people are' ('The Novel' 182). However accomplished he finds the prose of his peers, Lawrence identifies their wordiness as detached from worldliness, complaining that 'you can get a James Joyce or a Marcel Proust to say as many words as they like – and they like to say a legion – yet they never say anything except the innumerable last words about their own specific case' ('Morality', first version 242). The failure Lawrence attributes to his contemporaries is reflected in the 'crustacean' novelist Clifford Chatterley of *Lady Chatterley's Lover* (1928), who, insulated in himself by his 'hard, efficient shell' (110), writes stories which similarly enclose their characters. Clifford's novels, popular with both readers and critics, are 'curiously true to modern life', yet there is 'no touch, no actual contact' in them (16), filled as they are with 'that slightly humorous analysis of people and motives which leaves everything in bits at the end' (50). For Lawrence, the problem stems from viewing consciousnesses as discrete. In his view, 'the *basic* state of consciousness which preserves the human being all his life fresh and alive' is that of being in a 'living continuum with all the universe' ('Galsworthy' fragment 249, emphasis from source). Rejecting the discrete personality, Lawrence's project as a writer centres upon reconfiguring how literature approaches character and development.

What Lawrence calls for is, in effect, the novel of psychic connection. Demanding novels which render character as developing unpredictably, in interconnection with other consciousnesses, human and otherwise, Lawrence requests the kind of challenge to established novelistic form which was to emerge across the twentieth century. Lawrence sees himself as unaccompanied in this project, though others in his time, like May Sinclair and Evelyn Underhill, also draw on telepathic speculation to imagine a connected individual. Moving on from nineteenth-century novels of complete psychic control like *Trilby*, each explores what happens to individual development if a person is seen to be ever open to an interplay of psychic transmission and reception. In light of psychical speculation precipitated by apparent proofs of telepathy, each questions how self is constituted, rejecting the search for an authentic, individuated core self as misguided and damaging. What results are novels of connected individuality, where the particularity is a function of a unique position in a psychic web of connections. It takes later writers, like Doris Lessing, to question whether the novel might disregard the bodily individual entirely.

Where criticism of Lawrence's work has long focused on his valorisation of individuality, what it tends to miss is that, for Lawrence, meaningful individuality is only achieved in through acceptance of psychic connection. For Lawrence, the only true individuality is arrived at through a person's particular interfusion with other people and with the universe at large; this, for him, stands opposed to a false individuality which resists these external forces in pursuit of a separateness which leaves a person null rather than individual. Lawrence's rendering of psychic connection directly inspires others to build upon his challenge to novelistic individualism. Aldous Huxley, one of Lawrence's closest friends in his later years, recalls of Lawrence that he 'could never forget, as most of us almost continuously forget, the dark presence of the otherness that lies beyond the boundaries of man's conscious mind' (117), a presence Huxley dedicates great energies to identifying in his own novels. Lessing, recalling reading Lawrence in her youth, credits him with having had 'an enormous effect on me because of the vitality of the man' (Ingersoll 48). While she explains that she 'never read him for his ideas', the likes of the *Canopus in Argos* series conceive of vitality very much as Lawrence did, offering the immaterial 'substance-of-we-feeling' as 'substance-of-life' (*Shikasta* 96): the suggestion that connectedness does not just elevate the quality of life but imbues life-force itself is Lawrencian, as is the implicit corollary that disconnection means nullity. Where Lessing goes further than Lawrence is to suggest that a person does not just contain those forces but is constituted by them.

Advancing a form of panpsychism, Lawrence insists that the novel must reproduce the relatedness he sees in the universe. A character, he asserts, 'must have a quick relatedness to all the other things in the novel: snow, bed-bugs, sunshine, the phallus, trains, silk-hats, cats, sorrow, people, food, diphtheria, fuchsias, stars, ideas, God, toothpaste, lightning, and toilet paper' ('The Novel' 183). This relatedness is not reducible to mere awareness – to a passive appreciation of the range of entities and concepts with which we share the planet – but is instead an interpenetration, whereby psychic forces resonate through all things and interact. For Lawrence, not only can unforeseen events precipitate unexpected psychic consequences, but psychic forces without clear physical correlates also shape his characters. The 'unknown, overwhelming insinuation' Anna Brangwen feels bristling in the darkness in 1915's *The Rainbow* (201) and the 'deeper than human' consciousness Richard Lovatt Somers feels under the full Australian moon in 1923's *Kangaroo* (340), like the many other irresistible pulls and obscure callings Lawrence's characters feel throughout his work, are impersonal resonances in the psychic domain. By nature beyond individual comprehension, these forces disrupt expectations that human events should reach conclusions explicable entirely in terms of human motivations and that characters should constitute discrete, coherent beings. As a novelist, Lawrence strives to show these forces as agents in themselves, demanding that they not be read as metaphors for desires and revulsions internal to individuated characters.

Lawrence's call for a new kind of novel with a new impulse is answered by the novels of psychic connection which follow his. By rethinking thinking they offer, on a fundamental level, new ways of considering the human condition. Novels of psychic connection – including Lawrence's – abound with the 'speculative effects' Pierre Macherey associates with literature at large (232). For Macherey, 'the work of literary writing opens up new prospects for philosophy, new fields of investigation that escape the strictly codified competence of professional philosopher' (232), with, in his view, 'the truly philosophical effect of literature' being that it 'breaks up all systems of thought' (233). The way in which he conceptualises that rupture is especially apposite for novels of psychic connection. Literature, for Macherey, introduces into systems of thought 'a collective and shared polyphonic reflection stemming from the free circulation of images and schemas of narration and enunciation': it, in effect, can break through to radical new truths freed from the iterative, reasoned approach of the philosophy. The novel of psychic connection, imagining new ways for ideas to circulate, is innately collectivist and polyphonic in and of itself. In this much, it not only provides the speculative effect of literature at large, but is also able to attend directly to that rupture in systems of thought in itself, directly provoking ontological speculation in the reader.

The fact so many novelists' challenges to the discrete, individuated character have been little addressed in accounts of their work can be attributed to what Nancy Armstrong identifies as liberal individualism's 'skill at defending the very concept of the individual against assaults on its universality' (11). Nancy Armstrong, in insisting the novel is inseparable from individualism, unwittingly participates in that defence. Albeit the Western novel emerges alongside individualism, there is no innate reason to hold the two to be indivisible from each other. The assumption of a lasting connection between the novel and individualism has obscured alternatives, leading novelistic manifestations of psychic connection to be read as figurative or metaphorical – as tools which ultimately say something about an individual underneath. Reading references to telepathy and collective consciousness literally is radical only because of the weight of individualistic assumptions readers and critics bring to novels. Likewise, address to instances in which narrative subjects think as one, or in which thoughts pass between subjects, tends to assume these are figurative devices which connote something about an ultimately individuated subject, overlooking the possibility that they more directly reflect underlying reality as the writer suggests it to be, whether with conviction or speculatively.

Characterising both the popular and literary novel of his time as comparably sick, Lawrence presents himself as unaccompanied in endeavouring to create an alternative novel of dynamic, interpenetrating consciousness – and perhaps sincerely believes himself to be. However, the early twentieth-century climate of psychical speculation sees other writers active at the time, including Sinclair, Underhill, Algernon Blackwood and J. D. Beresford also approach character as permeable and as affected by opaque, impersonal psychic forces. Openness to the possibility of psychic forces enjoyed cachet – at least for some – as a marker of an enquiring mind, in the last decades of the nineteenth century and first decades of the twentieth, thanks in large part to the Society for Psychical Research, presided over by the likes of future prime minister Arthur Balfour and developer of wireless telegraphy Oliver Lodge. The work of contemporaries like Sinclair and Underhill shares with Lawrence an anxiety that the individual who lives open to unpredictable psychic forces risks estrangement from society, taken as eccentric and potentially dangerous. What Lawrence does to offer more, especially in his later novels, is to imagine how communities might be reconstituted to embrace and empower the psychically connected individual, be it on the small scale of the workers' movement in *Kangaroo* or the national scale of the Mexican revolutionary movement in *The Plumed Serpent* (1926).

Sinclair, herself a member of the Society for Psychical Research from 1914, sees the self as expansive and sees need for literature to reflect this. Her unqualified assertion in 1917 that 'telepathy is a fact' is illustrative of an intellectual climate in which the detailed reports of supposed psychic phenomena produced by members of the society convinced many that telepathy had been demonstrated beyond doubt (*Defence* 313). Lawrence, for his part, speaks to telepathy as fact in *Kangaroo*, its narration asserting that 'the communication between the individuals in a herd [. . .] is telepathic' (298): the novel's further contention that 'powerful influences are emitted by men like Gladstone or Abraham Lincoln' makes telepathy central to its account of the attraction of a charismatic leader (300). For Sinclair, psychic connection means that the self 'is something over and above its own experience, its own memories, and its own organism' (*Defence* 313). The conviction informs her novels on a fundamental level. Sinclair renders the mind as porous and apt to be affected by forces of unknown origin. *The Flaw in the Crystal* (1912) endows its protagonist, Agatha Verrall, with the 'gift' of supporting others through psychic contact and, moreover, reflects upon the lived consequences of psychic porousness. Agatha, it is explained, has 'had to destroy not only the barriers of flesh and blood, but those innermost walls of personality that divide and protect, mercifully, one spirit from another' in the use of her power (153). This erosion of boundaries marks a significant change from nineteenth-century stories of mesmerism. When effecting change in others, Agatha does not project her will in a determined dependable form and does not override the will of her counterpart. As Agatha explains, 'any substitution of self for self would be useless, for there is no more self there. That is why the Power cannot work that way' (160). Unlike in late nineteenth-century stories of mesmerism, where the gift of mesmerists like Arthur Conan Doyle's Miss Penclosa from *The Parasite* (1894) consists in projecting their will as an individual 'into another person and superseding his own' (42), the action of psychic force has become more nebulous and nuanced and the individual mind is no longer conceived of as an indivisible, necessarily discrete entity. With telepathy displacing mesmerism as a pervasive paradigm, psychic connection comes to be conceived as more dialogic, involving the blurring of subject and object.

Like Lawrence, Sinclair expressly sees need for the novel to change, in order to encompass a broader consciousness and to treat of character in connection. Suggesting that 'there is nothing more fundamental than the unity of consciousness', she offers that 'the analytic psychological novel is becoming a thing of the past' and that 'the synthetic psychological novel is taking its place' ('Future' 7). Sinclair is more prepared than Lawrence, however, to see modernist contemporaries as offering psychological syntheses. In identifying a 'mysticism apart' in Richardson's *Pilgrimage* ('Dorothy Richardson' 59), Sinclair finds the direction of that pilgrimage 'transparently clear' when, in *Honeycomb* (1917), Miriam

> gathered up all the sadness she had ever known and flung it from her. All the dark things of the past flashed with a strange beauty as she flung them out. The light had been there all the time; but she had known it only at moments [. . .] Something that was not touched, that sang far away down inside the gloom, that cared nothing for the creditors and could get away down and down into the twilight far away from the everlasting accusation of humanity. . . Deeper down was something cool and fresh – endless – an endless garden. (qtd in 'Dorothy Richardson' 59)

For Sinclair, what is significant is that even from the intensely personal, individual perspective of *Pilgrimage* external, eternal presences are fleetingly discernible. Where, for Lawrence, the synthetic character should continually and explicitly be drawn in its breadth of interfusions, in the work of Richardson, Sinclair finds a constricted introspection able to expose how syntheses underscore ostensibly individual experience. By attending to the minutiae of an individual life as closely as she does, Richardson, for Sinclair, casts light on aspects of experience neither explicable in terms of sensory stimulation nor in terms of innate, individual mental structures: Richardson's work is, for Sinclair, suggestive that there are channels into the individual other than the senses. Notwithstanding their greatly differing evaluations of the current health of the novel, Lawrence and Sinclair alike perceive the novel's future as a movement beyond the individuated character.

Blackwood, like Sinclair, associates psychic force with the destruction of the boundaries of the discrete self. In *The Centaur* (1911), travel writer Terence O'Malley finds a pair of fellow passengers on a steamship to the Black Sea to feel curiously inhuman and curiously expansive (albeit with nothing concretely identifiable as unusual in their appearances). In their presence, he comes to sense greater reaches of consciousness, experiencing the 'revelation that the Consciousness is not contained skin-tight around the body' (154). Blackwood, confident that human possession of faculties which 'register beyond the normal gamut of seeing, hearing, feeling' is 'beyond the denials to-day of the petty sceptic' (Introduction xiv), attends in his fiction to the moments of terror or beauty in which psychic forces are first perceived, interested in the rupture of the ordinary understanding of the world. This focus precipitates a predilection for shorter fiction, in which the flash of realisation can be centred. However, *The Centaur* engages in a more complex reflection upon how the personality is articulated after such ruptures, when there is cognisance of vast but dimly known parts of self. Describing O'Malley's written and oral accounts of his experience with the strange passengers, the narrator of *The Centaur* notes the unorthodox structure of his account but praises it as fitting. 'Climax,' the narrator asserts, 'in the story-book meaning, there was none', but contends that the 'very incoherence conveyed the gorgeous splendour of the whole better than any neat ordered sequence could possibly have done' (235). However, *The Centaur* itself mediates O'Malley's story through the narrator, who has filtered and organised it, and adopts an approach which largely follows the chronology of his physical voyage. In this much, the narrator rejects the incoherence he supposedly found fitting to O'Malley's story. The novel becomes the story of O'Malley, rather than O'Malley's story, holding on to the physical person as the unit of self, centring on the physical health of the bodily individual and ending when that body perishes.

For S. T. Joshi, 'the incommunicability of extramundane experience' is at issue throughout Blackwood's work and the weird tales of other writers (108). As Joshi sees it, the problem inheres in the use of language, which is bound to the expression of the mode of being it evolved alongside. O'Malley's exasperated declaration that 'language cannot seize a mode of life that throve before language existed', for instance, presents the articulation as entirely impossible (129). However, the narrator's suggestion that O'Malley's original incoherence was fitting and expressive suggests that narrative tools rather than language might be the more precise nexus of communicative frustration. While Lawrence and Sinclair can easily express rejection of novelistic individualism in essays and can have narrators in their novels proclaim that characters are apprehending impersonal forces, the degree to which the novel accommodates unindividuated subjectivity is contestable. Much criticism of the novel offers that an essential aspect of the form is the reading of the individual subject for its universality. For Armstrong, no innovation is capable of changing this. She asserts that 'new varieties of novel cannot help taking up the project of universalising the individual subject. That simply put, is what novels do' (10). So wedded does she see individualism and the novel as a medium that she claims she 'cannot quite believe that any novel can reach in and modify the ideological core of the genre and still remain a novel'. This is largely mirrored by Eric Bulson, who, in *The Cambridge Companion to the Novel*, suggests that 'the trick for novels has involved navigating between characters that can seem like real individuals (with souls and hearts) and those that are merely one-dimensional types' (11). While Bulson's reference to the 'individual' character is explicable as a function of the usual synonymity assumed between 'individual' and 'person', it speaks to the scale of the task facing writers who contest individuated selfhood (and, given Bulson is writing a century after Lawrence, Sinclair and Blackwood, to the degree to which they and others since have failed to overturn the pervasive assumption that the novel, by nature, deals in individuals). Comparably, when Marta Figlerowicz offers that in novels 'characters are aesthetic compromises with reality' who 'convey *both* the uniqueness and autonomy of individuals *and* certain types or generalizations through which one can zoom out of these individuals' lives' (123, emphasis from source), the contract between writer and reader is seen to be founded on the individual, individuated character as the centre of gravity around which the rest of the reader's interpretative apparatus orbits. It is through reliably offering the stories of characters conceived as discrete individuals that a novel is supposed to gain a foothold to speak its generalisations, to offer its contribution to the broader understanding of human nature. Stylistically or structurally a novel may innovate, it may speak to a part of the world unfamiliar to the reader, it might describe unfamiliar positions in society, or a period of history outside the reader's experience, but the assumption is there that the interface between novel and reader is established on the basis of the individual character as a shared unit.

However, in what Figlerowicz offers is also the suggestion that the value of a novel, whatever way it thinks of character, depends in large part on the generalisability of the stories and characters it presents. Even in the most personal, local story the reader is expected to read for broad, potentially universal, patterns of thought. In effect, the identification with characters as individuals sits in uneasy but productive relationship with an approach to characters as translatable types. When the novel offers panpsychism or other configurations of psychic connection, then that relationship is reversed. The pattern of thought is no longer a function of individual characters, but instead the ostensibly individual character is a function of the patterns of thought. As such, there is impetus to switch the readerly attention to thought as primary, with character an offshoot from it. This refocusing is something Doris Lessing speaks to when she reflects in the Afterword to her *The Making of the Representative for Planet 8* (1982) that 'there must be definite lifespans for ideas or sets of related ideas. They are born (or reborn), come to maturity, decay, die, are replaced' (129). That novel and others of hers limit the usual readerly approach to character by mapping names to roles rather than bodily individuals, obfuscating whether the figure present in any given episode is the same bodily individual as in other episodes. Notwithstanding the fact that the lifecycle Lessing ascribes to ideas humanises them – and, indeed, attributes character development to them – the sense is that ideas exert forces which shape people, more than the reverse, and the attempt should at least be made to recalibrate the novel to reflect this. Lawrence, invested in character as connected, ever subject to psychic forces, offers generalisation as not just a writerly or readerly ascription, but finds a generality, beget by unindividuated forces, already permeating the individual.

At stake is both what readers can make of novels, as well as what novels can make of readers. Where Armstrong observes that the individual has passed 'from a novel-made discourse into a self-perpetuating one' (9), criticism of the novel – including Armstrong's itself – plays a role in perpetuating the impression that the individuated character is required by the novel even when, as in much of Lawrence's work, the opposition to individuated character is explicit. This has fed into an overwhelming refusal to countenance novelistic engagements with psychic phenomena, including Lawrence's. When Clifford Chatterley proffers that the 'whole problem of life [is] the slow building up of an integral personality, through the years' (45), he encapsulates the effect of reading the novelistic development of character as identical with the process of development in life. The contention that a stable and discrete personality should be forged in life is at minimum limiting and likely demands an invalid closure of the space between self and personality. The full self will never align with the way the personality is read – whether or not psychic extension is canvased as feasible. The self is more than character, a fact to which the novel of psychic connection is especially attuned.

Self-Realization and the Universal Consciousness

Lawrence and contemporaries like Sinclair write at a time when there is considerable speculation about the philosophical implications of telepathy being real. This seeps into Lawrence's thinking during his education. Among Lawrence's earliest surviving writings is a letter in which he outlines a sense of the self as fundamentally connected. In 1907, at the age of twenty-two, three years prior to the publication of his first novel, Lawrence writes to the Reverend Robert Reid, the minister at Eastwood Congregational Church – then his local church. In it, he expounds upon his personal faith, asserting that he 'believe[s] that a man is converted when first he hears the low, vast murmur of life, human life, troubling his hitherto unconscious self'. For Lawrence, 'most are born again on entering manhood', when, he contends, 'they are born to humanity, to a consciousness of all the laughing, and the never-ceasing murmur of pain and sorrow that comes from the terrible multitudes of brothers' (Boulton 39–40). As such, the human belonging Lawrence describes is one which is founded upon an invisible communication, whereby expressions of emotion emanate and are received, the process being what gives meaning to being a member of the species. Michael Levenson's observation that, for Lawrence, 'no individual can constitute a kind', and that 'a conception of humanity can never emerge from within the self; it can only derive from our participation with others in a common life', is already in evidence (149). Later in 1907, in a letter to Louie Burrows – a childhood friend and fellow student at University College, Nottingham – Lawrence proposes 'a discussion among ourselves on the ultimate questions of philosophy raised in the education class' (Boulton 42). He specifies the matter of 'a "Universal Consciousness"' as one he particularly wishes to address. Lawrence's quotation marks and capitalisation suggest he has in mind a specific theory of consciousness to which he wishes to respond. However, the phrase is not easily pinned down – a function of the widespread speculation about the nature of consciousness under way at this time. It may be that Lawrence and his class read Arthur Balfour's *The Foundations of Belief*, from 1894, which identifies a universal consciousness with God. For Balfour (who was president of the Society for Psychical Research in 1893), 'it is difficult or impossible to conceive the relations between the pure, though, limited self-consciousness which is "I" and the universal and eternal Self-consciousness which is God' (152). However, 'universal consciousness' as a concept also appears in occult and theosophical writings. Annie Besant, for one, identifies the self as 'a fragment of the Universal Self', and proposes that 'in the Universal Self is present all which has taken place, is taking place, and will take place in the universe; all this, and an illimitable more, is present in the Universal Consciousness' (265). For Besant, who Lawrence would eventually encounter in person when, in 1922, she travelled to Australia on the same ship as him (Roberts, Boulton and Mansfield 235), no 'memory of events [is] stored up in the individual consciousness' (277). Instead, she offers 'every event is a present fact in the universe-consciousness' (277–8) such that apparent recall consists in 'tak[ing] out of the universal consciousness that of which we have already had experience in our own' (279). Besant thus offers individual identity as epiphenomenal; any personal memory at all draws from the collective consciousness, rather than constituting the content of an individual mind. If the universal consciousness Lawrence refers to was encountered in assigned reading from the University College, the writer is likely to have been one with conventional credibility, but the impossibility of identifying the concept with a single writer speaks to a climate in which the idea of individuated selfhood is being contested from multiple directions.

The universal consciousness remains accepted as a baseline assumption throughout Lawrence's life, ever underpinning his enquiries into selfhood and self-actualisation. Where, in his work, Lawrence speaks to the unconscious, it is impersonal and dynamic, informed by the notion of the universal consciousness. Although Lawrence's two book-length psychological essays are named *Psychoanalysis and the Unconscious* (1921) and *Fantasia of the Unconscious* (1922), he suggests the word 'unconscious' to be ill-formed, it being in his view 'a mere definition by negation' with 'no positive meaning' (*Psychoanalysis* 13). Attempting to redefine the term, Lawrence offers a formulation which recasts the unconscious as a creative force, generated prior to individual mental activity and thus uncoloured by it, rejecting the Freudian idea of an unconscious formed as a repressed underside of consciousness. For Lawrence, 'the first bubbling of life in us, which is innocent of any mental alteration, this is the unconscious' (15), thus being 'a very different affair from that sack of horrors which psychoanalysts would have us believe' (12). Recasting the unconscious as a purer precursor to mental consciousness, Lawrence challenges the logic of the 'un-' prefix.[1] Although he does not forgo the term 'unconscious', his attempted redefinition draws it close to a universal consciousness – or, at least, the manifestation of it on a personal level.

In Lawrence's fiction the referent of the 'unconscious' is often explicitly broad and impersonal. When, in *Women in Love*, Gerald experiences psychological trauma on seeing Gudrun scratched by a rabbit, it seems to 'let[] through the forever unconscious, unthinkable red ether of the beyond' (242). Elsewhere in the same novel, when Birkin feels 'violent waves of hatred and loathing of all he said' coming from Hermione during a conversation with her, the loathing itself is said to come 'strong and black out of the unconsciousness', (104), the definite article and the suffix '-ness' combining to evoke impersonality. As in Blackwood's work, moments of trauma precipitate puncture of the limited, individuated self. In Lawrence's fiction, however, the spurs of this experience are more unpredictable than in Blackwood's; the incidents which trigger awareness of the porousness of the local self are often very minor (like the rabbit scratch). Moreover, there is not the narrative framing to foreshadow transgression. In *The Centaur*, mystery accumulates around O'Malley's fellow passengers long before he becomes aware of their true nature, and across Blackwood's work foreboding accumulates in sites of potential rupture, as in, for example, the woodland of 'The Willows' (1907). Making the causes of rupture unpredictable and mundane, Lawrence reflects a sense that the psychic forces at work are in dynamic interplay, the logic of their interaction and accumulation alien to the reasoning of the everyday self.

The penetration of psychic forces into everyday awareness may provoke trauma or rapture, depending on the level of attachment to the individuated self. For Hermione, the assertion of herself as a distinct, individuated being is undermined by a gnawing but unclear fear that the conviction has no foundation. She, it is said, 'always felt vulnerable, vulnerable, there was always a secret chink in her armour. She did not know herself what it was. It was a lack of robust self, she had no natural sufficiency, there was a terrible void, a lack, a deficiency of being within her' (16). This disposition primes Hermione to experience the influx of impersonal consciousness as negative, so antithetical is it to her established conception of herself. By contrast, Tom Brangwen in *The Rainbow*, a figure 'inferior in almost every way of distinction' (40), who does poorly at school because 'his mind had no fixed habits to go by' and 'nothing to get hold of' is entirely more ready to accept an irruption of impersonal consciousness into his awareness and so experiences delight rather than terror when it occurs (18). When Tom meets Lydia Lensky and feels an immediate attraction to her, he experiences a 'loss of himself' which puts him 'on the brink of ecstasy' (38). The compulsion towards her, founded upon an 'invisible connection' (38), precipitates 'queer little breaks of consciousness' which 'rise and burst like bubbles out of the depths of his stillness' (41). Given Lawrence's belief in a universal consciousness, Tom's epiphany, taken by itself, might be seen to reassert the favourability of an open understanding of self. However, prior to meeting Lydia, Tom's lack of a distinguished, fixed sense of self is shown to leave him poorly equipped for everyday life. He turns to drink to achieve a 'kindled state of oneness with all the world' but in doing so 'obliterat[es] his own individuality' (28). The figure who is primed to accept the penetration of impersonal unconsciousness is at risk of lacking what is necessary to survive, never mind succeed, in day-to-day existence. Individual integrity is immensely important, for Lawrence, even as the individual exists in connection with impersonal forces.

A tension between universal consciousness and desire for selfhood forms a cornerstone of Lawrence's interpretation of other writers' literature. In the commentary on Dostoevsky he offers in a 1916 letter, for example, he characterises the Russian writer as wanting to be self-less and live in 'the universal consciousness', while simultaneously wishing to be 'a pure absolute self' (Zytaruk and Boulton 543). A great novel, for Lawrence, must speak to the conflict between narrow and encompassing understandings of self. As such, for Lawrence, 'all the ramblings of Dostoevsky are only accumulated evidence of what is [. . .] succinctly, symbolically stated' in Nathaniel Hawthorne's *The Scarlet Letter* (1850) (*Studies* 313), which, he contends, 'contains a marvellous and perfect exposition of the deepest soul-processes, and is one of the world's wonder-books'. That exposition, for Lawrence, consists in the interaction between representatives of two worlds, one of mental, 'limited' knowledge and one of 'direct vibrational-contact' in the form of Chillingworth and Dimmesdale respectively (309). The pair, for Lawrence, are representatives of two aspects of reality which struggle against one another. In Lawrence's work, that struggle is often localised within a single figure. In *The Trespasser* (1912), Siegmund – the first of a number of Lawrence's protagonists in an unfulfilling marriage – becomes drawn to another woman, Helena, who spurs in him a feeling of connectedness. Helena, it is explained, 'seemed to connect him with the beauty of things, as if she were the nerve through which he received intelligence of the sun, and wind, and sea, and of the moon and the darkness' (76). However Helena cannot release Siegmund from the limitations of bodily existence. When Siegmund, while with Helena, bangs his elbow against a rock and initially denies the pain – telling himself that 'it is impossible it should have hurt me' – he belies false expectations for what a connected being can be. Wanting concert with the world to dissociate himself from the needs and discomforts of his bodily existence, Siegmund, like Blackwood's O'Malley, cannot resolve awareness of the expanded self to the limitation of bodily existence. That both Siegmund and O'Malley escape by choosing bodily death for themselves has the effect, however, of centring their narratives around the narrower, bodily self; as such, the conventional literary centre of gravity ultimately presides.

Evelyn Underhill's *The Grey World* (1904) is narratively bolder in balancing bodily and expansive selves, quickly throwing aside the initial bodily form of its protagonist. Jimmy Rogers, a child sick with typhoid, dies in the opening pages. Passing into a realm of spirits overlaid upon the physical world, Jimmy is able to muster the will to wish himself back to life, resulting in his consciousness being transferred into the body of a new-born child, Willie Hopkinson. The result is that Wille grows up with 'a puzzled self-consciousness, in which present realities were always tempered by the memory of a confused but unforgettable past' (20) and the reader, likewise, is confused in their sympathies. Where in *The Trespasser* the reader is above all invested in the health of Siegmund as a bodily individual, in *The Grey World* it is not obvious whether Willie's physical well-being should be privileged, or the health of the consciousness within him (which was, after all, introduced first and is inarguably distinct from the bodily individual). *The Grey World* appears to settle on a complete inversion of the usual balance between individual and impersonal. When Willie comes to hold that he 'daren't live the conventional life' as it 'makes me forget the real things' (303), that reality is the expansive, psychic one. Ultimately, determined to 'live the Imaginative Life' (302), Willie walks through a forest which becomes ever more fantastic until he realises he has 'burst, in fact, from the woods to the downland; from inclusion to infinite space' (308). The spatial dissemination of his being following his embrace of reality, Willie exemplifies a relationship identified by György Lukács, for whom 'attenuation of reality and dissolution of personality are [. . .] interdependent: the stronger the one, the stronger the other' (26). The personality, requiring as it does consistency in the face of continual flux, is inimical to underlying reality if not outright opposed to it; the novel favouring an expanded self has to accept that not only the bodily individual but also personality at large are problematic vectors for readerly investment. *The Grey World*, however, does not end with Willie's dissolution. One more chapter follows, the perspective shifted from Willie's to that of Elsa, the older woman who has been a guide to him, with her being told how Willie is happy and healthy having taken to bookbinding in an isolated cottage in the woods. Displaying to the reader that the bodily Willie has survived the dissolution of the expansive entity, there is a sense of *The Grey World* giving away the personal motivation underlying its interest in expansive selfhood – that is, the favourable effect on the local individual of the dedication to the expanded self.

Lawrence's *Sons and Lovers* (1913) provides a more cautious, more nuanced reflection on the effects on the bodily individual of compulsion towards transcendence of the local self. It suggests the local self to be a contingent formation, Lawrence innovating with narrative ambiguity to communicate fluid, overlapping subjectivities. For Helen Baron, one feature of *Sons and Lovers* is that Lawrence 'demonstrably uses different styles' with the effect being 'to scatter the ego-centric "I" of perception and wreck the illusion of a rational consciousness that steadily filters and controls experience' (361). She highlights Lawrence's use of ambiguous and idiosyncratic constructions to obscure who is thinking a given thought or experiencing a given sensation. For instance, when Lawrence writes of Paul and his mother that 'a tinge of loneliness was creeping in again, between her and him' (77), there is no clear origin for that feeling in either character – and, indeed, 'between' may imply it is experienced by both, or that it occupies a liminal hinterland, an obstruction in an impersonal area of mind. When Lawrence leaves ambiguous who experiences given feelings or thoughts, it is in part a function of representing the blurred boundaries of the self, but also a function of the fact that consistent, precise awareness is incompatible with a world in which consciousness exists in a multi-layered domain of fluctuating forces. A variable strength of feeling, or a variable level of awareness, is fundamental to a world of mental forces, and a narrator with consistent, precise knowledge cannot help but neutralise this and thus distort even while narrating in good faith. For Baron, however, while Lawrence enacts 'the dissolving of identity and consciousness, [and] the capacity for individuals to fuse with or be altered by each other and their environment' (361), he 'does not discuss and expound a *concept* of the "Unconscious"' (377, emphasis from source). Such didactic discussion, however, abounds elsewhere in Lawrence's work (in his essays, especially) and is unsuited to either the sensing, sympathising narrator of *Sons and Lovers*, or to Paul as a figure. Closely attentive to his mental existence, Paul strives to deduce the nature of his mental being from what he feels, rather than what he thinks. Paul identifies recurrent patterns of feeling, with limited imposition of reason; he, like Lawrence, distrusts thought (as opposed to feeling), as unverifiable on a personal, subjective level.

Aware of consciousness as overflowing the apparent boundaries of the individual, Paul confronts existential doubt – to identify with his bodily self, or to embrace a wider being and face dissociation from the bodily self. Wrestling with Hamlet's great dilemma, Paul determines to be, but associates being with inertness and loss of self. As he reasons, 'night, and death, and stillness, and inaction, this seemed like *being*. To be alive, to be urgent and insistent – that was *not-to-be*' (331, emphasis from source). Contradictory on the surface, Paul's sense is that individual resistance to impersonal forces means a more limited existence – a lesser being. For Paul, 'to be rid of our individuality, which is our will, which is our effort – to live effortless, a kind of conscious sleep – that is very beautiful, I think – that is our afterlife – our immortality' (331–2). The problem Paul's reasoning runs into is that an individual effort to be effortless is self-defeating by nature – the stronger his will to be will-less, the further Paul himself gets from the immortality he identifies. This seemingly intractable tension is one Lawrence suggests can be resolved through cooperation with other bodily individuals. Psychic efforts producing, for Lawrence, forces, interaction with a counterparty or counterparties can allow the expression of will to be balanced. As Lawrence contends in *Psychoanalysis and the Unconscious*, 'no human being can develop save through the polarized connection with other beings' (40). Paul's sense of purposelessness after the death of his mother, with whom he had 'shared lives' (142) and 'knitted together in perfect intimacy' (172) – in neither case metaphorically – is suggestive of the fact that expansive self is given definition by interactions and concentrations of psychic force which depend on others. Without his mother, the expanded self he had identified himself with can no longer exist. To go on living requires living as a new person. His decision in the final paragraph of the novel to turn away from darkness and to turn away from his mother brings about his personal ending, just as his Hamletian reflections expect: Paul choses life and ceases to be.

The Bodily Effect of Psychic Forces and the Connected Individual

Rendering consciousness as diffuse across the universe, Lawrence often draws upon the terminology of psychical speculation when articulating the means by which psychic forces interact, including both mesmerism and telepathy. Lawrence's work resembles nineteenth-century mesmerist fiction in evoking a 'magnetic' energy which can engender the enrapture of one party by another, differing from his contemporaries who offer a telepathy which exists as a metaphysical phenomenon, thoughts and feelings floating between minds without direct effect on the physical world. However, unlike in nineteenth-century mesmerist fiction, Lawrence's mesmerism is multipartite and multipolar, the magnetism he sees between people requiring opposed poles, both pushing one another. Lawrence's psychic forces, delicate in their balance, fluctuate in response to the changing intensity of the wills of the parties, generating tremulations which constitute a form of communication Lawrence sometimes addresses as telepathic, albeit generally with qualifiers marking it as independent of the mind, a communication of drives rather than thoughts.

By the first decades of the twentieth century, psychical speculators tend to estrange telepathy from the physical world. In a 1915 volume of the *Proceedings of the Society for Psychical Research*, Eleanor Sidgwick suggests that the view that telepathy between the living is physical is 'more and more improbable as our knowledge increases', her contention being that 'telepathic communication between spirits in the body is similar in kind to communication between spirits out of the body', with, indeed, 'the body [. . .] a great hindrance to any awareness, or full manifestation, of such communication' (318). In 1918, W. F. Barrett contends that 'telepathy cannot be explained by any known method of mechanical transmission of "brain-waves" through the ether, or other forms of radiant physical action' on account of the fact that the intensity of telepathic transmissions do not diminish with distance (257), offering instead that telepathy may be 'the direct operation of a transcendental part of our being which is not conditioned in matter or space' (259). This informs telepathy's typical depiction in literature of the day, wherein the absence of physical evidence for apparent telepathic occurrences sees it conceptualised as metaphysical. In Underhill's *The Grey World*, telepathy is a feature of the distinct spiritual domain. Jimmy, after his death, finds that between him and other spirits 'a mysterious telepathy seemed to be established' as he can 'read deeper and deeper into the unhappy minds that were travelling beside him' (14). Having experienced this metaphysical connection motivates his inattention to the physical after his rebirth in Willie. Focusing on the mind to the exclusion of the body empowers him; it is by going 'to a place of pure thought' (364) that he is able to hear his mother 'like a voice within his own mind' after her death (262–3) For Sinclair, telepathy is also without grounding in the physical world, being associated with a motionlessness. In *The Flaw in the Crystal*, to use her power Agatha tunes in on a part of herself 'poised in the ultimate unspeakable stillness, beyond death, beyond birth, beyond the movements, the vehemences, the agitations of the world' (62). From her exalted perspective, she sees the ordinary physical world as permeable, finding it 'radiant, vibrant, and, as it were, infinitely transparent' (74–5). Telepathy for Underhill passes over, for Sinclair it passes through, unlike for Lawrence, for whom it shakes and even breaks, involving the 'sending out [of] intense vibrations' with 'telepathy, like a radium-effluence, vibrating fear principally' (*Kangaroo* 299–300). Telepathy is, for Lawrence, 'not brain-power' but 'in some ways, the very *reverse* of brain-power: it might be called the acme of stupidity' as an expression of 'the pre-mental form of consciousness' (299, emphasis from source). When, then, Thalia Trigoni suggests that for Lawrence 'a body is an intelligent cognitive agent capable of performing complicated cognitive actions of which the conscious mind is unaware' (n.p.), it loses the key particularity of Lawrence's bodily consciousness and the 'vertebral telepathy' it engenders (299) – that it is consciousness entirely without intelligence.

Writing against his peers' emphasis on the mind in transcending individuated selfhood, Lawrence sees the mentalising of consciousness as an arrestation of the flows needed to maintain psychic connection. Thus, in *Psychoanalysis and the Unconscious* he identifies the brain as 'the seat of the ideal consciousness', which is 'only the dead end of consciousness'

(19), contending that 'we cannot, even with the best intentions, proceed to order the path of our own unconscious without vitally deranging the life-flow of those connected with us' (24). As a result, states of mesmerism (or near-mesmerism) are often desirable in Lawrence, arresting the mind's insistence upon imposing order. Thus, Kate Leslie in *The Plumed Serpent* (1926), 'almost mesmerised' at a mass Mexican dance (130), is animated to feel connection. She, it is said, 'felt her sex and her womanhood caught up and identified in the slowly revolving ocean of nascent life' (131). The quiescence of the mind also animates sexual connection. In *The Rainbow* (1915) Ursula, enjoying a brief romantic liaison with Anthony Schofield, finds herself 'aware of him as if in a mesmeric state' (384). Her mind consequently 'an extinguished thing', she finds that 'she was all senses, all her senses were alive' (384). Seeing submission as an escape from overbearing mental consciousness ignites some of Lawrence's most offensive writing, including an exhortation to spousal abuse in *Fantasia of the Unconscious* (197–8). Indefensible whether intended seriously or as provocation, the rhetoric masks the fact that the submission Lawrence most demands is that of a given individual's mind to their own body, that being a means to attain heightened awareness.

Insomuch as Lawrence's vertebral consciousness is not the product of repressed mental desires, then it cannot be understood through analysis of the mental self. In *Psychoanalysis and the Unconscious*, Lawrence characterises the relationship between aspects of a person as an antagonism, offering that 'every man and woman grow[s] and develop[s] as a result of the polarized flux between the spontaneous self and some other self or selves' (41). The interaction between aspects of self is a physicalised one: when they pull in different directions, the person is stretched, as might be expected when a pliable object is subject to tension. There is little, however, Lawrence feels that the mental self can do to assure growth, insomuch as there is no innate need for mental and vertebral forces align productively. As such, when N. Katherine Hayles offers that, in Lawrence's work, 'the body centers of one person engage those of another in a fierce dialectic', the process is also one identifiable on the level of a single person (86). For Hayles, Lawrence's 'metaphysical scheme' is one whereby the purpose of 'the dualistic to-and-fro' between people 'is to reach the unconscious, that part of the psyche which is able to hold opposites in a continuing tension without needing to resolve them' (89). In Lawrence's scheme of the unconscious, more physical than metaphysical, reaching the unconscious is a question of attaining a state, rather than a question of knowledge: it is not a matter of knowing the content of an unconscious part of the mind, but of finding a way to resist consciousness. For him, 'the true self is not aware that it is a self' (Review of *The Social Basis* 336); the conscious person, in Lawrence's work, must struggle intensely for even momentary dissolution of the barriers between it and the unconscious self (or selves). However, where Hayles contends that 'Lawrence struggles to move from this abstract scheme to its application in family relationships' (89), there is an implicit assumption that there should be an application in family relationships in the first place. Instead, Lawrence tends to reject the family unit – and other social units – as constrictive to the flowering of the self, most explicitly in *Aaron's Rod* (1922), in which Aaron walks out on his wife and children on Christmas Eve. No explanation for the act is provided, with Aaron's need to escape from 'the horrible, stinking human castle of life' (228) as much justification for his behaviour as is provided. Lawrence favours the establishment of personally productive bonds, which may potentially be sexual – heterosexual, homosexual or otherwise sexual – or non-sexual, but will be contingent and temporary, the development of the self the goal above lasting interpersonal relationships.

Being reactive to the impulses of vertebral telepathy may, as in the case of Aaron, set the individual on selfish paths. That Aaron's approach to life is broadly supported in *Aaron's Rod* is suggestive of Lawrence's attitude to individuality, which, for him, is not only compatible with psychic connection, but requires it. For Lawrence, the novel arrests life when it presents the personal psyche as disconnected from a wider consciousness and thus he finds the novel's usual understanding of individuality to be an artifice. Addressing John Galsworthy, whose *Forsyte Saga* renders being a Forsyte synonymous with being an individualist, such that the 'first interference with the free individualism of a Forsyte drove him almost frantic' (599), Lawrence contends that 'in all his books I have not been able to discover one real individual' ('Galsworthy' fragment 251). Lawrence finds the Forsytes' aloofness incompatible with what he sees as a more genuine individuality. For Lawrence the delineation of boundaries between the self and other is, counterintuitively, fatal to what he considers being a 'true individual' (249). He writes that 'as soon as the conception *me or you, me or it* enters the human consciousness, then the individual consciousness is supplanted by the social consciousness' (249, emphasis from source). Galsworthy, for Lawrence, is aware of the artifice underlying the Forsytes' presumptions of distinction; Lawrence suggests that Galsworthy's aim is 'to show that the Forsytes were not full human individuals, but social beings, fallen to a lower level of life' ('Galsworthy' 212). Certainly, when Galsworthy writes of 'the irritation and regret which all Forsytes feel at what curtails their individual liberties' (536), the sweeping stroke with which the members of the family are rendered as identically individual belies the conformism needed to uphold the family name.

In Lawrence's view, the introspective modern novel also only appears to be centred upon the individual. As Lawrence contends, 'the more one reads of modern novels, the more one realises that, in this individualistic age, there are no individuals left', as people 'are *not* thinking their own thoughts, they are *not* feeling their own feelings, they are *not* living their own lives' ('Galsworthy' fragment, 249, emphasis from source). In Lawrence's view, the self-conscious, inward-looking novel enacts a fixation not on the self, but on the site of a lost self. Contending that 'the moment the human being becomes conscious of himself, he ceases to be himself' (249), Lawrence finds the modern novel engaged in a morbid and misguided project, that of trying to reclaim the self by ever more microscopic reflection on the 'I'. The isolated individual mind is, for Lawrence, both a simplification and a distortion. For him, not only is every person animated by a 'pulsing union with mankind', but it is through this union that a person can become aware of and develop their particular essence and ultimately be 'perfected in his individual being' (*Kangaroo* 302). Lawrence does not understand individuality as a matter of separateness: indeed, separateness is inimical to it. Instead, individuality is a matter of particularity, with development into a singular being dependent, in his view, on connection to humanity at large. Studying the individual without attending to connection is comparable, as Lawrence sees it, to studying a corpse in order to understand the living creature. The notion of the discrete individual allows delimitation of the object of investigation, but at the price of misconceptualising it. The boundary of enquiry becomes mistaken for a quality of the object of study: discontinuity between one individual and another is taken as an essential truth. In effect, the study of individuals in isolation creates the isolated individual.

In this much, Dorothy Richardson's claim that 'only in individuality carried to its full term can we find the basis of unity' (*Gleanings* 9) is antithetical to Lawrence, insomuch as the unit to be integrated, for Richardson, is 'the single human soul faced with its individual consciousness'. Lawrence's sense that modernist contemporaries distort what they purport to give focus to anticipates Lukács's criticism of modernism, for whom the modernist individual, 'alone in the universe, reflecting only itself—takes on [. . .] incomprehensible and horrific character' (38). In Lukács's view, human character, composed of potentialities, can only be made sense of in the interaction between individual and environment, as it is in this interaction that manifested potentialities can 'be singled out from the "bad infinity" of purely abstract potentiality' (24). For both

Lawrence and Lukács, a turn inward is a turn towards a void. Deeper elements of self are not more authentic or more eternal, but instead are less connected to material realities; they are possibilities of being not called forth by current conditions. This connected individuality underscores Birkin's image of

> a lovely state of free proud singleness, which accepted the obligation of the permanent connection with others, and with the other, submits to the yoke and leash of love, but never forfeits its own proud individual singleness, even while it loves and yields. (254)

Individuality is promoted by connection, cycles of feedback particularising. By contrast, isolation is null and unfree. Connie in *Lady Chatterley's Lover*, who has 'willed herself into [. . .] separateness' but feels herself now 'condemned to it' (126), demonstrates that, for Lawrence, there is no freedom in separateness. At the remote Wragby Hall, she not only lives 'in the void', but, individuated on the wrong terms, she is like a character in one of Clifford's stories. Feeling herself 'a figure somebody had read about', there is 'no substance to her or anything . . . no touch, no contact' (18). Individuation by isolation estranges from the flows of consciousness, precipitating the experience of non-existence.

Lawrence's connected individuality can misdirect critics who associate individuality with separateness, in spite of figures like Connie. Offering individuality as a 'doctrine' for Lawrence (237), George J. Zytaruk frames this in terms of the discrete, suggesting that for Lawrence 'we as individuals are to come to our separate fulfilment' (251). As a result, Zytaruk offers a reading whereby Lawrence is seen to suggest that 'to become one with God is a violation of the individual self', and whereby we must 'struggle not to achieve oneness with the rest of creation but to bring to flower the individual, spontaneous self' (241). The nourishment Lawrence sees in connection is not just excluded from this account, but reversed. Similarly, Michael Levenson suggests that Lawrence desires 'an individuality so radical that it no longer falls within the boundaries of humanity' (150), in light of what he sees as the 'vivid possibility' of Birkin in *Women in Love*'s 'non-human singleness' (317). Levenson's interpretation puts little stock in the redemption Birkin experiences in permitting himself to form a bond with Ursula, as well as the considerable body of Lawrence's writing in which he associates true individuality with connection. Fiona Becket, suggesting that Lawrence 'exploit[s] the subtle differences between "singleness" and "individuality"' (*Thinker* 24), points towards why the critical conflation occurs. The difference between singleness and individuality is ultimately not subtle for

Lawrence – the two are opposed in his view – but his novels frequently present figures like Connie who misguidedly pursue singleness while desiring individuality. Narrating their mindsets, Lawrence channels their terminology, with faulty thinking exposed primarily by its consequences, rather than through direct narrative rebuke. To the extent that decisive developmental events are seldom clear in Lawrence's fiction – a function of the unpredictability of psychic forces – the error of isolationist individualism is rarely signalled strongly in a single work (though *Lady Chatterley's Lover* is unsubtle in this regard), but is exposed in the aggregate, as multiple characters suffer through seeking separation.

At stake in how the novel understands the individual is what it can hope to achieve. For Lawrence, the novel should favour the extraordinary over the ordinary. He points to the Gospels as examples of a more vital literature, describing them as 'novels with a clue for the future, a new impulse, a new motive, a new inspiration' ('Future' 154). In taking the Gospels as a model, what is clear is that Lawrence sees exceptional rather than mundane human experience as better placed to distinguish the essential from the circumstantial in human nature. The story of Christ, and the suggestion that death may be defied, inspires in Lawrence the conviction that the most irresistible rules of human existence are open to transgression. The novel, in Lawrence's view, can effect change in perception and can show apparent boundaries to be illusory. Belief in the connected individual as the true individual undergirds Lawrence's project. His quarrel with his contemporaries is not merely a matter of focus, whereby addressing the minutiae of daily existence is rejected as a project of lesser value. Instead, the failure to examine other possibilities for existence is seen as a betrayal of literature's purpose and a closure of possibility, creating the limits it takes as essential. The novel, for Lawrence, may do much more. By looking beyond the limits of everyday being, the novel can expose the artificiality of those limits and, Lawrence hopes, summon a selfhood unbound by them. In this much, Lawrence advocates a speculative approach to the novel, surpassing recognised limits meaning, necessarily, speculation about the possibilities beyond. In *Aaron's Rod, Kangaroo* and *The Plumed Serpent* especially – which is to say, in the novels Lawrence produced in the years immediately before and after his essays on the novel – he experiments with the modelling and depiction of an unrestrained self, each novel imagining the development of the extended personality differently, thereby testing the efficacy of respective models. They instantiate what Lawrence proposes in 'The Future of the Novel', where he argues that the novel has 'got to present us with new, really new feelings' (155). New feelings will not happen in old social formations, so Lawrence presents new alternatives, like the extreme independence of Aaron. Interested in the potentialities of the human character more than in examining the physics of psychic connection in itself, Lawrence never drifts into science fiction, but when Lessing describes science fiction as 'exploding out of nowhere [. . .] when the human mind is being forced to expand' ('Remarks' 9), she locates the impulse for science fiction in the same place as Lawrence's impulse for his redefined, speculative novel. Moreover, for Lawrence, the novel – as a channelled product of consciousness – can itself stimulate psychic development in readers. As the narrator of *Lady Chatterley's Lover* offers, 'the novel, properly handled' can 'inform and lead into new places the flow of our sympathetic consciousness, and it can lead our sympathy away in recoil from things gone dead' (101). To the extent that the novel itself is losing vitality for Lawrence, then it must change or be one of the objects to be recoiled from.

Psychic Connection and Unpredictability

There is a contrary, counterintuitive relationship between the presence of psychic connection in a novel and the readability of character. In spite of the direct interface with other minds (or other centres of consciousness) that psychic connection implies, its presence in a novel consistently coincides with character being presented as indeterminable – even when psychic connection is conceived as enabling mind-reading. Rather than the open, porous character being marked by readability, they are instead given to unpredictable, outwardly incoherent behaviour. If psychic forces are conceived of as ever-present, ever-active, across all people, then they represent an incalculably complex influence on the flows of any given person's development. Reference to a person's established character weakens considerably as a guide to their future behaviour. Otherwise, in cases where psychic reach is conceived as an exceptional faculty, the tendency is to depict it as dissociating its possessor from ordinary paths of personal development, leaving the possessor (and others) with limited reference points for understanding their own growth. Lawrence's contemporaries regret this unpredictability, finding reason for the individual to lose motivation when development is uncertain and guided in large part by external forces. Lawrence, by contrast, sees it as activity desirable for the psychically connected individual to pursue unpredictability as elevating awareness.

In Blackwood's *The Centaur*, O'Malley's experiences are seen to render him unpredictable. He is, it is said, a man 'of deep and ever-shifting moods, and with more difficulty than most in recognizing the underlying self' (6). Impersonal psychic forces are identifiably behind those shifts. Conversing with the mysterious passengers on his voyage, O'Malley feels something rise 'out of the abyss of the subconscious', following which 'something touched a button and the whole machinery of his personality shifted round noiselessly and instantaneously, presenting an immediate new fact to the world' (29). Unpredictability is a function of reading the limited, everyday self as a whole, self-contained character. When it is said of O'Malley's mysterious fellow passengers that 'the little point of their personalities they showed normally to the world was but a single facet, a tip as it were of their whole selves' (131–2), this has been shown to be true of O'Malley likewise and, by extension, of people at large. When impersonal psychic forces are seen to be able to effect immense and immediate change in the local self, then the extent to which any decision is locally self-willed is suspect (whatever agency a person reckons themselves to have). The 'freedom in a larger consciousness' which seduces O'Malley and which leads to his neglect of his bodily self (321) consists in foregoing resistance, accepting that compulsions which feel external are attributable an encompassing universal consciousness, taking any self-interest in it to also be his.

In J. D. Beresford's *The Hampdenshire Wonder* (1911), psychic penetration is conceived as particular – as a rare, seemingly unique power – but is still associated with unreadability. The novel depicts the childhood of the psychically gifted, prodigiously intelligent Victor Stott and renders Victor as an innately inexplicable figure. Victor, possessing 'an extraordinary, and [. . .] altogether unprecedented power of enforcing his will without word or gesture' (231), is also marked out by 'the strange individuality of his thought' (231). That individuality not only thwarts others in understanding and predicting his thoughts and actions, but also frustrates Victor's attempts to understand himself. The narrator, an acquaintance of Victor's father who takes it upon himself to steer Victor's education, fails in efforts to have Victor shed light on how he understands himself. Having given Victor a range of philosophical texts – partly to stretch Victor's understanding and partly to deepen his own understanding through Victor's responses – the narrator attempts to discuss Hegel. Frustrated at a lack of direct engagement with his enquiries, he expresses to Victor that 'I wish you could explain yourself; not on this particular point of philosophy, but your life' (240). When Victor asserts that he cannot explain himself because 'there are no data', it speaks to the fact that his psychic faculties stand him in a different relationship to the universe from that of the philosophers the narrator admires. The philosophical texts, written by people without Victor's psychic faculty, employ a reasoning which is not only more limited than Victor's, but alien to his. However much the philosophers had intended to speak to underlying reality, their work reflects the world as it is perceived by ordinary human cognition. Even the dictionary and the encyclopaedia – which Victor has also been given and read voraciously – reproduce the embedded assumptions of their numerous contributors. No fiction is recorded to have been included in Victor's education; whether novels and other stories would give better, more translatable devices to understand himself is left unaddressed.

Among the philosophy Victor reads, only Henri Bergson's *Creative Evolution* draws anything other than immediate rejection: he reads it in its entirety, albeit at great speed, before adding it to a pile of discarded books including works by Kant, Hegel, Nietzsche and Hume. Bergson (who served as president of the Society for Psychical Research in 1913) is marked out in *The Hampdenshire Wonder* not only by Victor's brief interest, but also by the fact that the novel opens with its narrator approvingly reading *Time and Free Will*. What he reads speaks directly to the question of individual autonomy, Bergson claiming in a quoted passage that 'we choose in defiance of what is conventionally called a motive, and this absence of any tangible reason is the more striking the deeper our freedom goes' (qtd in Beresford 4). Victor, possessing 'a mind unbound by the tradition of all the speculations and discoveries of man' (132), appears to exemplify the narrator's conviction that 'the great restraining force in the evolution of man has been the restriction imposed by habit' (66). His lack of account for himself is a motivelessness per Bergson's scheme, his unprecedented power of reason giving him less reason to favour one understanding of himself over another. However, the elevation of Victor's mental faculties is not wed to bodily strength. His death by drowning, whether the result of crime or accident, mirrors *The Centaur* and *The Trespasser* in suggesting that psychic freedom is apt to be undermined by physical limitation.

For Lawrence, like Blackwood, unpredictability is, to some extent, a function of the unreadability of impersonal psychic forces. This is manifest in the case of Tom and Lydia Brangwen in *The Rainbow*. Tom, increasingly estranged from Lydia in their relationship, comes to feel 'a solid power of antagonism to her', which is associated with 'a curious communion with mysterious powers' (60). Those powers, strong enough to drive 'him and the child nearly mad', shift abruptly in their polarity. Tom, while working in the fields, physically alone, finds that 'suddenly, out of nowhere, there was a connection between them again', which produces 'a tremendous, magnificent rush' and leaves him feeling 'he could snap off the trees as he passed, and create the world afresh'. No dialogue is part of Tom's conciliation with Lydia when he returns home – the understanding, formed at distance, that connection has been re-established is known to be legitimate, without the need for spoken confirmation. When, as David Trotter records, the change in Lydia 'has no content' (79), the ungovernability of psychic forces is made transparent. It is nothing Tom or Lydia has done which revitalises the connection between them. On either side, the connection is not constituted by a feeling about the other party; the psychic forces underlying it do not carry reason within them.

However, Lawrence does not only attend to unpredictability as a consequence of psychic forces. He, moreover, suggests that there is a motivation for the individual in panpsychic conditions to choose to be unpredictable. This is the product of a sense that an attenuated consciousness actively accrues in conditions of uncertainty and indeterminacy, such that seeking those conditions is motivated by the search for enhanced understanding. *Aaron's Rod* most fully manifests this among Lawrence's work. Aaron, having cast away a predictable path through life by walking out on his family, wrestles with the inrush of 'a new and responsible consciousness into his mind and soul' (151). After shedding his predictable life, Aaron allows immediate stimuli to guide him, moving to London and then to Italy without premeditation, an approach to life encouraged by the mentor figure, Rawdon Lilly, for whom the form of your 'developing consciousness' is something 'you don't know beforehand and you can't' (296). Lawrence, counting himself among those who 'those who work forever for the liberation of the free *spontaneous* psyche' (*Psychoanalysis* 32, emphasis from source), sees psychic awakening as the opening of 'a whole new field of consciousness and spontaneous activity' (29). The joint awakening of the consciousness and a capacity for spontaneity speaks to a tight binding. Enhanced consciousness in the impersonal field is, for Lawrence, not only recognised, but defined by the capability to act spontaneously. In this much, Lawrence seems to articulate a relationship between consciousness and freedom which resembles the relationship Bergson perceives. For Bergson, consciousness and freedom are fundamentally bound to one another, such that he defines consciousness as being 'synonymous with invention and freedom' (*Creative* 278). The reason, for him, that they coincide is because consciousness has evolved specifically to animate choice, such that 'consciousness corresponds exactly to the living being's power of choice; it is coextensive with the fringe of possible action'. Lawrence, like Beresford, follows Bergson in identifying consciousness as the substance of freedom, but in *Aaron's Rod* the relationship is the reverse of *The Hampdenshire Wonder* – freedom comes first and an elevation of consciousness results.

When Aaron resolves to live heedless of expectations, he expands the range of his possible action. This brings, at least at first, a number of rewards. The mode of being empowers him to move away from his uninspiring colliery town and his job as the secretary of the Miners' Union, enabling him to make a profession of his previously amateur flute playing. His openness is, it seems, so compelling as to inspire a stream of figures to afford him opportunities for which he never asks. His lack of planning might appear unthinking – and, in that regard, limited in consciousness – but passivity coheres with Bergson's understanding of the interface between freedom and the concentration of consciousness. For Bergson,

> where many equally possible actions are indicated without there being any real action (as in a deliberation that has not come to an end), consciousness is intense. Where the action performed is the only action possible (as in activity of the somnambulistic or more generally automatic kind), consciousness is reduced to nothing. (152)

Bergson's understanding is tied to a sense of consciousness as pervasive and unbound from minds, diffuse but not equally concentrated, such that it is able to accrue at nexuses of possibility. Seeing the 'human consciousness [as] related to a higher and vaster consciousness' ('Intuition' 109), Bergson describes the brain as 'the sharp edge by which consciousness cuts into the compact tissue of events', holding that 'the brain is no more coextensive with consciousness than the edge is with the knife' (*Creative* 277). Open-minded and pliant, Aaron makes a maximal range of possible actions possible. His established persona discarded on leaving his family, he deliberately refuses the fixity of adopting another. Aaron, it is said,

> had wilfully, if not consciously, kept a gulf between his passional soul and his open mind. In his mind was pinned up a nice description of himself, and a description of Lottie, sort of authentic passports to be used in the conscious world. These authentic passports, self-describing: nose short, mouth normal, etc.; he had insisted that they should do all the duty of the man himself. This ready-made and very banal idea of himself as a really quite nice individual: eyes blue, nose short, mouth normal, chin normal; this he had insisted was really himself. It was his conscious mask.
>
> Now at last, after years of struggle, he seemed suddenly to have dropped his mask on the floor, and broken it. (163)

Aaron's apparent freedom does not consist simply in no longer being seen through his past actions and, with it, judged by a self he has grown away from. More fundamentally, he achieves the situation of not being an object of thought at all. No longer having a mask, he finds himself an unthinkable subject; counterparties, he finds, '*could* not really think anything about him because they could not really see him' (163, emphasis from source). That removal from the interplay of thought favours rather than mitigates an elevation of consciousness, by Lawrence's scheme. For him, thought is largely antithetical to consciousness. He holds that 'the moment an idea forms in the mind, at that moment does the old integrity of the consciousness break' ('Pictures' 171). Thought is conceived of as creating fixity and, for Lawrence, consciousness is necessarily dynamic. Indeed, the narrator of *Aaron's Rod* takes pains to point out that the verbalisation of Aaron's sentiments is a transcription of 'his deep conscious vibrations into finite words' (164). Fluidity is conceived as foundational to Aaron's being. He is a being of Lawrencian speculative fiction – a maximal instantiation of a mode of being which might, Lawrence hopes, open humanity to a better, healthier existence.

In identifying freedom with the absence of constraint, Bergson substantially accords with an understanding of freedom which László Földényi contends has only recently come to appear natural. By his understanding, Enlightenment secularisation led to an understanding of freedom which 'more than anything else could be designated *unrestraint*', this 'proceeding from the hypothesis that civilizational fate is the function of human intelligence, free of prejudice, perception, and thought' (*Dostoyevsky* 55, emphasis from source). The maximal creative potential exists with the fewest restrictions. For Földényi, the contrast is with a pre-secular freedom, wherein '*constraints* and *embeddedness* made the human being free' (59). By Földényi's account,

> With the advent of secularization, the sense of human embeddedness within the cosmos – or the sense of one's being cast into the cosmos – was eliminated from civilization's range of vision. And thus the traditional concept of freedom metamorphosed. To be free now meant that the human being wished unequivocally to be the master of not only his or her own self but of all existence. *Cogito ergo sum* is the motto of secularization, as it were reversing the earlier formulation (Which of course was never stated in these terms): *I am thought of, therefore I am.* (55–6, emphases from source)

In effect, for Földényi, faith in gods or God coincides with a belief in an order to nature, such that freedom is conceived relationally, the gods or God animating humanity to act and to interact with the cosmos. For Földényi, 'what is in play here is the much-mentioned rootlessness of the modern individual' (56). When the sense is lost that there are innate relationships between humanity, nature and the cosmos, then humanity becomes unembedded, its meaning – if there is any – no longer explicable through its apparent relationship to the entities it has been placed alongside. Maskless, and therefore without a fixed persona for others to interpret, Aaron is freed from thought, but not to feel free in thought. That he confesses to not feeling free (267), in spite of the much expanded possibility space he has come to live in, is suggestive that, for Lawrence, the freedom in separation is by nature a null freedom. If others no longer truly see him, no longer truly think of him or have feelings about him, then there is no way for Aaron to *feel* the freedom he has.

For Lawrence, unlike Bergson, embeddedness remains vital. He, in particular, insists on the need for the human being to have roots. In *Kangaroo*, Lawrence asserts that even 'the greatest of great individuals must have deep, throbbing roots down in the dark red soil of the living flesh of humanity' (*Kangaroo* 302). The unconscious, or universal consciousness, being, for Lawrence, not 'a homogeneous force like electricity' (*Psychoanalysis* 16), an embeddedness remains essential to give form to the human individual and to the consciousness accruing around them. Just as his invocations of mesmerism attribute physical presence to psychic forces, consciousness is not, for Lawrence, to be imagined floating insubstantially, irrespective of surroundings. That is especially clear in *Kangaroo*, set in Australia and informed by Lawrence's four-month stay there. In it, his nervousness at what he perceives as the 'vacancy' of Australia precipitates the fear that it leaves a risk of a dangerous psychic shapelessness. Claiming there is a 'great relief in the atmosphere' of Australia, the narrator of *Kangaroo* terms it 'an absence of control or will or form', and suggests it to be productive of 'the sense of irresponsible freedom' (27). As such, one of the chief questions of the novel can be seen to be one of how distinction as a (connected) individual can be maintained in conditions taken to be innately inimical to psychic definition. English writer Richard Lovat Somers, visiting Australia for a similar duration to Lawrence, soon worries that he is 'drowning in this merge of harmlessness' (279). However a mechanistic interpretation of psychic forces inspires in him the conviction that it is 'inevitable' that 'there will come a reaction and a devastation' to the 'freedom absolved from control' (351). The rendering of a 'volcanic pitch' rising in Somers, with eruption also 'inevitable', takes that apprehension and makes it the reality of the novel. The human being is, in effect, embedded in the environment and the environment in the human being. That interaction implies, for Lawrence, that the conditions of Australia would, inevitably, produce a very different human nature from England, Italy or elsewhere in Europe.

In *Lady Chatterley's Lover*, Connie encapsulates the sense that underlies Lawrence's fiction that the idea of predictable, stable character disregards embeddedness. Her claim that 'the human consistency and dignity one has been led to expect from one's fellow men seem actually non-existent' (266) reflects a sense always present in Lawrence's work, but especially manifest as he travels the world, that character is not only forged in an environment, physical and psychical, but continually negotiated with external conditions. Being true to oneself, for Lawrence, is ever-evolving, and it is 'vivid rapport with the mass of men' which drives that change (*Kangaroo* 302). Freedom, for Lawrence, is promoted by embracing these changes, even when they are experienced as irruptions from without. That unpredictability sits at odds with what fiction – and in particular the novel – typically approaches as characterisation, at odds with the knowability and consistency traditionally expected in characters. Even when a character acts in a surprising manner, there is an expectation that the surprising action can be fitted with what the reader has already seen, with comprehensible motivations for even surprising actions being taken as indicative that a character is well realised. As E. M. Forster writes, 'the test of a round character is whether it is capable of surprising in a convincing way' (*Aspects* 54). For Forster, 'a character in a book is real [. . .] when the novelist knows everything about it' (44); for Lawrence, a character is real, by contrast, when practically nothing can be known, when chance encounters and impersonal flows of consciousness frustrate demands for coherence.

Lawrence embraces the spontaneous and unpremeditated, not only in the spontaneous approach to life of characters like Aaron, but also in a spontaneous approach to the construction of the novel itself, allowing the coincidental and the spontaneous to inform his work. This is true with respect to telepathy. The first of Lawrence's completed novels to explicitly mention telepathy (as opposed to mesmerism) is *Kangaroo*,[2] and the first direct mention of it is the product of chance, but precipitates an extended gloss on human nature in which psychic interconnection is offered as fundamental. Somers is reading the Sydney *Bulletin* and encounters an article which offers that 'there can't be much telepathy about bullocks' (278) as it recounts an incident in which a group of twenty had been placed in an unfamiliar paddock, only for them all to fall into the same hole overnight and drown. That article, quoted almost in full, is not Lawrence's invention: it appeared in the 22 June 1922 edition of the Sydney *Bulletin* – one of eleven passages from the *Bulletin* incorporated into *Kangaroo*. Allowing these circumstantially seen articles to inform the novel as they do is tacit admittance from Lawrence that his thoughts are shaped by others in a way that is beyond his control. It also signals rejection of the idea of the novel being the creative product of a single mind, making explicit that the final form of any novel is subject to unpredictable forces and cannot be preordained. Thereafter, telepathy becomes part of the novel's explanation for the appeal of charismatic leaders – including the novel's own revolutionary leader, Benjamin Cooley.

Similarly, chance brings the concept of volcanism into *Kangaroo*, only for it to provide a model for the development of human personality returned to across the rest of the novel. An extended interpolation from another newspaper, this time the Sydney *Daily Telegraph*, sees Lawrence reproduce almost all of a 1,300-word article entitled 'Earthquakes: Is Australia Safe?' Presented as part of protagonist Somers's morning reading, the article suggests that large areas of basalt in Queensland point not only to past volcanic activity but also imply a potential threat of future volcanic activity. Finding the article 'thrilling' (168), Somers feels a permission in it to accept nature's forces as irresistible, including on a personal level: as he asks himself, 'what can a man say to himself if he *does* happen to have a devil in his belly!' (168, emphasis from source). Subsequently, an internal volcano does erupt; when Somers finds himself troubled by the once suppressed trauma of his near conscription to serve in the First World War, it is 'like a volcanic eruption in his consciousness' (259), one which he expects to have a persistent after-effect as it 'sets in hot black rock round the wound of his soul' (260). This idea, that mental consciousness is shaped by unpredictable spurts from beyond the day-to-day, is approached as universal. Somers suggests that 'the lava-fire at the bottom of a man's belly breeds more lava fire, and more, and more – till there is an eruption' (262), following which the intruding material will likely 'set[] into rocky deadness'. The chance behind the entry of this volcanic model into Lawrence's thought is not masked: not only is the *Daily Telegraph* article repeated verbatim, but the name of its author, A. Meston, is mentioned and, while its date is not provided, its publication on 11 May 1922 shows it must have been read by Lawrence while writing *Kangaroo* and immediately incorporated into the novel. The engagement with these ideas being itself the consequence of an irruption from without, their incorporation accepts – and indeed embraces – the fact that creativity is in large part driven by unpredictable, external stimuli.

Universal Consciousness and Society

In early twentieth-century novels centred on psychic connection, psychic faculties perversely isolate. *The Grey World*, *The Flaw in the Crystal* and *The Hampdenshire Wonder* all offer exceptional individuals who are either marginalised by society or choose themselves to occupy the fringes. Willie in *The Grey World*, content in his isolated life as a bookbinder, is happy that his 'Star is carried and hidden' (318). Agatha in *The Flaw in the Crystal* needs to close herself off from the world to use her power, the narration shifting to the second person to explain that 'you made everything dark around you and withdrew into your innermost self' (54). As her powers are associated with the metaphysical domain, engagement with the physical world is antithetical to their operation. Victor, finally, in *The Hampdenshire Wonder* is viewed by his father as 'incomprehensible, some horrible infraction of the law or normal life, something to be condemned' (104). After his faither deserts him, Victor's life is spent almost entirely in the hamlet of Pym, 'the most perfectly isolated village within a reasonable distance of London' (49). Even there, he is a marginal figure; educated almost entirely by books, he does not seek the company of others and is taciturn when company is present. The socially isolated positions of Willie, Agatha and Victor allow the novelistic interest in the individual to be maintained, even as the novels they feature in problematise the most basic foundation of individualism. Cloistered, wider society is not affected by their powers and nor are they able to contact others like them.

A sense that interpersonal psychic forces permeate society is more likely when such forces appear as subtle, ambiguous presences in a novel. The very fact of being in the background rather than the foreground engenders the sense that these forces are, or may be, constant presences. This can be perceived in James Joyce's *Ulysses* (1922) – particularly, for Charles Ko, in the 'Circe' episode. For Ko, the way 'Circe' recirculates words and thoughts from earlier in *Ulysses* – with little regard for their prior ownership – suggests connection between the minds of characters (749–50). Stuart Gilbert, similarly, identifies an 'intermittent telepathic communication, a seepage of current' between Bloom and Stephen in his 1930 study of *Ulysses* (57) – a study produced with Joyce's collaboration. Joyce's initial schema for *Ulysses* describes 'Circe' as 'hallucination' (Gilbert 313), with Gilbert identifying that in it 'inanimate objects, unuttered thoughts take life, speak and move as independent, zoomorphic beings' (318). Agency is granted to thoughts, albeit their incarnation implies that the thought requires substantialisation to act. As it is, 'Circe', presented in the style of a playscript, with dialogue and stage directions, excludes a knowing narrating consciousness – a 'telepathic narrator' as Nicholas Royle puts it (*The Uncanny* 45) – such that the mechanism of its flow of thoughts is unaccounted and unaccountable. Casting telepathy as a ghostly presence is suggestive of the sense that, if it is real, it may very well be unproveable and its nature essentially inarticulable in individualist discourse.

Comparably, the faint suggestion of telepathy in E. M. Forster's *A Passage to India* (1924) is sufficient to shade the novel at large. In it, telepathy is offered by Cyril Fielding as an explanation for how Mrs Moore knows, without having been there, what happened to Adela in the Marabar Caves. Albeit telepathy is a 'pert, meagre word' to describe what happened and Cyril feels the desire to withdraw it after it passes his mouth, he cannot reject the possibility that there were 'worlds beyond which they could never touch', and that 'all that is possible enter[s] their consciousness' (238). Indeed, for Nicholas Royle, telepathy is significant enough in *A Passage to India* as to be described as 'the very oxygen' of the novel. In his view, the novel functions through 'the uncertain, telepathic mixing of points of view, voices, feelings and identities' (*E. M. Forster* 83), with Royle seeing novels at large as 'fundamentally telepathic structures' for Forster. He cites *Aspects of the Novel* (1927), in which Forster describes novels as offering 'people whose secret lives are visible or might be visible' (qtd in *E. M. Forster* 84). However, when Forster adds that 'we are people whose secret lives are invisible' and that novels 'give us the illusion of perspicacity and power' (*Aspects* 44), the sense is that, even if telepathy might have real existence, its novelistic function deviates from reality, making a faculty at best fleeting and uncertain dependable in what it shows and persistent in its operation.

For Lawrence, in his call for re-energisation of the novel, insinuation of connection is inadequate. As a novelist, he suggests, his task 'is to know the feelings inside a man, and to make new feelings conscious' ('State' 221). Explicitly, he claims that 'we have to be sufficiently conscious, and self-conscious, to know our own limits and to be aware of the greater urge within us and beyond us' ('Pornography' 251). Effectively, Lawrence suggests the novelistic project should be one of revising our understanding of the geography of human feelings, including identifying impulses with origins beyond the individual. In this project, it is not sufficient to suggest the existence, or possible existence, of psychic connection – the specific fabric of connections should be articulated, even if that articulation is, by nature, speculative. Impelling this, for Lawrence, is a sense that society needs to be reconfigured, with psychic connection not only recognised but made central to a restructured society. For Lawrence, 'this doom of self-enclosure [. . .] is the doom of our civilisation' ('Pornography' 250). Speaking to the fact that 'great social change interests me', Lawrence argues that 'we must have a more generous, more human system, based in the life values and not on the money values' ('Funk' 221). This social dimension of psychic connection takes prominence in *Kangaroo* and *The Plumed Serpent*. *Kangaroo* has Somers encounter an imagined fringe political movement, the Diggers, who wish to wake Australians from their apathy. *The Plumed Serpent*, more ambitiously, imagines a revolutionary movement which succeeds in gaining traction in Mexico, drawing on Mexica gods as focuses for an awakening of the spirit of followers. In each case, it is the leaders of these movements who hold the greatest interest for Lawrence, as he engages above all with how authority can be commanded in conditions of psychic connection.

Kangaroo and *The Plumed Serpent* each imagine a good-willed authoritarian leadership, but neither finds a formulation to overcome the estrangement of the leaders from the people. Cooley, the leader of *Kangaroo*'s Diggers, articulates a Lawrencian vision in suggesting that a person who resists 'life's ever-strange new imperatives' will be damaged, claiming that 'most men bruise themselves to death trying to fight and overcome their own new, life-born needs' (112). His role as a leader, he claims, would be, as a filter for a greater voice, a greater consciousness, with 'no creed' of his own. In this much, the subservience Kangaroo expects he would encounter as leader would be founded upon the recognition of him as a conduit for a higher authority. The natural leader is, for Kangaroo, made by an ability to transmit, the narrator identifying 'the magic of a leader like Napoleon' as being 'his powers of sending out intense vibrations, messages to his men, without the exact intermediation of mental correspondence' (299). Given this kind of attitude, Michael Bell offers that for Lawrence 'the leadership ideal [. . .] was a misplaced image for something [he], quite rightly, did not reject: the more subtle and problematic "authority" of the prophetic artist' (187). The novel, which for Lawrence should carry a new impulse but not be self-conscious, becomes a conduit like Kangaroo and the writer of the Gospel-like novel must absent filters from their process. The imperatives issued by either leader or didactic novel are optimistically absolved of authoritarianism by the sense that the issuer is sufficiently able to absent personal disposition as to be a true channel.

In *Kangaroo*, Lawrence identifies two 'great telepathic vibrations which rule all the vertebrates' (300). The first of these is a 'most intense enveloping vibration of possessive and protective love' with which the leader of a herd generates a oneness within the group; the other is 'the intensest vibration of power' which the leader uses to keep the herd 'subdued in awe in fear'. This vision implies a fixity to roles: most members of the group are the receivers of telepathic vibrations, the leader the transmitter. Conformity is demanded; there is no opportunity for the group to respond to the leader, and there will be no refinement of the leader's signals in accommodation of the group's needs or wants. Unlike in earlier novels, wherein conscious connection is rarely harnessed and depends on the establishment of an equitable partnership, *Kangaroo* conceives of telepathic vibrations as continual, such that powerful transmitters cannot but impress themselves widely. Lawrence's engagement with strong leadership, which Cornelia Nixon associates with a turn in his thinking between *The Rainbow* and *Women in Love*, can be tied to an increased sense of the power of psychic transmission. For Nixon, 'in the eternal war between body and mind, his allegiance tilted noticeably, if not toward the mind, then away from the body, toward transcendence of the very physical being he had glorified in his early works' (4). However, while Lawrence divides body from mind, not only does he see the body as conscious, but it is the bodily consciousness through which a natural leader can transmit power and love – as explicitly asserted in *Kangaroo*.

The truly powerful individual, for Lawrence, is not empowered on a social level, recognised as powerful by dint of wealth, familial heritage or other socially sustained marker; instead, that leader is endowed with substantial physical power, a vector for the consolidation and potential control of, psychic forces. In this much, the natural leader Lawrence invests in at this point is not merely a figure with innate, natural charisma, but a figure so naturally designed to lead that resistance to that leadership is in opposition to physical laws. Thus he exhorts in his school textbook *Movements in European History* that

> every youth, every girl can make the great historical change inside himself and herself: to care supremely for nothing but the spark of noblesse that is in him and in her, and to follow only the leader who is a star of the new, natural noblesse. (266, emphases from source)

For Barbara Mensch, Lawrence's recognition of the authoritarian personality 'does not constitute an endorsement' as 'whenever Lawrence draws an authoritarian personality type he counters it with another personality that is honest, feeling, and what might even be defined, in the fullest sense of the word, as "liberal"' (2). However, at this point in Lawrence's thinking the linkage of the dominant personality with a more feeling personality type is a function of the physical necessity that the natural leader must have followers; it is not in service of showing an alternative to authoritarianism.

The Plumed Serpent is a more self-conscious as an attempt to write a Gospel-like novel, its ambition underscored by the fact that, in the year following its publication, Lawrence repeatedly claimed it to be his most important novel (Boulton and Vasey 371, 320, 332). Written in the same period as Lawrence's spate of essays on the health of the novel, it can be said, in Lawrence's own terms, to succumb to self-consciousness, too intentional and too artificial in its attempt to present a new geography of human feeling. As Jeff Wallace puts it, Lawrence's approach to the novel has become, at this point, programmatic, a function of which, he considers, is that 'the novel cannot avoid thinning out into a series of rigidities or postures' (226). While, to some extent, *The Plumed Serpent*'s failings can be associated with the flawed project of the revolutionary leaders it offers, the result is nevertheless a novel which is both heavily invested in psychic connection and fatally disconnected from lived human experience.

Like Cooley in *Kangaroo*, the leaders in *The Plumed Serpent* see a difference between themselves and the bulk of humankind. Revolutionary spearhead Don Ramón terms himself a 'Natural Aristocrat' – a member of an elite subset of humanity he sees as uniquely capable of being 'international, or cosmopolitan, or cosmic' (248). However, Cooley, who offers himself as 'a quiet, gentle father' (113), sees himself in a familial bond with humankind at large, whereas Ramón and co-leader Cipriano see, and deepen, a gulf between themselves and others. Claiming to be the living embodiments of Mexica gods Quetzalcoatl and Huitzilopochtli respectively, they are marked as inhuman and separate: Ramón has an 'inhuman gaze' (295); Cipriano possesses 'an inhuman assurance' (323) and 'inhuman black eyes' (444). Cipriano occupies 'a dusky world of his own, apart' (313), while Ramón drifts into a 'state of extreme separateness which makes it very hard to come back to the world' (181). Much followed though they may be – to the point that Mexico closes its churches and the religion of Quetzalcoatl is declared the national faith – they are in many respects condemned to a similar fate to Victor Stott, isolated by a power supposed to engender connection. Ramón's project sees him, and Cipriano likewise, 'isolated' and under 'deadly strain' (428). Albeit *The Plumed Serpent* ends inconclusively, with Kate's decision to leave Mexico, Ramón and Cipriano's separation manifests great damage to them and their movement can accordingly be seen as unsustainable.

While *The Plumed Serpent*'s revolutionary leaders set themselves apart from the crowd to achieve their 'cosmic' consciousness,[3] a counterpoint is offered by the protagonist, Kate. Initially attracted to Ramón and Cipriano's project, she comes to understand that expanded awareness explodes the very idea of apartness. Having identified the spirit of Mexico as 'down-dragging, destructive' (50), finding in the country a similar effect to that which Somers finds in Australia, she initially sees this as leaving the Mexican people without integral personalities. However, with reflection, she appreciates that her outside perspective has instead shown her a universal fact – that no person, anywhere on Earth, has a singular, solid existence. As she comes to understand, 'the individual [is] an illusion and a falsification', and something which 'does not and cannot exist' (390). Considering the exhortations to be a true individual Lawrence would make both before and after this – including the Galsworthy essay of 1927 – it may be best to view Kate's realisation as a quiet corrective to Lawrence's more strident rhetoric elsewhere, rather than a wholesale recantation.

Both *Kangaroo* and *The Plumed Serpent* presents the wider population as a 'mass', *Kangaroo* rendering them as automations, 'scurrying and talking in the sleep of death' (266), possessed by a '*collective consciousness*' which pushes the individual consciousness into abeyance (298, emphasis from source). Telepathic vibrations corral a unity in the mass, for Lawrence. When a Napoleon-like leader sends out a vibration, it 'encloses his herd into a oneness' (300). Lawrence's mass is like Gustave Le Bon's crowd, in whom 'the sentiments and ideas of all the persons in the gathering take one and the same direction, and their conscious personality vanishes', such that 'a collective mind is formed [. . .] presenting very clearly defined characteristics' (2). For Le Bon, the 'psychological crowd' not only manifests a separate consciousness (6), but it is a consciousness which incorporates orders of thought and feeling not found in the mind of the individual. As he writes, the crowd becomes 'a provisional being' in whom 'there are certain ideas and feelings which do not come into being, or do not transform themselves into acts except in the case of individuals forming a crowd' (6). Lawrence, similarly, finds the contents of the collective mind are not readily processed by individual minds. He offers that 'there is no Morse-code for interpreting' the 'throb-throb-throb' which is 'always at the doors of the innermost, sentient soul' (*Kangaroo* 296). In this much, the mental state of a crowd, for Lawrence, should be interpreted in terms of bodily consciousness overcoming mental consciousness; the crowd, unreasoning, is driven by a purpose transcending not only any given member, but all members, save the leader. A function of this is that, for Lawrence, 'the study of collective psychology to-day' is 'absurd in its inadequacy' (294). By his understanding, the study of collective psychology consists in outlining chain reactions of individual responses, taking the assumption that the members of the crowd are, in the first place and above all, individuated beings. The approach is unable to speak to qualities which only emerge through interpersonal interaction, or to characterise the crowd as anything other than a confluence of discrete individuals.

Lawrence's crowd, resembling Le Bon's in possessing a collective mind which cannot be analysed as the product of constituent individual minds, could be a vehicle for contesting the investment in the bodily individual as the novel's unit of character. For Michael Tratner, Le Bon's crowd has literary interest, defying, he suggests, the conventions of realism by 'merging the subjective and the objective' (2). However, Lawrence's masses are consistently objects of fear. For Lilly in *Aaron's Rod*, 'all that mass-consciousness, all that mass-activity' is 'the most horrible nightmare' (119), while for Gudrun in *Women in Love* the prospect of 'sinking into one mass with the rest' is a horror (118). They fit a formulation Armstrong offers, whereby 'the modern individual could only define him- or herself as such in opposition to an engulfing otherness, or mass, that obliterated individuality' (25). For all that Lawrence reconceives individuality as consisting in particularity rather than separation, the mass remains menacing: connection with an apparently undifferentiated populace is seen to homogenise, nullifying both individuality as separation and as particularity alike. The exaltation of human belonging and of participation in a universal consciousness does not, in practice, see the human aggregate embraced. Lawrence's novels problematise the nature of the individual and emphasise psychic connection, but they also follow so many of the previous century in having the novelistic subject use the power of narrative to articulate distinctions between themselves and the mass.

Returning to home territory in *Lady Chatterley's Lover*, Lawrence's credulity that there can be a natural class of leaders diminishes. He has Connie express regret at what aristocrats, natural or otherwise, have done to her country. Picturing industrialised England as inhuman, she wonders 'what have the leaders of men been doing to their fellow men?' answering to herself that 'they have reduced them to less than humanness; and now there can be no fellowship any more!' (153). The elevation of an aristocracy has to have a counterbalance, that being the degradation of the working classes. There is also a corrective to *Kangaroo* and *The Plumed Serpent* in the fact that Connie and Mellors are content for what they create to be personal and private, known only to them during their secret encounters. Identifying sexual desire as the 'flame of another consciousness' (221), *Lady Chatterley's Lover* recentres physical intimacy as a precipitator of connection. Unlike in *Kangaroo* and *The Plumed Serpent*, there is no call to restructure society to promote greater interpersonal connection. In restricting his focus, Lawrence avoids the social consciousness supplanting the individual consciousness, the failure he diagnoses in Galsworthy and which he unselfconsciously repeats for much of the 1920s. The stratified social systems of *Kangaroo* and *The Plumed Serpent*, whatever underlying intent there may be, each oppose 'true' individuality as Lawrence had long understood it. His own caution that 'the novel can help us to live as no other utterance can help us', though 'it can also pervert us as no other can' ('Morality' 245) is demonstrated by those novels. In them, Lawrence comes to privilege the visionary over the vision and with it manufactures a separation of the visionary from humanity as a whole.

By retreating from the grand visions of his preceding novels, Lawrence reconnects with the personal as valuable. His desire for reinvention of the novel with 'a new impulse' and 'a new motive' having propelled the generation of artificially distinct figures in *Kangaroo* and *The Plumed Serpent*, in *Lady Chatterley's Lover* he accepts the personal new impulse and motive of Connie and Mellors's intimacy as sufficiently significant, even as the spark their sexual connection generates resembles billions in human history. He avoids specifying how the 'flame of another consciousness' which is kindled through Connie and Mellors's intimacy should be conceived (212): where previous novels provided explicit, extended accounts of telepathy and bodily consciousness, the sexual connection in *Lady Chatterley's Lover* offers sufficient relatability for this to be excluded. Only in the sense that this bodily connection rouses a consciousness does Lawrence show that it remains for him an item with content – content he now does not attempt to verbalise, cognisant of its untranslatability.

Across Lawrence's fiction, however, the emphasis on connected individuality opposes the universalising of the individual subject which Armstrong suggests novels cannot avoid. For Lawrence, an individual who is universalisable dissolves; Lawrence's most fully realised characters, including Paul Morel, Ursula Brangwen and Rupert Birkin, are not easily read as types, with learning embedded in their particular life situations. Lawrence's individual being defined by particularity rather than by separateness, idiosyncrasy amounts to a defence of the self. As the boundaries of consciousness are seen as porous, sharing characteristics with others implies not just resemblance, but more substantive fusion. Figures like Birkin or Cooley strive for self-definition as explicit defence against subsumption into the universal. What the likes of Paul Morel and Connie Chatterley recognise is that this dissolution is not obliteration: the thoughts and feelings which had been identified with the individual self persist even as a new form of being is generated. This also paves the way for a new form of novel, one in which agency is dissociated from the bodily individual, attributed instead to thought itself. As Stapledon, Huxley, Lessing and others take the novel of psychic connection through the twentieth century, the assumption that the bodily individual must be the novel's primary unit of character is rejected. While Lawrence is not alone in the early twentieth century in probing what a psychically connected novel can be, his sense that the unpredictability of connected development is to be embraced rather than feared sees his work energise subsequent writers convinced there is no self other than the connected self.

Chapter 2

Olaf Stapledon and the Scope of Interpersonal Connection

Across the 1930s, Olaf Stapledon produced three novels of unprecedented scale – 1930's *Last and First Men*, 1932's *Last Men in London* and 1937's *Star Maker*. Each spans billions of years, imagining potential trajectories for the development of humankind and its relationship to the universe at large. In so doing, Stapledon probes the limits of the novel as a form, testing the binding of the novel to individualism through rescaling far away from the lifespan of the individual, to cover the rise and fall of species and solar systems. Zoomed out to this degree, Stapledon's cosmic novels challenge the most basic interpretative apparatus. For Frederic Jameson, the scale of Stapledon's cosmic novels means that 'human beings can scarcely even recognize themselves any longer' (168), meaning, in his view, that the novels must 'be allegorized [. . .] in order to bring such figuration back to any viable anthropomorphic and Utopian function' (168). In effect, for Jameson, the absence of individuated human beings in these novels implies a need to read as if there were individuated human beings, that being how novels are read. However, while there is mirrored exploration of the cosmos and the self in Stapledon's work, underlying this is not allegory, for Stapledon, but interfusion of humanity and cosmos. Not only, in his view, can human thought be transmitted, but moreover that possibility speaks for a universe structured, perhaps designedly, to make that transmission possible. Telepathy, taken by Stapledon as real, allows for human thought to exist outside human minds, and so, he finds, the universe must contain something human across its expanse. Stapledon's project, then, points at a core question underlying a literature of psychic connection: that of how we are to read the spaces between people if thought can fill them. Stapledon's optimism that the cosmos is innately knowable and accommodating to the human is a vision rejected by later novels of cosmic exploration offered by the likes of Naomi Mitchison, Stanisław Lem and Doris Lessing.

Writing at a time when J. B. Rhine's experiments at Duke University were giving telepathy the veneer of academic backing, Stapledon follows the Rhines in taking as possible not only the emanations of psychic force, but the transmission of thought with content. When, for instance, Louisa Rhine contends that 'in telepathy at its best, the individual [. . .] may get an item, a fragment, but rarely if ever the connected whole of another person's thought' (260), there is concession that the transmitter's thought might be imperfectly received, but also confidence that thoughts with content can pass between minds. That assumption is also made in a large portion of science fiction featuring telepathy, but where many novels focus on the telepath as a person – as, that is, an individual character – attending to how the telepath comes to terms with the difference of their mind, Stapledon's interest is in the space between minds. As such, the assumption of a cosmos able to house thought outside minds matters more in Stapledon's case. Rendering a human element omnipresent, his novels are fundamentally flawed in their enquiry as to the limits of the cosmos, but they are revealing about the limits of the novel: bodily individuals de-emphasised, collectivities acting with common will, his novels remain cogent and coherent (albeit sometimes inelegant), belying essentialist claims that the novel is innately and exclusively fitted to speak to individual development.

An impetus for Stapledon's literary project is, explicitly, the incompleteness he sees in the individuated novelistic self – particularly the Freudian self governed by inborn internal drives. He finds that much celebrated literature of his time – including Lawrence's work – profoundly misrenders human thought by reflecting individualist psychology. In his final novel, 1950's *A Man Divided*, Stapledon has the protagonist, Victor, introduce his lover, Maggie, to Lawrence, Joyce, Eliot and Wells. Reading their work, she experiences 'a vague feeling that the whole of this "modern wisdom" was somehow incomplete, perhaps superficial' (84). Maggie, a waitress with limited formal education, is deployed by Stapledon to embody an unaffected insight: her feeling is Stapledon's, presented through a vehicle wherein substantiation need not be offered. When writing in his own person, Stapledon also speaks to incompleteness in literature. In 1934's *Waking World*, he offers that Wells 'adopts a position from which it is impossible to see things whole' (10). It is, specifically, the full power of human thought which Wells is seen to miss. Wells, for Stapledon, 'does not take the whole of man's nature into account' and therefore fails to recognise 'that the gifts of intelligence and imagination open up for man vast spheres of activity which cannot in the present state of knowledge be fully understood' (*Waking* 12).

In correspondence with Wells, Stapledon is prepared to assert something similar. In a 1939 letter, he tells Wells that he

> take[s] into account aspects of experience which you are inclined to underestimate, mainly because in your early days it was *necessary* to underestimate them, whereas in my early days it became necessary to recover the essence of them without the silly wrappings. (*Dialogues* 46, emphasis from source)

The vagueness with which these sentiments are expressed is symptomatic of Stapledon's writing outside his fiction. Sceptical of religion, but finding those who approach telepathy as a science too cautious in fitting it into a moral picture, Stapledon tends to stick to a suggestive register when advancing his own position.

Maggie's sense of modern thought being built upon an incomplete truth is compounded by reading Freud. While she is persuaded that 'we are more or less what Freud says we are', she 'just can't believe that is *all* there is to us' (84, emphasis from source). In his own words, Stapledon contends that Freudian theory 'clings to the concept of an individual whose fundamental nature is fixed at birth and incapable of any real enlargement' (*Modern* 259). That enlargement Stapledon feels is missing is an expansion in which the self is formed by interaction with the universe at large. Stapledon holds that, while an individual has innate dispositions, environmental effects 'may build thereon a nature whose capacities are no more discoverable in the primitive nature than a symphony is discoverable in the mere instruments of the orchestra that plays it'. Beyond a claim that nurture trumps nature, the idea is that environment engenders in the individual modes of being unknowable and incomprehensible on the individual level.

For Stapledon, only in the totality of relations is selfhood coherent. Not only is 'each active self an approximation to a universal self which should include all actual selves as members within itself' (21) but 'anything less than [. . .] a universal self is inherently self-contradictory' (40). In Stapledon's view, the actual self, formed and developing through a web of relations, takes as its content 'a mere ragged abstraction from the whole of things; and its values are, so to speak, nursery approximations to the only values which are coherent and final' (41). As such, a living self is not unlike a literary character: each is bound into a wider, complete existence, the values of which they incompletely reflect. Both living selves and literary characters abstract, each being a filtered element of the whole acting as a whole. As Stapledon puts it, abstraction 'consists of drawing something away from something else which is left behind.

When we abstract we attend to and think about certain characters within a complex mass of characters, and we ignore the rest' (*Waking* 116). To render the personality readable, exclusions are made, fating any reading to be a misreading. For Stapledon, the individuated literary character excludes impersonal, interpenetrating layers of self, such that any stories generated are incomplete fictions, unable to speak to imperatives emerging from the wider, interconnected self. As such, for Stapledon, there is a need for a new kind of novel and with it a new kind of reading, invested in the relation between bodily self and a broader, collective being. Little traction as Stapledon's ideas may have had in their time, they ultimately feed into the injunction behind the twenty-first-century network novel, which, for Mark McGurl, arrives in part to address 'the nesting of individual and corporate identity' in an age of social media (212). However ill-conceived the foundations of the telepathy Stapledon believed in, the imperfect identity he speaks to between an actual self and a far-reaching virtual self has become a facet of ordinary existence. The early twentieth-century novel of psychic connection anticipates a situation whereby virtual selves transmit thoughts far beyond the reach of physical selves, and develops forms suited to narrating the connected existence of today. In this regard, Stapledon's novels – and other novels of psychic connection – have, in many respects, more value than they did in their day, given that technology has made real much of the connected, extended selfhood they hinge upon.

The human possibilities Stapledon's cosmic novels present are diverse. *Last and First Men* imagines eighteen successive human species (and a number of offshoot species) stretching two billion years into the future. Among successors to our species are avian and aquatic humans and species both of much greater and much lesser intelligence than ours. *Star Maker* takes a broader perspective still. Where *Last and First Men* invests in a biological lineage from *Homo sapiens* in identifying humanity, *Star Maker* rejects biological form as a defining aspect of the human, instead focusing upon similarity in mental life. It identifies intelligent plant species as 'vegetable humanities' (131) and likewise allows that symbiotic and composite beings might also manifest human nature: on one planet, the novel's unnamed narrator witnesses flocking birds electromagnetically connected to each other, who he considers collectively constitute 'an individual approximately of our own spiritual order, indeed a very human thing' (116). The discontinuity between what these two novels consider humanity speaks to a difficulty at the heart of Stapledon's literary search for the boundaries of the human. The outcomes of his explorations of what it is to be human are, effectively, determined at the moment the terms of inquiry are fixed. They are exercises in mental speculation, in which one and the same mind determines limits and probes them.

Nevertheless, in spite of the marked differences in how *Last and First Men* and *Star Maker* define the human, the novels share an approach to probing the limits of the novel as form. Covering timeframes far beyond a human lifetime, distances far beyond the range of even the most powerful telescopes, they ask if it makes sense to think of the interplay of cosmic forces in developmental terms – whether the rise and fall of planets, or even galaxies, fits narration as a story; whether the translation of these events into language induces too significant a misrepresentation; and whether there is any legitimacy to finding meaning in the patterns which are discerned.

While *Last and First Men* and *Star Maker* conceive the human very differently, there is significant similarity in the ultimate direction these novels suggest for human development. Among the human possibilities these novels offer, telepathy stands out. Stapledon finds human development (however humanity is defined) to be oriented towards enriched understanding, and telepathy, he offers, affords almost limitless potential in this regard. As well as colouring Stapledon's challenge to the limits of the human, telepathy colours his challenge to the limits of the novel. In stretching the timeframe and spatial range of the novel far beyond any previous maximums, he demands that the reader identifies the novel's elements with alternative figurations. When *Last and First Men* and *Star Maker* describe whole species of human without discriminating individuals within them, or even groups (either subspecies or societies), then conflict and motivation cannot be located on the level of the individual. Nor, more fundamentally, can the unit of character be found in the individual. Development has to be read in terms of the collective, and desires and fears have to be ascribed to masses rather than single minds. Telepathy means collectives can constitute characters with substantively shared motivations. For Charles M. Tung, the scaled-out viewpoint of Stapledon's space fiction is used 'to generate distant views of human life' (528). However, Stapledon's universe is one in which the range of human thought is, potentially, limitless. Personal struggles may be miniscule, but, for Stapledon, human striving resonates widely, far beyond the physical reach of our species.

Such is Stapledon's willingness to go beyond the novel's apparent limits that he himself does not label his works of space fiction as novels: the preface to *Last Men in London* asserts that 'though this is a work of fiction, it does not pretend to be a novel' (333) and the preface to *Star Maker*, similarly, offers that 'judged by the standards of the Novel, it is remarkably bad' and 'in fact, it is no novel at all' (9). Approaching a century later, a change in expectations is under way. Stapledon's space fiction has attracted the attention of critics like Ursula Heise and Timothy Wientzen as a precursor to an Anthropocene novel, invested in humankind's far-reaching impact – with successors including Doris Lessing's *Shikasta* (1979), Stephen Baxter's *Evolution* (2002) and Adrian Tchaikovsky's *Children of Time* (2015). For Heise, the Anthropocene can be expected to precipitate 'stories of large-scale change and forces influenced by and yet not controlled by humans, stories about the emergence and demise of communities that relate in different ways to the planet's changing ecology' (301). For Wientzen, 'Stapledon's modernism offers a particularly apt way of modeling the scalar dilemma that Chakrabarty sees as constitutive of the Anthropocene' (80). The scale of Stapledon's space fiction is fitted to this kind of story, but the interaction between human agency and wider forces is not of the kind Heise describes. Stapledon's interest, especially as his career progresses, is in humanity's immaterial connections with the universe, rather than its material interactions with its environment. The pervasive spread of human thought is also fundamental to the way Stapledon structures and narrates his space fiction: his appeal to think collectively is a literal one. Unpacking the implications underpinning Stapledon's work gives chance to consider how much there truly is a model for an Anthropocene novel in Stapledon's example. Whatever attitude is taken to the classification of his work, Stapledon's cosmic literature, being fiction, will be read using established tools for processing long-form fiction: in this much, these works are read *as* novels. For Nancy Armstrong 'reading novelistically [. . .] mean[s] that one identifies a lack in the protagonist that he must overcome' (139). Stapledon, in his cosmic fiction, connects individual protagonists to humanity at large, or indeed the cosmos at large. By so doing, Stapledon suggests that the one true lack any individual can be said to manifest is a lack of perspective: everything is interfused with the individual if they can but see it.

Telepathy as Fundamental to Human Potential

Telepathy gives Stapledon's exceptional, expansive novels cohesion. Firstly, it offers the means by which characters are able to communicate with one another across vast spans of time and space. In *Last and First Men*, Stapledon's first novel, telepathy allows the last human beings in a dying Solar System to listen to the stories of their ancestors and also allows a representative to tell the compiled story of humankind to a twentieth-century recipient. Telepathy enables *Last and First Men* (and, similarly, *Last Men in London* and *Star Maker*) to cohere with at least some basic expectations of a novel: it lets characters, albeit almost all unnamed, from across the novel's timespan interact (sometimes one-sidedly, sometimes two-sidedly), learn from one another and, as a result of this, develop.

Over and above this narrative unity, telepathy is distinguishable from other human possibilities in these novels by dint of the interpersonal cohesion Stapledon associates with it. This is most marked in *Star Maker*, in which intelligent lifeforms from across the entire universe become connected to one another through the merging of consciousnesses. This ultimately culminates in the generation of a 'communal mind' (246) which encompasses the whole cosmos, across all of time. To be part of this communal mind is to be 'awakened into a mode of perception and thought and imagination and will more lucid than any experiencing known to any of us as individuals', a mode of perception 'of higher order' than that of the individual (125). Telepathy is, for Stapledon, the key to escaping individual limitations.

Stapledon draws upon two models of telepathy. The first is an ether model, whereby psychic waves are transmitted across great distances through the space between matter – this speaking to the kind of willed transmission J. B. Rhine's research presumed to report. The second bears a specific debt to the model of telepathy offered in J. W. Dunne's 1927 book, *An Experiment with Time*. Dunne sees telepathy as a means to communicate across time as well as space and posits the existence of a 'general observer' overseeing all thought – a figure analogous in many respects to Stapledon's Star Maker. Stapledon himself is explicit that two different processes might be encompassed by the word 'telepathy'. In *Star Maker*'s glossary, Stapledon offers that 'a distinction may be made between "one way" telepathy and "reciprocal" telepathy' (269–70). While the glossary does not address the mechanical operation of either variety, telepathy on the ether model is largely reciprocal in Stapledon's novels and telepathy, following Dunne's model, is largely one-way.

Dunne's serialism is based almost exclusively upon the experience of its own author. Nonetheless, the personal quality of Dunne's account sees it resonate widely, with many readers – including a number of literary figures – considering themselves to have had analogous experiences. Mary Butts writes in 1931 that she feels herself to manifest a 'future awareness', 'sometimes very strong, on Dunne's pattern' and 'sometimes frequent, insignificant' telepathic ability (Blondel 370–1). In the introduction to his dream diary, *A World of My Own* (1992), Graham Greene similarly sees his own experience accounted for by Dunne. Suggesting that 'time and again incidents of the Common

World [. . .] have occurred a few days after the dream', Greene asserts that, because of this, 'I am convinced that Dunne was right' (xxi). J. B. Priestley terms Dunne's theory 'not only the most fascinating, but the most satisfying' theory accounting for how dreams might presage future events (255). Others credit Dunne, albeit without having had dreams of the kind Dunne describes. T. S. Eliot nods to Dunne's *An Experiment with Time* in a 1927 letter to R. L. Mégroz, noting the 'good deal of interest' Dunne's book has aroused, and suggesting that Mégroz might put together an anthology of anticipation dreams. For his part, Eliot records that he has 'never had any such myself', but asserts 'I think that they are not uncommon' (Eliot and Haffenden 783). Dunne, then, convinces significant parts of his readership that a breakthrough in the understanding of the mind is not merely immanent but has arrived.

The enormous scale of Stapledon's cosmic works is tightly wedded to the telepathy they contain. For Stapledon, it is telepathy that dissolves distance in both space and time and thereby brings faraway beings into the range of apprehension. As such, for those attracted to Stapledon's work as potential exemplar of how literature and art at large might process human smallness and localise the human, this investment in telepathy might be problematic: there is, Stapledon's cosmic fiction suggests, little or nothing beyond human reach. In criticism of Stapledon's work, however, the presence of telepathy is consistently treated as insignificant: it is taken as predominantly a structural tool, or as a knowing departure from the credible. This fits a pattern Susan Stone-Blackburn recognises in science fiction criticism as a whole. She suggests that 'when critical attention has been focused on telepathy in science fiction, the conventional or metaphorical functions of telepathy have most often been emphasized' (241) – which is to say, it is read as a figurative rather than fundamental component of the literature in which it is encountered. What is more, Stone-Blackburn – writing in 1993 – finds much science fiction theory 'openly hostile to psi', suggesting that a field at the margin of literary study seeking credibility will not find this by engaging with fringe science with a credibility problem of its own. The situation has changed to some degree: as science fiction study has become more academically established, this has allowed research to address science's margins with more confidence, precipitating greater exploration of the place telepathy and ESP have in science fiction. Damien Broderick, in 2018's *Psience Fiction*, finds that place to be a central one. He offers that ESP is among 'three major icons' in the Golden Age of science fiction of the 1930s and 1940s, alongside space conquest and the command of atomic forces (1).

The presence of telepathy in Stapledon's cosmic novels informs how science fiction in his wake interfaces with the vastness of time and space. As the twentieth century continues, scientists advocating telepathy become fewer and more remote from the scientific mainstream, but science fiction writers nevertheless continue to pair deep space exploration with discoveries of new mental faculties. In part, it is thematically fitting that as great distances in space are explored, great discoveries in human nature also occur. At the same time as they lean into this thematic correlation, however, Stapledon's successors are doubtful that mental connection might be anything other than faulty or illusory. Thus, in Lessing's *Shikasta*, the telepathic link across the cosmos from the galactic empire of Canopus to Earth proves to distort and misrepresent – leading the colonising Canopus into complacence, as it falsely perceives cultural compatibility with the Earth it is colonising. Meanwhile, in Lem's *Solaris*, human beings intent upon establishing connection with an alien existence can apprehend nothing of its nature and instead begin to see material manifestations of remembered human loved ones. The Stapledonian wish to connect with something 'human' in the far reaches of the cosmos is, as such, fulfilled in *Solaris* in a corrupt form. In the work of Stapledon's followers a greater self-consciousness develops with respect to the relationship between cosmic fantasy and the fantasiser.

Among those who find telepathy to be a device of literary convenience in Stapledon's fiction is Robert Branham. He characterises Stapledon's use of telepathic phenomena as a means to escape a 'paradoxical bind' whereby visionaries are impelled to communicate their visions accurately, but language is too limited and too ambiguous (252). Telepathy, by Branham's understanding, is effectively a shorthand for a perfected linguistic interaction and, indeed, he links it to the enriched, subtle language of the fifth of the eighteen species of humankind in *Last and First Men*, describing telepathy as a device through which 'formidable communicative obligations' may be fulfilled. As such, telepathy, according to this account, functions as a vehicle for the communication of the truth rather than a part of the truth in itself. For Stapledon, however, visionary clarity is engendered by telepathy. *Last Men in London* (the sequel to *Last and First Men*, which offers much more detail as to how the last humans harness the power of telepathy) proposes that 'through the cumulative effect of constant telepathic intercourse, the mind comes into such exact understanding and vivid sympathy with other minds' (356). Surpassing language is required not only in communicating visions, but also in precipitating them: the understanding they are founded on in itself requires more direct knowledge of others.

This optimistic vision of frictionless communication is later contested by Stapledon's long-time friend Naomi Mitchison.[1] Mitchison's 1962 novel *Memoirs of a Spacewoman* reflects upon the possibility and desirability of more perfect communication. The protagonist, Mary, is a specialist in communicating with newly discovered alien species. Mary, Gavin Miller writes, 'seems to have telepathic abilities' (254), though her means of interacting with species who may not even make audible utterances is never defined as such, and considerable reflection and interpretation is required to achieve even limited comprehension of the species she encounters. Mary's communication is not the immediate knowing of other subjectivities witnessed in Stapledon's cosmic novels. It requires adaptation and letting go of parts of herself – of, it may be said, aspects of her nature as a human. As Mary reflects, one 'will be altered by the other forms of life with which one will be in communication, and [. . .] these bio-psychical alterations must be accepted' (18). She further offers that 'thinking oneself into the shape of one's contact was elementary when considering communication techniques', though 'one had to be very careful to think oneself back' (35). Unlike *Star Maker*'s protagonist, then, Mary does not seek the human in other beings, hoping for something recognisable to connect with: she lets the alien become a part of herself, meeting her interlocutors (who, after all, are on their own planets) on their own terms.

For Mary, the learning process has spiritual value. When she reflects that 'some day I suppose we shall be able to communicate instantaneously between galaxies' (85), she offers that work done on this has mostly been 'singularly useless', and moreover wonders 'if I really want quite that amount of communications efficiency'. In what feels like a direct rebuff to Stapledonian thinking, she contends that such instantaneous communication would 'take something out of exploration', and might remove 'some spiritual tension that comes only in isolation'. The spirit, it seems, is only ever developed in the individual. A Stapledonian meeting of minds is rejected as a fantasy – one which disregards the learning inherent in processing thought into linguistic expression.

Telepathy in Stapledon's work has also been read as a hypothetical example of a future product of human evolution. Jonathan Goodwin offers an analysis of this kind. He proposes that Stapledon 'invokes telepathic development as a consequence of the evolution of intelligence' (83), the formulation of which suggests that evolution is Stapledon's guiding concern, with the invocation of telepathy an offshoot. There is, though, reason to distinguish telepathy from other future possibilities Stapledon offers in *Last and First Men*. Humanity's achievement of telepathy is artificial in *Last and First Men* – the result of the fourth men implanting a specially bred Martian parasite in their brains. That it is telepathy, rather than any other hypothetical ability, which is cultivated by the intellectually developed fourth men is suggestive of its significance to Stapledon. It is a prospect sufficiently attractive to compel humanity to remake itself and a possibility monumental enough to give humankind a common purpose.

The idea that telepathy is an incidental feature of Stapledon's work is, though, ostensibly endorsed by Stapledon himself. In the preface to *Last and First Men*, he suggests that the novel's use of telepathy may seem to the reader a 'barren extravagance', and declares that it 'might easily have [been] omitted without more than superficial alteration to the theme' (xiv). The claim that telepathy could have been excluded from the novel without difficulty is, on a practical level, easily supported. The novel as it stands is narrated by one of the last men (that is, the eighteenth and final human species) telepathically accessing the past of all human species. However, *Last and First Men* could have been narrated by an external omniscient narrator, a change which need not have great impact upon the plot (although a narrator who knows the entire history of Earth might carry a resonance of divinity troubling for the agnostic Stapledon). However, if it would have been simple to exclude telepathy and Stapledon was conscious of this, then the question arises why Stapledon nevertheless includes it not only in *Last and First Men* but in all of his major works of fiction in some form. Stapledon's justification with respect to *Last and First Men*, that telepathy is a 'trick' – a 'radical and bewildering device' to suggest 'our whole present mentality is but a confused and halting first experiment' (xiv) – undersells his investment in telepathy: it is not a neutral choice of one potential human capacity from many. Telepathy is more fundamental to his vision of the universe than Stapledon felt prepared to admit. Telepathy appears for Stapledon to be not just a means for beings to connect more meaningfully with one another, but the means. His work can be found to suggest that there is no alternative to a literal meeting of minds if real understanding is to be achieved.

Throughout his life Stapledon shows signs of a preoccupation with the possibility of telepathy. The oldest surviving essay by Stapledon is a 1908 paper he produced while an undergraduate at Balliol College, Oxford, in which he suggests that the voices heard by Joan of Arc might have been telepathic events (Crossley, *Speaking* 82). Underlying this is a reasoning which would remain part of Stapledon's thinking with respect to extrasensory phenomena: that the most vivid of the apparent products of the human imagination may, indeed, be too rich to have been generated within the mind of an individual. A similar idea is voiced in a

1916 letter to his then fiancée, Agnes Miller (whom he would marry in 1919). Writing a year into what would be a four-year separation due to the First World War, Stapledon explains to Miller that his mental picture of her is 'so vivid and detailed and springs from such a multitudinous sense picture' that he finds himself 'tempted to believe that two minds can even pierce the sense curtain and apprehend one another directly' (130).

Following this, telepathy is present across Stapledon's novels and shorter fiction, be it uniting the universe in his cosmic works, or distinguishing exceptional individuals from the populous at large in *Odd John* (1935) and *Sirius* (1944) (the former concerns a child prodigy, the latter a chemically enhanced dog able to speak and to communicate telepathically).[2] That difference – telepathy as uniting, or telepathy as distinguishing – does suggest that there is fluctuation in the value Stapledon ascribes to the power. Addressing *Odd John* and *Sirius*, Charles Elkins offers that these novels see Stapledon, despairing of 'man's inability to overcome his nature and nurture, [. . .] move[] towards embracing the "myth" of the superman' (147) – a figure Elkins associates with telepathic ability. *Sirius*'s identification of its numerically small elite as 'wide-awake people' in communion with the spirit, able to 'hear its voice' (154), presents a less inclusive and optimistic picture than Stapledon's cosmic novels, wherein inclusion in telepathic communities stands to be universal. This is reinforced by the fact that possession of telepathic ability should, *Sirius* suggests, distinguish a class of leaders from humanity at large – a proposal which, for Elkins, indicates Stapledon's 'acceptance of biological determinism' (147). There is also an echo of the class of natural aristocrats Lawrence offers as leaders in *Kangaroo* (1923) and *The Plumed Serpent* (1926), whose superiority likewise consists in psychic ability unmatched in the wider population. However, in mitigation to this, the metaphor of wakefulness implies that others could be woken – that telepathy is a latent faculty in the wider population, rather than an absent one. That the faculty manifests in an artificially bred dog moreover reveals that telepathic potential should not only be associated with the biologically human. The benign leadership Stapledon expects from his elite also suggests that in his view a good is intrinsically associated with telepathic ability: either the spirit itself or the act of communing with it can lead a varied group to a common (and apparently valid) understanding of what is morally right. As such, even in these more pessimistic novels, the sense remains that mental communion should be associated with enlightenment.

Aside from its recurrent appearance in his novels and short stories, telepathy is often addressed in Stapledon's non-fiction. In particular, his

1939 book *Philosophy and Living* shows an excited credulity towards telepathy. While Robert Crossley suggests Stapledon manifested 'determined skepticism' towards telepathy and other paranormal phenomena in the 1930s (*Speaking* 352), this is not in evidence in *Philosophy and Living*. In it, Stapledon contends that 'there is some evidence that at least a few individuals, perhaps all to some extent, are capable of "telepathy,"' a conclusion he finds to be 'strongly suggested by recent experiments' (233). In light of this, he proposes that 'no serious student of human nature can afford to ignore' claims of super-normal powers. While he does concede that the field is 'intellectually disreputable' (457), he finds in its general dismissal a spur to probe into the area – to give it a fair trial where he feels others are not giving it one. At this point in time, telepathy has become a matter of popular excitement and academic controversy in large part thanks to Rhine's purported findings, whose experiments appeared to represent an increase in systemic rigour from the generally informal investigations conducted by various members of the Society for Psychical Research. Rhine carried out many experiments using cards with simple shapes (now known as Zener cards), asking participants to either try to perceive the cards a counterparty was looking at (testing telepathy), or to perceive the picture on face-down cards (testing clairvoyance). The apparently exceptional performance of certain participants (which many have since attributed to deep methodological flaws) was greeted by an excited press, with *New York Times* science editor Waldemar Kaempffert writing in 1937 that Rhine offers 'an avalanche of evidence which prove[s] that some of us at least are not dependent on the senses alone for our knowledge of the external world' (2). Rhine also found an enthusiastic champion within the academy in the form of Ernest Hunter Wright of Columbia University, who wrote two very enthusiastic articles on his experiments for *Harper's Magazine* in 1936. However, Wright, as a professor of English Literature, was an advocate invested in the implications of ESP for the understanding of human nature with little qualification to assess the evidence in its favour. Nevertheless, Wright was prepared to assert that 'we have formidable evidence that in a goodly number of us an extra-sensory gift has now been demonstrated' (583) and that 'after long and painful scrutiny' he sees ESP as supported by 'indubitable' facts (575). For Wright, the upshot is that 'we may be traveling toward a revolution in the realm of the mind more or less comparable to the revolution effected by Copernicus in the universe of matter' (586). Insomuch as extrasensory perception promises radical re-evaluation of humanity's capabilities, it stands, by extension, to reformulate the discipline of the humanities. The embrace of this speaks to excitement at broaching a new frontier, mixed perhaps with a fear of being left behind. Aldous Huxley also contributes to the embrace of telepathy by literary figures, writing two articles in 1934 which hail the value of Rhine's work, 'Mind Reading' and 'Science Turns to the Supernatural', claiming the Duke experiments 'seem[] to leave no doubt as to the reality of telepathy on the one hand and clairvoyance on the other' ('Supernatural' 169). There are also many voices of caution, including that of Chester E. Kellogg, who, in *The Scientific Monthly* criticises Rhine's handling of statistics, suggesting he greatly underestimates the possibility of high scores occurring by chance and highlights operational issues, including the fact that participants were frequently permitted to shuffle cards themselves (337). Having handled a set of the Rhine's cards, Kellogg also claims that the heavy printing of the symbols makes it possible 'with at least 50 per cent accuracy' to discern the symbol on a face-down card by touch ('Letters' 24).

Stapledon, long disposed to believe in human mental connection and collectivist in his political bent, betrays his desire for telepathy to be real in his dismissal of criticism as intellectual elitism. Like Wright and Huxley and the many writers persuaded by the more anecdotal investigations which precede Rhine's, it seems that, for Stapledon, telepathy's humanisation of the immaterial cosmos is sufficiently attractive, and feels sufficiently emotionally true that reasoned criticism is treated as the reaction of an establishment flailing at a threat to its status. Rational objections, however intellectually well founded, are taken as categorically unconvincing in addressing phenomena which employ neither the recognised senses nor ordinary individual cognition. Just as Lawrence deems collective consciousness 'vertebral', excluding the brain from its operation, for Stapledon telepathy is by nature beyond logic. Arguing that 'the scientist works by the method of abstraction' (*Waking* 116), he finds scientific argument calibrated to a certain sphere of existence, but unequipped to speak to or even recognise elements of existence beyond the scope of its systems. In Stapledon's view, 'as things stand, they do suggest that in the psychical sphere we are overhung by unexplored immensities' (*Youth* 111), and he proposes that psychology might 'triumph over the other sciences' if it could show 'biology and physics [. . .] to be really dealing with the physical manifestations of striving minds' (*Waking* 124). Albeit this victory of psychology is only a hypothetical one, the way Stapledon imagines it implies that for him psychology is by nature at odds with the physical sciences, with thought assumed immaterial.

Stapledon is confident enough in the power of mental interaction to assert that a person's 'dealings with others call forth in him many kinds of activities which otherwise would be impossible' and that 'not merely his *knowledge* of his own person but the actual *character* of his own person is very largely the product of his relations with others' (*Waking* 71, emphasis from source). As a medium, the novel, albeit it draws its subject in her or his social relations, does not necessarily reinforce this: it frequently presents a person's true character as constituted by a core inner self. It is this paradigm which has George Eliot's Romola feel that 'transient emotion, strong as it was, seemed to lie quite outside the inner chamber and sanctuary of her life' (235) and this paradigm which has Anthony Trollope assert that in his Lady Anna 'so did persecution with her extract from her heart that strength of character which had hitherto been latent' (284–5). In the nineteenth-century novel, experiences in life might provoke innate qualities to be expressed or repressed, but the underlying character is fixed. As such, the novel of the nineteenth century concerns itself with the constriction of an innate character rather than its construction. For Armstrong, the subject 'redirects presocial ambitions at socially acceptable goals', with the result that the 'subject adapts to a position more limited than its subjectivity, which constitutes an inner world apart and only partially expressed in social terms' (56). Growing more adapted to the world thus constitutes a contraction of possibilities. Stapledon's cosmic novels, *Star Maker* especially, present fully expressed personal subjectivity not as the unimpeded expression of an innate individual self, but as the maximisation of contact with other selves and with it the maximisation of different configurations of being. As the unnamed protagonist of *Star Maker* defines it, 'to be true to oneself, to the full potentiality of the self [. . .] demands the discipline of the private self in service of a greater self which embraces the community' (85). Through his first mental union, with Bvaltu, an 'other man' on a distant planet, he finds their 'two minds together became a new, more penetrating, and more self-conscious mind' as 'all experience of each took on a new significance in the light of the other' (70). The ability to have both inner and outer perspective on personal experience means a clearer appreciation of the personal position and a better appreciation of how that personal position limits the possible interpretations of external phenomena.

For Stapledon, the significance of the universal perspective is that establishing multiple far-reaching, diverse connections might allow aggregated patterns to be perceived, most frequent repetitions noted and thus the cosmos's predilection deduced: its structure should, for Stapledon, show the modes of being it favours. However, as the protagonist of *Star Maker* experiences mental communion with ever more beings across the cosmos, the linguistic difficulty of speaking his subjectivity becomes clear. He tells the reader that 'it must not be supposed that this strange mental community blotted out the personalities of the individual explorers', but instead that, 'though there was only the single, communal "I," there was also, so to speak, a manifold and variegated "us," an observed company of very diverse personalities, each of whom expressed creatively his own unique contribution to the whole enterprise of cosmical exploration' (134–5). Stapledon is cognisant that narrating the collective requires acknowledgement of the position of the speaker within the collective. As a literary narrative subject, 'we' challenges established modes of thought. However, when Monika Fludernik asserts that we-narratives 'force readers into accepting vague or even quite un-verisimilar situations of narration' ('The Many' 150), there is an expectation that the reproduction of everyday experience should be the benchmark for that verisimilitude. For Stapledon, the human individual is interpenetrated by the cosmos, impelling narration which speaks to both integrated and individual perspectives. *Star Maker*'s protagonist acknowledges the challenge of speaking simultaneously to these orders of being, noting that

> I am well aware that this account of the matter must seem to my readers self-contradictory, as indeed it does to me. But I can find no other way of expressing the vividly remembered fact that I was at once a particular member of a community and the possessor of the pooled experience of that community. (135)

Where Philip Weinstein contends that 'drama requires a projective narrative of "I" moving through lawful space and ongoing time' (11), Stapledon finds drama in the 'I' confronting its own contingency and its inadequacy as an articulator of connected selfhood.

Stapledon, writing in the wake of modernism's peak, shares a modernist concern that the integral personality is a conceit. As Omri Moses puts it, modernists 'felt that overemphasis on personality limited the possibilities for imagining human beings because it prevented self-invention and enforced critical paradigms that looked for secret unmovable centres guiding and motivating behaviour' (2). For Stapledon, the individuated personality is a fiction, but, given a psychically connected universe, he sees creation of the self as necessarily collaborative. As such, the individual must find acquiescence in a larger will, rather than seeking means to control creation personally. Where, for Moses, 'modernists felt that individuals can change themselves while engineering their own affirmed forms of continuity with the past without falling back on a substantive underlying sameness at their core' (6), for Stapledon a common substance does underscore human belonging. *Death into Life* (1946), which imagines the after-death experience of a group of airmen killed during the Second World War, offers that, immediately after death,

> the whole company of spirits was a strange quivering flux, criss-crossed by ever-changing new patterns of individuality and communion. Individuals coalesced with one another or broke apart to merge themselves in new corporate beings, which might presently be once more disintegrated, or engulfed in greater beings. (37–8)

Freed of their bodies, the common underlying substance allows integration into a greater self. That this induces new individuality rather than erasure implies a Lawrencian sense of individuality as particularity. Increasingly addressed in connection with the modernist moment, Stapledon does not share the sense of being as discontinuous which characterises modernism for Moses.

Stapledon and Contemporary Telepathic Speculation

Philosophy and Living cites three specific texts as valuable with respect to telepathy and extrasensory perception. Stapledon recommends that 'those who are interested in the question of super-normal powers should read J. B. Rhine's *Extra-Sensory Perception*, J. W. Dunne's *An Experiment with Time*, and A. W. Osborn's *The Superphysical*' (456). The first of these, Rhine's *Extra-Sensory Perception*, primarily details the Duke University experiments. These experiments Rhine finds indicative of 'unrecognized boundaries and reaches of the human personality' (2). He further suggests that 'a deep consciousness' of the hidden extension of the human personality might pave the way to 'a larger factual scheme for a better living philosophy'. In effect, then, Rhine espouses a vision of enhanced human sympathy through telepathy of a kind comparable to Stapledon, offering this with the anchorage of experimental support obtained at a reputable academic institution. Among Rhine's apparent findings is that physical distance between participants 'is no barrier' (46) to telepathic communion, and he speculates that separation in time may also pose no impediment to ESP subjects (though this is offered only as speculation). As such, not only does Rhine provide support for Stapledon's investment in human telepathic potential in general, but he also reinforces Stapledon's sense that it can allow transgression of the limits of both space and time.

Stapledon's next recommendation, Osborn's *The Superphysical*, was first published in 1937, the same year as *Star Maker*, and after both *Last and First Men* and *Last Men in London*. While, then, not a source for Stapledon's ideas concerning telepathy in those works, there is a common flavour in how telepathy is conceptualised. Osborn does not hedge regarding the likelihood of telepathy being real, asserting that 'it is certainly proved beyond reasonable doubt that telepathic communication does occur' (115). For Osborn, 'telepathy proves that we live in a world wherein we establish subtle *rapport* with one another' (115), a form of connection he holds 'may operate as a species of psychical gravitation which binds individuals into groups and brings them into reciprocal relationships in a series of embodiments' (117). Osborn's rendering of telepathy as a binding force, acting across serial embodiments, in particular resembles *Star Maker*, wherein minds from across the universe coalesce into ever greater unities, towards an all-encompassing collective consciousness, a 'minded cosmos' (228). The final significance of this coalescence is also similar. For Osborn, it leads to a possible 'World-Soul' (105), a culmination of all consciousness akin to Stapledon's Star Maker.

Osborn's World-Soul and the Star Maker each have a defining role as ultimate observer, though they differ in their relationship to time. Stapledon's Star Maker is an entity for whom contemplation is 'absolute' (256) and observation is also primary for Osborn's World-Soul. Osborn suggests that 'the process we call creation' might be equated to 'com[ing] into the focus of attention of the World-Soul' (122). By this, Osborn means that a future which 'may exist in thought' becomes actual under the attention of the World-Soul. Stapledon's Star Maker, by contrast, 'timelessly contemplate[s]' (233), witnessing all things simultaneously, seemingly disallowing the kind of momentaneous selection among forked futures which Osborn attributes to the World-Soul. Nevertheless, in each case ultimate truth is found on the plane of thought, and the integration of consciousnesses can, theoretically, continue limitlessly until that truth is apprehended directly.

The third of Stapledon's recommendations in *Philosophy and Living*, Dunne's *An Experiment with Time*, has particularly close coherence with Stapledon's work in its rendering of telepathy: the mechanism by which Dunne suggests an individual might perceive events distant in time resembles one Stapledon develops across his cosmic fiction. Stapledon's debt to Dunne is even made explicit in *Last Men in London*. That novel's future messenger suggests that Paul, the twentieth-century human he contacts, should read *An Experiment with Time* because it can 'help to understand the incursion of future events into the present', albeit he concedes that 'to the Neptunian mind it was philosophically naïve' (554). It does not require a far-future perspective to see methodological flaws in *An Experiment with Time*. The book is bad science, even when the contrast is with other works invested in telepathy as real. It teases local, anecdotal experience – Dunne's own dreams – into a theory of the entire cosmos; a theory wholly inelegant in its continual recourse to the invention of new concepts and new layers of reality to address the deficiencies of those preceding. Stapledon's recommendation of Dunne's *Experiment* in *Philosophy and Living* (and his embedded recommendation in *Last Men in London*) speak therefore of a failing in his philosophical acuity. However, it is only transposed into fiction that Stapledon explores Dunne's ideas (the recommendation in *Philosophy and Living* being offered without elaboration), allowing that Stapledon is at least somewhat conscious that the greatest value in Dunne's thought is as an imaginative stimulus.

Dunne's initial goal in his *Experiment* is to account for his own experiences of apparent precognition through dreams. Dunne considers himself to have foreseen both world events and personal experiences. From the former category, for instance, Dunne recounts a dream in which he was on a French-speaking volcanic island, trying to warn the residents of an impending eruption; this, he claims, preceded by a few days his reading of a newspaper report concerning a major eruption on the French island of Martinique. A more local episode sees Dunne claim to have had a dream in which a horse escaped from its field, a night before witnessing a horse escape (with similar details) during a real-life walk with his brother. Based upon experiences such as these, Dunne proposes that dreams contain fragments of both past and future experience, usually so mixed and distorted that we do not recognise this quality in them. This is possible, according to Dunne, because our consciousness exists upon a plane of time removed from that in which we have our bodily existence and is therefore not bound to a specific point in space-time. Wakeful mental activity blocks this freer perception of past and future, while the sleeping mind removes filters. Explicitly, Dunne writes of a 'dream field' which is 'something quite other than the waking field', offering 'a degree of temporal freedom denied to the waking individual' (164).

Dunne supports his claim about consciousness by appeal to the idea that an individual's movement in time (or, more precisely, space-time) is observable. The conscious experience of that movement, for Dunne, must therefore exist in a 'Time behind Time' (96). This can be linked to the approach taken by Stapledon's last humans when establishing communion with their distant ancestors, insomuch as it also involves observation from a perspective removed from normal time. In *Last Men in London*, Stapledon writes that a state of trance is entered in which the entranced 'see in a flash, as though from another dimension of time, the whole historical order of events' (363). The process of discovering the past is, moreover, described in terms associated with sleep. The narrator claims that when 'the higher centres of my brain were wholly possessed by the past' to an onlooker 'watching me during these routine activities, I should have appeared as a sleep-walker' (362). Not only, it seems, would an outsider have this impression; the telepathic explorer also experiences the 'summation of all happening, of all physical, mental and spiritual flux [. . .] as a vast slumber of the spirit, punctuated with moments of watchfulness' (363). It is rhetoric which echoes Dunne, privileging a dreaming or dreamlike state as one in which perception is freer. More broadly, the focus here is on vision rather than connection: these explorers strive to take up 'the point of view of eternity', momentarily exiting the 'stream of time' to do so (364). Though they might attempt to influence past minds, this is explicitly 'carried out from the point of view of [the explorer's] own experience' (373). Just as Dunne's observing self, operating on another dimension, can be conscious of events distant from his bodily self, removal from space-time allows these explorers to influence certain suggestible parties remote from themselves.

In *Last Men in London*, the other dimension is rendered as figurative, rather than literal. By *Star Maker*, though, Stapledon more explicitly endorses the existence of extra dimensions beyond those ordinarily recognised. In it, the unnamed human narrator, having achieved telepathic communion with beings across the galaxy, finds himself 'out[growing] the three-dimensional vision proper to all creatures' (226) – this enabling the narrator to see the Star Maker for the first time, as an 'effulgent star' at the 'centre of a four-dimensional sphere whose curved surface was the three-dimensional cosmos' (227). As such, the Star Maker is recognised by an ability to perceive all of the universe simultaneously from a dimension outside it (and, it would seem, from a perspective equally removed from any given point).

There is, though, a problematic implication to Dunne's theory that an observer on a level above is required to record progression in time – one which appears to inform *Star Maker*. Dunne himself recognises that on the second level of time, that of the observer of ordinarily experienced time, there is also a discernible progression: the movement from one state of observation to the next also takes the quality of a recognisable passage. By Dunne's understanding, this therefore necessitates another level of observer witnessing the changes in the observer below. This does not stop at the third level. Changes in each observer's state of observation imply a witness on a higher plane, to infinity.

Having thus conjured infinity, Dunne allows strange things to happen there. From extrapolation to infinity, Dunne finds a 'general observer'

(203) – an omniscient figure, identified at once as being at the centre of all consciousness and as being external to all dimensions of time. Those qualities are mirrored by Stapledon's Star Maker. Where Dunne's general observer is 'the unknown element which lies at the bottom of consciousness and mind' (204), Stapledon's Star Maker is 'the source and goal of all' at the 'depth of my own nature' (223, 224). Dunne's general observer is 'Space-filling' and 'observes everything that exists' (204, 203), while the Star Maker is said, comparably, to witness the whole sequence of events within the cosmos (and, indeed, within multiple cosmoses) not only from within, but also externally, at which level he (Stapledon's choice of pronoun for the Star Maker) sees 'all the cosmical epochs co-existing together' (233). What is more, while he is nominally identified as the creator of the cosmos, the Star Maker's major quality is that of a perceiver. The narrator, having connected telepathically with intelligent beings from across the universe, comes to find that he 'feel[s] something of the eternal spirit's temper as it apprehend[s] in one intuitive and timeless vision all our lives' (256). The narrator experiences from the Star Maker 'no pity, no proffer of salvation, no kindly aid'. Though the Star Maker has lived all lives, 'with complete understanding, with insight and full sympathy, even with passion', the narrator comes to understand that 'sympathy was not ultimate in the temper of the eternal spirit; contemplation was. Love was not absolute; contemplation was.' The Star Maker is, then, ultimately a general observer. He has passion but delivers no message to show it: the universe he created, however, is one that allows deep connection between individuals to exist: telepathy is, for Stapledon, the purest manifestation of this.

For Lem, there is literary power in Stapledon's recognition of 'the terrible disproportion between human effort, no matter how intense it is and the infinite indifference of the universe that accompanies humanity's historical struggles' ('On Stapledon's *Last and First Men*' 284). Lem, though, identifies fundamental flaws in the assumptions which underpin the Star Maker as creator. He offers that, because the Star Maker acts imperfectly (early universes created by the immature Star Maker contain 'irrevocable flaws' (*Star Maker* 220)), 'the question immediately arises: What constrains, what injures Its perfection?' ('On Stapledon's *Star Maker*' 4). To this, Lem answers that an 'even higher authority' is implied. As such, Lem induces a pattern of maker above maker which echoes back to the infinite layers of observers in Dunne's *Experiment*, albeit without the suggestion that infinity offers an outlet for ordinary logic to cease applying.

Lem's own fiction, written on the other side of the Iron Curtain, belies sympathy towards Stapledon's striving for connection, at the same time as it rejects as naive his vision of the universe as intrinsically compelling connection. His novels reflect upon the human urge to explore the universe and to experience connection to something greater as a result. However, for Lem, the existence of this compulsion in humankind does not imply the cosmos holds any reward for it. *Solaris* is the most powerful manifestation of this. In it, humanity's efforts to connect with the living ocean surrounding the planet Solaris yield frustration. While it is determined that the ocean has 'psychic' functions, and also that the ocean has 'noticed' the human travellers above it (171), they can make nothing of the ocean's character, no matter what signals are sent to it, or what instruments are used to read its activity. So impenetrable is Solaris that it provokes the conclusion that 'there neither was, nor could be, any question of "contact" between mankind and any non-human civilization' (170). However, the communicational failure may be largely on the side of humanity. As protagonist Kris Kelvin reflects in *Solaris*, 'Man has gone out to explore other worlds and other civilizations without having explored his own labyrinth of dark passages and secret chambers' (157). Humanity has turned to the cosmos for answers, incognizant of how great are the unanswered questions which still lie in it its own nature.

Indeed, a large part of the planet Solaris's fascination comes from its reflection of the human mind. In one sense, the travellers do find what they desire at Solaris. For reasons unknown memories of loved ones generate physical, incarnate beings when in the vicinity of the living ocean. As such, the ocean frustrates the ostensible reason for visiting: the possibility of connection with a non-human intelligence is ever tantalisingly close, but ever unachieved. However, in another sense, Solaris affords the opportunity for tactile, physical contact with the most deeply desired objects of fantasy – other human beings. The creations are incomplete, uncanny – built from the material of the travellers' individual memories – but nonetheless these partly human beings come to dominate each traveller's attention, ahead of the ocean. Lem, then, intensifies an implication of Stapledon's work Stapledon himself appears unselfconscious of, however conspicuous it is: that humanity's fascination is with itself rather than the outer universe and that it is harmony with itself humanity ultimately desires. In *Star Maker*, it is not so much the alien which is compelling, as the 'human' in the alien (it is, after all, the 'human' aspect of alien beings the narrator is able to connect with). While *Solaris* may not support the identification of any familiar, 'human' quality in its alien, it is the alien's reflection of humanity which fascinates. The ocean is 'psychic' to the extent it can discriminate memories from the rest of the mental landscape and can generate manifestations of them, but it is not obvious that this is anything more than an automatic process, or that any comprehension or consideration is involved. The interaction spurs no connection and certainly no validation. While Stapledon finds validation in observation by the Star Maker, Lem offers a formulation wherein observation by a creative force carries with it no discernible appreciation whatsoever.

In essays, Stapledon postulates that direct mental connection does not constitute a mode of apprehension of an entirely distinct kind. Instead, it resembles the writer's ability to identify with others. For him, telepathy and clairvoyance are 'merely strange modes of perceiving events of commonplace order', and he likens them to the 'distinctively human' apprehension 'of another individual as an active conscious person' which 'literature is largely concerned with' (*Philosophy* vol. 2, 254). For Stapledon, like Lawrence, the possibility of a direct connection with others means that individualist accounts of human psychology are to be distrusted. Stapledon contends that 'many of those who have keen sensibility in the most developed spheres of human experience, in literature, art, the appreciation of personality, and in moral perception, find the psycho-analytical account [. . .] ludicrously inadequate' (*Philosophy* vol. 1, 198). Instead, for Stapledon, 'there can be no personality save that of persons in community with one another' (*Youth* 80). Much like Lawrence's idea that true individuality is only engendered in community, for Stapledon the group cannot be removed from the individual.

Stapledon finds literature successful when individual independence is shown as untenable, either through characters enriched by connection, or through the presentation of individuation as dehumanising. He praises Thomas Hardy's *Jude the Obscure*, contending that between Jude and Sue, 'cousinship seemed to add a sympathy to their love unattainable by others', with 'their minds [. . .] very closely akin' (Crossley, *Talking* 318). This potential for mental connection contributes to 'a grandeur and a truth' Stapledon finds in the novel. Aldous Huxley's *Brave New World* (1932) he finds 'a brilliant caricature of the kind of society which is likely to result' when 'the individual becomes more and more a cog in the machine, and power lies more and more with those who plan and organise the whole great system of processes' (*Youth* 72–3). Stapledon's own novels, both the space fiction and other works, endeavour to reconfigure literature's tools, such that an enlarged understanding of selfhood is not undermined by the abstraction he sees in the crafting of character through filtering and excluding. Blowing up the novel to unsurpassed scale is, for Stapledon, not about showing the smallness of the human individual (in contrast with a possible ideal for the Anthropocene novel), but about showing the largeness each character is encompassed by and encompasses.

Scale in Stapledon's Work

The Star Maker's split relationship with time – being both within it and external to it, seeing both momentaneously and holistically – can be brought into conversation with a critical perspective invested in deep time. The immense scale of Stapledon's cosmic works can be valued for exposing the contingency and impermanence of the most ostensibly definite of items (physical objects and mental concepts alike), but it can also be valued for its interface with the aspect of human experience constituted by the clashing of scales. The mind accommodates fleeting whims, day-to-day reflections, memories accumulated across a lifetime, historical knowledge, and also an awareness of the epochs and eons our existence is situated within – categories of experience which overlap and interface with one another. As such, the difference between the Star Maker's multiple experience of time and a human individual's may be more quantitative than qualitative. He exaggerates a multiplicity already within us. For Charles M. Tung this makes telepathy a 'heterochronic device[]', insomuch as it 'trouble[s] the ultimate historicization that might integrate and make coherent the entirety of time' (531). The fact, then, that Stapledon's telepathy works across not only space but also time is vital for this effect. It problematises linear understandings of progress and development, as well as their narration: a fact hinted at by the ordering of elements in the title *Last and First Men*. As Lessing observes, reading Stapledon's fiction in itself is disorienting. She suggests that reading his novels 'means taking a leap out from our provisional and temporary sets of mind into a realm that is beyond current notions of space and time' (Afterword 307). Joining Stapledon in his cosmic striving amounts, it seems, to a mental exercise, one which takes the mind beyond its perceived limits. Thinking towards the limits of time and space entails questioning the limits of the conceptual apparatus used to think. Asking what happens to a given concept – such as, say, harmony – beyond the Earth, beyond the timescale of human life, has value, even if the answer cannot meaningfully be found when it is a terrestrial, human mind inquiring.

Not only can telepathy be termed 'heterochronic' for the reason Tung identifies, it is, on top of this, heterogenous: two differing approaches to telepathy exist in *Last and First Men* and *Last Men in London*, depending upon whether communication will be across time or solely across space. The mechanism for communion across time, which follows Dunne, can be distinguished from another form of telepathic connection which does not require dimensionally removed observation.

When communion is with a being or beings at the same point in time, *Last and First Men* instead characterises this as a process of 'transmission and reception of ethereal vibrations from brain to brain' (360). This is also a formulation with antecedent. Though the classical roots of the word 'ether' might appear to suggest Stapledon is myth-making, physicists of the late nineteenth century offered the ether as a substance of uncertain form – an apparent necessity for electromagnetic or gravitational forces to pass through seemingly empty space. With this background, the chemist and physicist turned spiritualist William Crookes offers that the ether might also transmit thought vibrations. He proposes that 'with every fresh advance in knowledge, it is shown that ether vibrations have powers and attributes abundantly equal to any demand – even to the transmission of thought' (8). Crookes was far from alone in holding such views. As Roger Luckhurst notes, 'telepathy prospered in ether-physics, because the "radiant matter" displayed by William Crookes, or the electromagnetic waves detected by Heinrich Hertz, or the demonstration of "X-rays," could all be interpreted as ethereal communications' (*Invention* 88). Stapledon's telepathy broadly follows this line of thought. However, with his major works all written in the 1930s, the appeal to the ether might be felt to have something of a different tenor from the late nineteenth century.

In 1905 Einstein declared the ether 'superfluous' ('Electrodynamics' 38), in light of the special theory of relativity. Relativity theory offered the speed of electromagnetic waves as a universal constant, which meant that the notion of the ether lost explanatory value as a determiner of their speed. This declaration quelled the first wave of voices espousing possible telepathic communication via the ether. Einstein's rejection of the ether was not, though, final. In a 1920 address at the University of Leiden, Einstein proposed that 'there exists an ether' ('Ether' 23) whose part 'in the physics of the future we are not yet clear' (20). The vague formulation provides little definitional value, effectively offering the moniker 'ether' as available for a future physics finding itself needing to label a substance between detectable matter. Of more importance, perhaps, is the implication Einstein could appear to be making, doubtless tantalising to some, that the material sciences are close to finding an immaterial substance. As such, as Massimiliano Badino and Jaume Navarro assert, 'far from killing the ether off, special and general relativity (and, to a less degree, quantum physics) caused an explosion of ether narratives into different directions' (2). Imprecisely defined, a provisional cipher for any of physical science's known unknowns, the notion of the ether could still be appealed to by advocates of telepathy:

indeed, while it remained scientifically resonant terminology, it was now freed from specific scientific definition.

Among those who did appeal to the ether deep into the twentieth century was H. H. Price, president of the Society for Psychical Research (1939–40, 1960–1). In a 1939 presidential address to the society, he proposes that there exists a 'psychic ether' which 'has mental properties' and is 'a certain level within a common unconscious mind' (31). Price's work was known to Stapledon, as eventually was Price himself. In *Philosophy and Living*, Stapledon cites Price's *Perception* as a 'classic' (451), while the two became acquainted through the Society for Psychical Research – albeit their first meeting was likely after Stapledon's cosmic novels were published (Crossley, *Speaking* 353). The praise for Price is understandable, given Stapledon's investment in a common unconscious in his novels. In addition to *Star Maker*'s 'communal mind', the idea of 'group mind' is explicitly raised in *Last Men in London* wherein a 'preparatory phase' of 'telepathic intercourse occur[ing] between individuals and between the group minds of various orders' is ultimately followed by 'a supreme moment, when, if all goes well, every man and woman in the world-wide multitude of multitudes awakes, as it were, to become the single Mind of the Race' (348).

Price grounds ideas of an ether of consciousness in quasi-scientific terminology, which sees Stapledon rating his work 'highly technical' (451). It follows a number of less scientifically inflected works comparably invested in the possibility of collective consciousness. Among those known to have been read by Stapledon and described by him as an influence,[3] 1929's *The Ascent of Humanity* by Gerald Heard offers that 'the establishment of telepathy reveals that there exists a field of consciousness which is impersonal' and collective (296). Heard suggests that 'individuality is but a boundary belt through which man is passing', and claims that 'ahead lies a new consciousness combining the peace of the co-consciousness with the intensity of personality' (297): in effect proposing the kind of mental integration described in *Last Men in London*. In *Philosophy and Living*, Stapledon also offers that the kind of progression Heard identifies is likely and not only in humankind. Stapledon writes that

> it seems more reasonable than unreasonable to believe that the ideal of progress in the direction of ever-increasing personality-in-community is not peculiar to man but is a very general characteristic of conscious beings and is in some manner deeply rooted in the nature of the universe. (403–4).

In this much, Stapledon appears to have moved in his thinking from the time of *Last and First Men*. Where in that novel the initial human development of telepathy is artificial, a fortunate acquisition from humanity's Martian neighbours, in *Philosophy and Living* Stapledon excludes a role for chance: consciousness innately and inevitably tends towards communion. By this time, not only does Stapledon's ether allow meaningful contact between minds, but it also impels it.

Problematic assumptions underlying this kind of conviction are exposed by Stapledon's followers. A connection is made to colonialist thinking, wherein suppression of existing cultures is justified on the basis that the colonised are being brought into contact with a more advanced, more universal culture. This is often achieved through plots which reverse the perspective of Stapledon's, whereby it is alien cultures that reach Earth and impose themselves upon humanity, as opposed to humanity discovering alien worlds. In Arthur C. Clarke's *Childhood's End* (1953), an alien civilisation places itself in control of humanity, stationing spacecraft with representatives above Earth's major cities. The alien rule leads to prosperity, with war ceasing, but human creativity is felt to be stifled. The aliens, termed Overlords, are accused of 'keeping us in the nursery' (141), an impression reinforced by the fact that their intentions towards humanity remain unrevealed for decades. The situation of humankind is described in explicitly colonialist terms. Groups opposed to cooperation with the Overlords are said to feel, 'with good reason, much as a cultured Indian of the nineteenth century must have done as he contemplated the British Raj' (25). These groups reason that 'even the most peaceable of contacts between races at very different cultural levels had often resulted in the obliteration of the more backward society' and that 'nations, as well as individuals, could lose their spirit when confronted by a challenge which they could not meet'. As such, Clarke implies that the creation of a universal spirit, so optimistically imagined by Stapledon, might in fact – intentionally or not – be achieved through the quelling of other spirits until only a single one remains.

Ultimately, the Overlords' purpose is revealed to be the engendering of telepathic and telekinetic powers in humanity, which will promote the generation of a group mind in humanity and enable it to join a cosmic Overmind. However, the Overlords are acting in blind faith in doing so: they believe themselves to be 'trapped in an evolutionary *cul-de-sac*' (206), unable themselves to connect to the Overmind they serve. As such, the Overlords are merely go-betweens: they provide a buffer between the Overmind and humankind, preventing humanity from addressing the Overmind regarding its intentions, even as the species is subsumed.

In *Childhood's End*, the incorporation into a greater collectivity, into what Stapledon would term a greater personality-in-community, is not associated with an enrichment of humanity, as Stapledon would offer, but with loss and incomprehension. As Overlord Karellen tells humanity in a radio broadcast, the advent of telepathic powers means that 'all the hopes and dreams of your race are ended now' (216). Only in the young will these powers develop, meaning an insuperable split from preceding generations. The young, indeed, are to become a 'single entity', whom the old will 'not think [. . .] human', and 'will be right'. Thus, the greater mind is not one humanity can meaningfully be said to contribute to, insomuch as connection to the Overmind is achieved only through the sacrifice of human nature. While protagonist Jan – ultimately the last surviving human not absorbed into the Overmind – considers the fate of the species 'not tragedy, but fulfillment' (241), *Childhood's End* offers much that makes this optimistic interpretation of events questionable. The Overlords may show faith that they are bringing betterment to the colonised group – in this case, humanity – but that supposed improvement is at the expense of existing identity and implies a traumatic, generational break in comprehension.

That there are two distinct forms of telepathy in Stapledon's novels is in large part a function of his engagement with differing understandings of the concept. However, including both in his cosmic novels, as Stapledon does, generates potential for confusion. *Last Men in London* mitigates this by localising the two, disallowing overlap. Access to the past in *Last Men in London* is associated with severance from the group mind. In it, those who work on the telepathic discovery of the past do so from a cavern a thousand feet beneath the Arctic, as 'only in a remote land, and beneath its surface, can we escape the telepathic influence of the world-population' (360). As such, the removal of these explorers is not only a physical separation from unwanted telepathic influence: it is also a conceptual removal to enact a wholly different telepathic process.

Star Maker, by contrast, allows different systems to come together. Stapledon offers the Star Maker as a contradictory entity – internal and external to individuals, internal and external to the universe, engaged and impassive – and lets him extend this through his multiple cosmic creations. The creator of innumerable universes, the Star Maker has 'conceived many strange forms of time' (251). He has created, for example, cosmoses with 'two or more temporal dimensions', with each inhabitant of such universes said to

> liv[e] for a brief period along one dimension, [. . .] perceiv[ing] at every moment of its life a simultaneous vista, which, though of course fragmentary and obscure, was actually a view of a whole unique 'transverse' cosmical evolution in the other dimension. (251)

He has also created cosmoses in which each being has 'sensory perception of the whole physical cosmos from many spatial points of view, or even from every possible point of view' (251–2). As such, the universe of *Last and First Men* and *Last Men in London* – that is, our own – has the quality of one of the Star Maker's experimental creations: a creation wherein telepathy refers to two distinct, separate abilities. Though Dunne's model of disembodied perception does not directly contradict ethereal telepathy (he does not engage with the idea of the ether), there is an awkwardness of interface. This is obscured by separation in *Last Men in London*. By contrast, the interaction between systems acts as a nexus of creative potential in *Star Maker*. As the narrator understands from his apprehension of the Star Maker, 'the goal which [. . .] the Star Maker sought to realize was richness, delicacy, depth and harmoniousness of being' (250), each new creative configuration a new form of dialogue between these elements, while the collective existence of these cosmoses constitutes a harmonic interface on another level. Of course, all this also speaks to Stapledon as a creator: he is, in a respect, as much the maker of these universes as the Star Maker – even if their existence within Stapledon's mind and Stapledon's works does not reach through to anything greater. Through overlapping these different modes of being, experimenting with time (like Dunne), Stapledon is similarly seeking harmoniousness. Mental communion, ethereal or otherwise, is key to participating in this harmony and across his writings Stapledon shows confidence that this is a key which humanity possesses (or, at least, which it can shortly acquire).

In practice, the project of exploding moral enquiry to a cosmic scale seems almost unavoidably to consist in imagining what it might be for humans to commune with other entities, so as to establish the existence of any common ground in values. However, from the start this exercise assumes humankind could connect with beings from other worlds and this assumption dictates the terms of further speculation. This is true with respect to Stapledon. In his cosmic novels, Stapledon finds that the ability to connect, to make telepathic links to one another, is the one universal and therefore constitutes the one great focus of the universe's moral system. The confidence Stapledon's cosmic novels show in building upon this foundation can be attributed to the quantity of material Stapledon encountered supporting the conviction that telepathy is real.

Towards the end of his literary career, however, Stapledon comes to show more cognisance that imagining psychic connection on a universal level means surpassing the human. In 1946's *The Flames*, he imagines a situation in which contact with other intelligences across the cosmos has been made, but not by humanity. In it, the protagonist Cass is pulled into psychic contact with a living flame, the flame having compelled him to pick up the igneous rock within which it has been trapped in a largely quiescent state. The flame informs him that it and other solar flames have 'made contact with more and more minded stars and planets of very diverse characters and psychical statures', a process which eventually saw them wake to 'be a single mind, a single-minded community of many diverse worlds' (77). Restaging the overarching trajectory of *Star Maker*, but with humanity not included, Stapledon implicitly recognises the faultiness of the sense that human consciousness must, innately, be reflected in a universal consciousness – and that the structures of that universal consciousness would be interpretable to an individuated human mind. Guided by the living flame, Cass develops telepathic power himself, but what is revealed on penetration of other human minds is the inhumanity of much of what they contain. Having 'often succeeded in observing continuous streams of thought in other human minds', he finds that 'this experience was remarkable both for its detail and the entirely nonhuman type of consciousness that it revealed' (15–16). Cass ultimately realises that reality is 'wholly alien to the spirit, and wholly indifferent to the most sacred values of the awakened minds of the cosmos', being 'Wholly Other, and wholly unintelligible' (79). Consigning Cass to the fringe, Stapledon shows tacit acceptance that narrativising the cosmos is, innately, an exercise in projection, the patterns observed functions of the patterns of human thought. While telepathy remains part of *The Flames*, it is, like the telepathy Rhine imagines himself to have proven, a near-blind groping to interpret faint patterns. Even Rhine's best participants are unsuccessful most of the time at an exercise built around receiving a minimal form of mental content (that is, the shapes on Zener cards).[4] Stapledon is still inclined to believe in telepathy at this time, claiming in a 1948 lecture that 'in view of recent spectacular but still very fragmentary discoveries in the field of paranormal psychology, it is just possible that communication with intelligent races in even the remotest planetary systems may be effected by a highly developed technique of telepathy' ('Interplanetary' 230). However, telepathy, as Rhine constructs it, is, literally, an exercise in wishing to pull symbols out of nothing, a fact which finds reflection in *The Flames*. Jameson's suggestion that Stapledon's space-and-time travellers 'gradually become aware that their receptivity to alien and exotic cultures is governed by anthropomorphic principles' (xii) misses the innately humane nature of his 1930s cosmoses, but in the case of Cass there is a stark realisation that the human mind only finds what the human mind is capable of finding.

In consideration of his work at large, the recognition that telepathy is not, for Stapledon, a structural convenience, or a 'barren extravagance', but is in fact a central aspect of his understanding of human consummation or fulfilment, could suggest the value of his vision is compromised. In that his cosmic reflections sit on such insecure foundations, their profundity can be felt to be limited. Certainly, writers in Stapledon's wake appreciate his ambitions, at the same time as they surface assumptions Stapledon makes. Mitchison demonstrates that communication, telepathic or otherwise, does not automatically imply connection; Lem and Clarke show that human nature in itself might not admit connection with alien intelligences, our minds and ways of thinking incapable of interface with alternative systems of thought. However, recognising what it is that compels Stapledon to invest in telepathy across his life also helps to secure the value of his work. The initial emotional pull of telepathy and collective consciousness is encapsulated by Gerald Heard. Heard offers that 'it is individualism that prevents men from realizing that as the new cosmology is larger than the old, so it results in a larger morality' (290). Stapledon's ambition can be characterised thus: not only does he offer fiction's first attempts to take on the full enormity of the cosmos, but he also speaks to the need for enlargement of sensibility (a need writers in his wake have continued to voice). In service of this, the unmediated meeting of minds facilitated by telepathy constitutes a symbol of a better, broader sympathy. It represents a sign writ so large that the direction in which it points should be unmistakable, albeit the destination Stapledon might have hoped for lies beyond human reach. It is this ambition that sees Stapledon's work lauded by succeeding writers of cosmic fiction (even those with reservations about his execution) and which secures the ongoing worth of his speculative work. Successors have demonstrated that Stapledon's emphasis on the human can be problematic, that it suggests an expectation other beings should meet us on our terms and that their level of resemblance to us determines their value. Underneath, though, is a desire to know how others think and feel – both humans and non-humans. The stretching Stapledon does in his cosmic novels, the reach to the most distant intelligences conceivable, remains a valuable exercise to join him in. Read against other novels of psychic connection, Stapledon's work is often naive in its assumption that there is a common material of thought capable of being formed in one mind and understood by another (a naivety much research into telepathy shares). Nevertheless, this assumption, considerable as it is, provides a footing for a scalar reach which explodes the idea that to be coherent the novel depends on individuating its subjects. However, while Stapledon is thinking telescopically, others are giving microscopic attention to that question Stapledon neglects – of what telepathy determines thought to be. Huxley, in his novels of ideas, explores what the relationship between thought and thinker must be if thought is transmissible, finding that thinking must consist more in apprehension than in generation, and thus that the novel must show ideas to create the self more than the reverse.

Chapter 3

Aldous Huxley, Telepathy and the Decentring of Personality in the Novel of Ideas

The Development of Character against the Development of Ideas

In Aldous Huxley's 1939 novel *After Many a Summer*, the intellectual Propter makes the claim that 'in so far as we're human, we're obsessed with time, we're passionately concerned with our personalities and with those magnified projections of our personalities which we call our policies, or ideals, our religions' (120). For Propter, politics, philosophy and religion do not captivate for their intrinsic worth – for the good or ill which may be achieved through them – but for the picture of ourselves which they provide. It is not only the implicit vanity of this which troubles Propter. More than this, the preoccupation with the personality and its products overlooks faulty foundations. Contending that 'individuality is not absolute', he claims that 'personalities are illusory figments of a self-will disastrously blind to the reality of a more-than-personal consciousness' (97). We should not, in effect, be trying to make more of ourselves, but less: to amplify the self obscures this other consciousness and by extension induces a failure to recognise reality. What Propter puts into words is what underlies the novel of ideas – both in Huxley's hands and in the hands of successors: ideas should be invested in above characters, because ideas shape characters, rather than the reverse.

Huxley's investment in a consciousness transcending individual personalities is wed to an intense belief in psychic phenomena. He is passionately convinced by J. B. Rhine's experiments and becomes both a friend of Rhine and a promoter of his research. Huxley's advocacy contributes to the mid-century prominence of telepathy in the public consciousness, which feeds back directly back into literature, as, in the 1950s and 1960s, stories of telepathic penetration and manipulation abound in science fiction. However, where Huxley follows Olaf Stapledon in seeing a moral imperative to harness telepathy in order to deepen interpersonal connections, the likes of *Telepathist* (1964) by John Brunner and John Wyndham's *The Chrysalids* (1955) associate the appearance of a new order of humanity with social upheaval and prejudice and question the innate superiority of the telepath.

Above and beyond this, psychic connection is an underappreciated component of the novels of ideas written in Huxley's wake. Iris Murdoch, often identified as a novelist of ideas, develops her skill as a young writer through working on 'a novel playing with Whately Carrington's [sic] theories on telepathy. Ideas. Ideas' (qtd in Lesson 50). Though that 1946 novel was not published, Carington's association theory of telepathy, whereby 'associations formed by me are effective for you, by virtue of a common subconscious' (58), speaks to a sense of psychic interdependence which informs Murdoch's published work. For Murdoch, because 'fantastic things happen all the time in ordinary life and people are very, very odd', there is 'some kind of air of open plausibility and open connection with life which I would want my novels to have' (Chevalier 72). Telepathy is directly referred to in many of Murdoch's novels, suggestive that there are linkages which fall outside ordinary systems of understanding. In *The Good Apprentice* (1985), for instance, Edward, attempting to process events following the death of his best friend, realises that he has been 'thinking about it in two quite different ways' (517). Viewed from an individual perspective, 'it's all a muddle starting off with an accident: my breakdown, drugs, telepathy, my father's illness, cloistered neurotic women, people arriving unexpectedly, all sorts of things which happened by pure chance.' Viewed holistically, by contrast, 'it's a whole complex thing, internally connected, like a dark globe, a dark world, as if we were all parts of a single drama living inside a work of art' (518). Many characters in Murdoch's work are seen to have the ability to manipulate these psychic bonds and so to enchant others. In *The Nice and the Good* (1968), John Ducane, investigating the death of his colleague Joseph Radeechy, reflects on his capacity to induce confidence in others. He has the sense that Radeechy is 'spinning in the quietness of the room a web of sympathetic atmosphere for the unwary', which the narrator identifies as 'a talent which depended upon all sorts of intuitive, perhaps telepathic, emanations of an almost physical kind' (67). Though hedged, the notion that the psychic acts like the physical reflects a wider sense in Murdoch's work that the novel interested in ideas must be prepared to speculate about ineffable, extralinguistic aspects of thought. This precipitates a conflict Murdoch claims she 'always feel[s] between character and plot' (Chevalier 72). If ineffable psychic forces are at play, their role in shaping the events of a novel will make characters less distinct and less predictable. The novel of psychic connection which focuses in on the movement of ideas rejects the individuated personality as illusory, per Propter, and with it the construct of individual motivation also falls apart.

A. S. Byatt, mentored in her early career by Murdoch, continues the novel of ideas' association with psychic connection. Her 1978 novel *The Virgin in the Garden* has schoolboy Marcus Potter and his biology teacher Lucas Simmonds 'practice the direct transmission of thought' together (149), with Simmonds convinced that Marcus has 'direct access to the thought forms, the patterns, that inform and control us' (64). When Murdoch praises Byatt for her 'excellent descriptions of the activity of thinking' in *The Virgin in the Garden* ('Force Fields' 586), it is directed at a novel in which multiple characters experience thought as at least partly transcendent of the individual. Byatt, who claims that 'I am a mystic, and I don't want to be', describes Marcus as 'a self-portrait: somebody baffled by things being far too much and not fittable into any of the languages you were offered' (Newman and Friel). For Murdoch and Byatt alike the idea of telepathy provides a means to speak to the incompleteness of linguistic and literary depictions of reality. Deployed in that capacity, the scientific credibility – or otherwise – of studies like Rhine's is largely irrelevant, save in cases like Simmonds's in which a character subscribes too doctrinally to a specific understanding of telepathy.

To operate as a novel, the novel of ideas is faced with the question of how to characterise the idea, both in the philosophical sense of identifying what constitutes an idea, and in a literary sense of how to represent an idea as an entity distinct from the thinker, developing beyond their control. This is especially true when the writer, like Huxley, sees psychic connection as real, but is still at issue in cases like Murdoch's and Byatt's, where the sense of a slippage of thoughts between thinkers is more cautiously advanced. What this tends to mean is that the person in the novel of ideas is diminished as a character, judged by established novelistic standards: with incomplete possession of their ideas, the person does not conform to an expectation whereby thoughts and feelings are explicable functions of individual experience. When Marta Figlerowicz contends that the novel's 'air of reality' comes, in part, from the 'self-sufficient complexity [its characters] seem to possess' (123), her view takes individuated readability as valid in both the novel and life. The novel of ideas, refuting this individualised self-sufficiency, is critically approached as less realistic, taken as reducing the fidelity of character to stage self-consciously artificial clashes of ideas. Thus claims like J. A. Cuddon's in his *Dictionary of Literary Terms and Literary Theory* that 'plot, narrative, emotional conflict and psychological depth in characterization are deliberately limited' in the novel of ideas (643) take the limitation of character – and other novelistic elements – as a necessary, unfortunate side-effect of the focus on ideas. Instead, the novel of ideas should be seen as refusing the delimitable character as a fiction and as exploring the possibility that the growth and movement of ideas in themselves might give the novel form – a form taken by writers like Huxley as more representative of the lived relationship between thinker and thought. Michael LeMahieu concedes too much when he offers that 'when it succeeds [. . .] the novel of ideas succeeds inasmuch as it is not quite a novel' (177): it is possible instead to hold that the conventional novel, in making plot a function of the discrete thoughts and actions of individuated characters, finds any successes it enjoys in spite of simplifying the elements it employs.

When *After Many a Summer* was published, shortly after the outbreak of the Second World War, the aloof Propter was not a well-received character. Albeit he considers himself a 'practical man' (129), his reflections on policies and ideals offer little to address the immediate crisis facing the world. Writing three years after the publication of *After Many a Summer*, William Tindall records that most readers he has spoken to 'either skipped the sermons of Mr. Propter or read them with pain' (452). Tindall also highlights the privileged position Propter speaks from, observing that his contemplations of eternity 'are assisted by his enjoyment of a private income – a prerequisite for spiritual enlargement' (461). However, while Propter's inattention to the threat of war may have alienated readers, *After Many a Summer* does, for Huxley, respond to pressing new knowledge. Huxley, like Propter, is convinced that unindividuated consciousness is real. In 1941 he asserts that there exists another 'mode of consciousness underlying, so to speak, the ordinary individualised consciousness of everyday life' (*Grey* 47). This conviction is primarily spurred by Rhine's experiments into extrasensory perception, which, for Huxley, prove the existence of telepathy beyond reasonable doubt. From the mid-1930s Huxley's understanding of personhood invests heavily in the idea that thoughts may exist outside of individual minds. That idea, a seemingly necessary condition for thought-transmission (if it is considered possible for a thought to pass from one mind to another, it must somehow cross the space between those minds), leads Huxley to view consciousness as multi-layered and to identify an underlying collective consciousness as the container of lasting truths and of undistorted perception of ultimate reality. This is a position he maintains until his death in 1963, and it substantially informs his writing across this period, as well as his approach to the novel as a medium. For Huxley, conveying this awareness has immense importance in pushing for a future less riven by power politics and less invested in absolutist ideologies: should collective consciousness be widely seen as real, a politics meaningfully dedicated to the common good might emerge. The novel is, for Huxley, a potent tool in reshaping the general understanding of personhood. As a medium, it has the potential to destabilise the idea of the individual personality and to show its boundaries as blurred and arbitrary. Even in his work of the 1920s, before Huxley gives explicit support to telepathy, there is doubt as to the existence of the stable, integral individual. The possibility to absorb ideas from others – via normal interaction, not only telepathically – leads Huxley to question the validity of individuated selfhood when individual identity is porous and contingent.

Huxley's promoters typically laud his contribution to the development of the novel by emphasising his novels of the 1920s. In this period, especially in 1928's *Point Counter Point*, Huxley offers ensemble pieces which stage conversations between exponents of diverse philosophies. In them, Huxley illustrates how point and counterpoint, thesis and antithesis, do not inevitably yield synthesis: often new ideas are either absorbed with little modification (and little regard for a person's existing beliefs), or rejected without reflection. However, while ideas saturate these novels, it is regularly offered that Huxley was, as a writer, uninterested in plot and characterisation. This critical tradition was established by Peter Bowering's landmark 1968 study of Huxley, which contends that the worth of his novels lies in 'the wealth of their ideas', a claim bargained for with the concession that 'for the traditional features of the novel, plot and delineation of character, he showed scant regard' (1). Many have since gone further, suggesting that Huxley's disregard for these features of the novel is so great that it is best not to consider him a novelist. While *The Columbia History of the British Novel* dedicates a chapter to 'Isherwood, Huxley, and the Thirties', Michael Rosenthal, the author of the chapter, expresses doubt that Huxley's place in the history is deserved. He writes that 'despite Huxley's enormous popularity, particularly among students and the young intellectuals of his generation, no lasting consensus has developed about his status as a novelist', and 'about whether he should be considered a novelist at all' (748). For Rosenthal, 'in his search to be interesting, Huxley eschewed the tightly wrought, highly conscious formal structures of, say, Henry James or Conrad or Virginia Woolf' (749), suggesting that instead 'what finally matters are the ideas themselves' (750). Harold Bloom, in a damning introduction to the volume on Huxley in his *Modern Critical Views* series, contends that Huxley was 'a superb essayist, but not quite [. . .] a novelist' (2). Aside from possible value as a rhetorical flourish, however, little is gained by discounting the writer of a dozen novels as a novelist. The gesture also does a significant disservice to Huxley's commitment to the medium: the notion that his formally distinctive novels are the product of a disregard for form is highly implausible.

Both Huxley's novels of the 1920s and his later mystically inflected work decentre the novel away from the development of the protagonist's personality. Across his career, Huxley exhibits the belief that the novel built around the development of a distinct, discrete individual is apt to present a false picture of the relationship between ideas and people. As it is traditionally understood, an individual's self-discovery is in large part constituted by the development and refinement of her or his own ideas. Characters, in a typical fiction of development, progress from being undistinguished as children, adolescents or young adults, becoming more and more individuated as their thoughts and actions set them apart. This may run in parallel with other self-realisation. Pip in Charles Dickens's *Great Expectations* (1861) rises from orphanhood to financial self-sufficiency, becoming independent in this sense, but his ambition to become a gentlemen is spurred more by a recurring feeling that his life is covered by a 'curtain dropped so heavy and blank', which shuts him 'out from anything save dull endurance' (97). To be a gentlemen, at least as Pip sees it, is to achieve individuation intellectually. The fear that individuation might not be achieved is often fuelled by a vision of undifferentiated masses. Charlotte Brontë's *Jane Eyre* (1847) has its narrator, when teaching at Morton village school, not only worry that her pupils are 'wholly untaught, with faculties quite torpid', but, moreover, that they are 'at first sight, all dull alike' (365). That Jane's perspective changes as she becomes more acquainted with the children is suggestive of the relationship between communication and individuation. Jane comes to realise that 'there was a difference amongst them as amongst the educated; and when I got to know them and they me, this difference rapidly developed itself' (365). Having the opportunity to have one's story seen and heard is central to the making of selfhood. The novel does not passively reflect the becoming of its protagonist; the telling of the hero's story is central to the generation of his or her identity as an individual. That Dickens's bildungsromans, *David Copperfield* (1850) and *Great Expectations*, are the only two of his novels to be wholly narrated in the first person reflects the degree to which the individuated self is a function of narration, rather than narration a function of the self. Likewise, *Jane Eyre*'s subtitle, *An Autobiography*, suggests a necessity to regard the protagonist as the author of her own self, the creator of the story as much as the teller.

For John R. Maynard, what is true of the bildungsroman is closely tied to what is true of the novel in general. He contends that, 'if in its central concern the bildungsroman is about the individual's situation in each coming generation, it really comes close to the normal concerns of the novel itself' (280). For Maynard, more is at play than set and subset resembling one another when defined broadly – instead, he considers the bildungsroman to constrict the potentiality of the novel at large. He offers that 'the conception of the bildungsroman genre not only keeps expanding as a set of possible meanings but also tends to process and colonize other genres' (280). The novel is expected to show character development, and the bildungsroman has sufficient force that its understanding of development as individuation permeates expectations for the novel at large. However, the bildungsroman's implicit understanding of human nature presents reason to explore a fiction less invested in the individual. To the extent that the bildungsroman conceives of individuality as something gained, as something which cannot be assumed, it implies not only that an undifferentiated personhood exists, but also that this is a default, more natural mode of existence.

For Huxley, as a writer who believes consciousness is more than personal, and as a writer convinced that telepathy is real, an individual's effort to achieve distinction can be seen to act against underlying interconnection. Indeed, individuation may be impossible. Beliefs or values are not the personal possessions they are apt to be taken for and, moreover, the flourishing idea is one which is shared and widely spread, not one which marks out an individual. A novel invested in this interconnection – that is to say, a novel of ideas in a strict sense – is, of necessity, substantially different from the novel which accepts the individual as its unit of character. Evidently, indeed, such a novel is different enough that significant temptation exists to discount it as a novel at all (an assessment also made of Olaf Stapledon's cosmic fiction, which, in a very different way from Huxley's work, prioritises the development of ideas over and above that of physical individuals). Responses like Rosenthal's and Bloom's belie the extent to which Huxley's novels, while not often linguistically experimental, push the medium – they are sufficiently radical in their structure that many critics are still uncomfortable accepting them as novels. Ideas loom larger than individuals in Huxley's novels, because, for him, ideas have more definite existences than the people who voice them.

Huxley's career as a writer makes clear his commitment to the novel as a medium. He enjoyed sufficient regard as an essayist that he need not have continued returning to the novel. Gerald Heard, for one, recalls that he 'would urge him to confine himself to his highly influential essays', but that Huxley would reply that 'novels pay far better' ('Poignant' 53). The glib response, apparently a repeated one, seems designed to stifle counterargument. True as it may have been, it is only a partial truth – this argument downplays the commercial potential of his non-fiction (Huxley was able in 1927, for example, to sell two articles for $1,000 dollars each (Grover Smith 284)). Instead, it is likely the novel as a medium does, for Huxley, have a special quality to be harnessed, that the medium is part of the message. Albeit in Huxley's preface to his own *Collected Essays* (1958) he finds similarity in the possibilities offered by the essay and the novel, suggesting that 'like the novel, the essay is a literary device for saying almost everything about almost anything', he ultimately attributes broader potential to the novel, claiming that that the essay collection can cover 'almost as much ground, and cover it almost as thoroughly as can a long novel' (v). For Huxley, the novel is a 'great orchestra' (ix), capable of generating harmony between voices encapsulating different facets of experience: as he writes in *Literature and Science* (1963), 'the possibility of shifting from objectivity to life's subjective meanings is built into the structure of almost every good novel' (18). It seems, then, that for Huxley the novel has structural compatibility with his convictions in key respects – it is almost inevitably polyvocal and it can distribute and interlayer ideas in a way which the essay is less equipped to facilitate.

Set against this, the lack of character development and concomitant paucity of dramatic plot in many of Huxley's novels need not be taken as a function of his limitation as a novelist, but can be seen to stem from the constraints his understanding of human nature impose upon his artistic composition: to the extent that he finds the individual personality illusory, his novels refuse to cohere with the expectation that personal development should be the novel's structuring idea. Instead, in Huxley's fiction, there is less delineation between characters than Bowering might desire not because Huxley is uninterested in delineating, or because of a want of capability, but because Huxley does not accept the reality of the isolated individual. Even without considering the telepathic transmission Huxley comes to believe is possible, ideas spread through the course of discussion, modifying and merging with others. If characters blend, momentarily or otherwise, it may pose difficulty for the reader during extended passages of dialogue, but it replicates the fluidity with which interaction informs identity.

The Protagonist as Medium

There is frequent discussion in Huxley's work of personality and identity, meaning that one of the main areas in which characters shift and mimic one another is in their understanding of character itself. While Huxley's characters occupy a continuum between committed materialism and advocacy of various forms of spiritualism, vitalism or philosophical idealism, his protagonists, like *Point Counter Point*'s Philip Quarles, are often experimenting with ideas they voice, rather than expressing something they have substantively absorbed. As Quarles reflects to himself, 'he had adopted other people's opinions, even their modes of life – but always with the underlying conviction that they weren't really his, that he could and certainly would abandon them as easily as he had taken them up' (375). Quarles, in short, voices ideas he has absorbed in large part to experience how it feels to give voice to them. To an extent, the experimentation might resemble that of a bildungsroman protagonist, seeking to understand herself or himself. However, Quarles's awareness that ideas entering his head have external sources precipitates a discomfort: he sees self-deception rather than self-discovery in treating acquired thoughts as his.

Point Counter Point suggests that, however unambiguous the distinction between self and other might seem, our unwitting absorption of the ideas of others should undermine our confidence in that boundary. The novel not only constitutes a collage of 1920s British literary society, but also a reproduction of Huxley's own mindset within that idea-rich environment. Quarles, a novelist and Huxley-like figure, is deeply uncertain with respect to his identity. So porous does he feel himself to the ideas of others, he is anxious that he cannot identify a definitive version of himself. As the narrator, channelling Quarles's inner monologue, asserts, 'this question of identity was precisely one of Philip's chronic problems', for the reason that 'it was so easy for him to be almost anybody' (253). Quarles, the narrator continues, 'had such a power of assimilation, that he was often in danger of being unable to distinguish the assimilator from the assimilated, of not knowing among the multiplicity of his rôles who was the actor'. In effect, a lack of stable identity is the characteristic through which Quarles defines himself: his mind is likened to 'a sea of spiritual protoplasm, capable of flowing in all directions' such that 'at different times in his life and even at the same moment he had filled the most various moulds'. Quarles's identity at a given moment hinges upon what books he might be reading, or what people he might be associating with, meaning that *Point Counter Point* as a novel of ideas is both an encapsulation of the society around Quarles, but also the society within him. He is a node in a web of transmission, with little pretence at control over the process.

Quarles is, in a sense, a medium, albeit without a performative effort in his channelling of ideas. He endures the entire series of anxieties Daniel Cottom identifies as provoked by spiritualism: that 'language, behavior, character, individual persons, and the entirety of culture' might be exposed 'as unfounded representations' (57). However, for Cottom, it is 'the extreme difficulty – even the utter improbability – of communication' which spiritualism indicates (56–7): the knocks and scratches of a séance, requiring the interpretation of a medium, suggest that 'words are never entirely present or self-evident' and that 'communication is always interpretation' (55). For Quarles, by contrast, it is the ease with which ideas are transmitted which is troubling: so many pass through him, in developed form and identifiable with their sources, that he feels unable to claim possession of any.

Quarles's misapprehension is that he is distinct in the way he takes on the ideas of others. In this, he is a voice of inexperience, unable to recognise that, while his interlocutors might articulate reasonably consistent positions, with reasonably consistent voices, underneath they share similar uncertainties to him and that underneath they would sometimes feel a disconnection between their public persona and their underlying self. Where, then, Jonathan Foltz worries that Huxley's 'novelist stand-in, Philip Quarles in *Point Counter Point* [. . .] openly espouses treating characters as "mouthpieces" for ideas rather than exquisite feeling' (167), this erases the doubt Quarles evidently experiences about the existence of character other than as a composite of ideas. Moreover, a novel, denuded, is comprised only of ideas: while characters can be objects of the reader's emotions and attitudes, they are, themselves, ultimately constructed as embodiments of a small set of ideas, known through a small stock of descriptors and tendencies. *Point Counter Point* offers that reading character in life is not so different from doing so in fiction: that it entails identifying and fitting together a number of discrete, disconnected elements, perhaps with artificial fixity. In life as well as fiction, identifying a person as, say, having a gregarious character is schematic: it simplifies and limits to make comprehensible. The apparatus for understanding character is not fitted to the underlying undifferentiated flow of being.

In addition to utilising uncommitted protagonists like Quarles, Huxley typically has his narrators interject little, a fact which contributes to the once common characterisation of Huxley as an 'aloof and fastidious ironist' (Joseph Bentley 143), or as a 'detached observer of the follies and foibles of his fellow-men' (Semmler 75). However, at no point in his career are Huxley's personal convictions truly absent from his novels. Though his earlier works place diverse voices into conversation with one another with little editorialising from their narrators, form lets Huxley's beliefs inform his novels. In his novels of the 1920s, in which the apparently impartial observation of diverse attitudes is most in evidence, Huxley challenges the tenet that the novel necessarily explores the development of an individual or multiple individuals. As László Földényi characterises it, a core principle of the novel, traditionally understood, is that it 'deals with individuals, that it contemplates the world from the point of view of subjectivity and not the individual in the light of the Universe' ('Novel' 5). The bourgeois novel, as Földényi terms it, takes the individual as its foundational assumption and builds outwards. Huxley privileges the maximal development of ideas over the refinement of a stable self. Anthony Beavis's proclamation in *Eyeless in Gaza* that it is 'one's duty to develop all one's potentialities – *all* of them' reflects this (97, emphasis from source). Characters' unconscious absorption of ideas from one another betrays that no individual controls the boundaries of herself or himself: personal change seldom follows a design and, indeed, is often only perceived from outside when it does occur.

Huxley's contestation of the reality of the integral individual spans a divide critics regularly draw in his life and career: routinely, a first phase marked by a commitment to rationalism is distinguished from a second marked by advocacy of mysticism – 1936's *Eyeless in Gaza* often being identified as the turning point. As Peter Bowering formulates it, 'the novels themselves, thinly disguised accounts of his thought, record the stages of Huxley's growth from the detached sceptic of *Crome Yellow* to the contemplative mystic of the later works' (3); he labels *Eyeless in Gaza* Huxley's 'conversion' novel (114). Jerome Meckier offers a similar account, albeit with an additional stage identified at the beginning of Huxley's career: he characterises Huxley's journey as one from 'poet of ideas to satirical novelist to perennial philosopher' (32). *Eyeless in Gaza* is again offered as the central point in a transition in his novels (210). However, this division of Huxley's career masks a continuing commitment throughout Huxley's career to contesting the reality of the integral individual personality. At no stage in his career does Huxley take individuation as either achievable or desirable. Where there is difference, it is that in the second phase of his career Huxley gives greater emphasis to the immaterial passage of ideas between people. The flow of ideas comes to be seen not primarily as a function of communication, but as a function of the nature of underlying reality, whereby thoughts have existence and motion beyond individual minds, such that their passage between people is inevitable. In short, the shift in the nature of Huxley's work in the mid-1930s correlates with his increasing conviction that telepathy is real.

The contestation of the individuated character marks Huxley's engagement with telepathy out from that of much of the mid-twentieth-century science fiction which incorporates telepathy. In it psychic ability is overwhelmingly seen as a binary, a product of evolution either present in an individual or not. As such, the novelistic concern with distinction is reinforced. Telepaths might form interpenetrating bonds with one another, but telepathic power provokes estrangement from the mass of humankind and is incompatible with existing social structures. In John Wyndham's *The Chrysalids* (1955), children in a post-apocalyptic society conceal telepathic powers which they consider will mark them for persecution as mutants. The telepathic youths interpret their faculty as conferring an advantage, Rosalind, for one, asserting that 'ours *is* a superior variant' (196, emphasis from source). In supporting her claim, she speaks to a psychic interfusion, but one which only incorporates those with the telepathic faculty. They are, she states, 'beginning to understand how to assemble and apply the composite team-mind to a problem' and are 'not shut away into individual cages from which we can reach out only with inadequate words' (196): in effect, greater interpenetration with one another, without the mediation of language, means, for Rosalind, that the youths are better equipped to understand and resolve societal difficulties. However, their mode of collaboration, unavailable as it is to the adults, necessarily implies exclusion would follow were the children to wrest power. Where the likes of Stapledon and Huxley see at least the potential for a psychic awakening in all beings, *The Chrysalids* offers no such hope.

Brunner's *Telepathist* likewise offers telepathy as alienating from the majority of humankind. Albeit the number of telepathists is said to be so small that 'few had formed lasting attitudes' about them, the experience of many telepathic children is likened to 'members of a family in Nazi Germany, who had just discovered that they had Jewish blood' (137). The difference between the nature of the telepath's mental processes and those of most of humanity entrenches that division; unlike in *The Chrysalids*, however, telepathy is seen as likely to engender refusal of society. In *Telepathist*, a telepath might read any mind, but the possibility to read less capable, less developed minds is unenticing. As Pandit Singh, an expert in telepathy (though not a telepathist himself) asserts, in many instances a telepathist 'prefers to retreat into fugue and make a fantasy world which is more tolerable' (65–6). This the telepathist can do 'on the grand scale', by providing 'himself with an audience – as many as eight people, if he's powerful – and tak[ing] them into fugue with him' (66). This audience, whom Singh terms 'reflective personalities' are seen to 'mirror and feed the telepathist's ego'. In effect, the accentuated mental existence of the telepath impels a predominantly mentalised being which devalues the physical world. The telepath's psychic concentration becomes a concentration on their own individuated psyche. In *The Chrysalids*, *Telepathist* and other fiction in which telepathy is a distinct faculty, possessed only by some, there are orders of psychic experience which, by nature, cannot be widely shared, and telepathy as a whole precipitates separation and discrimination.

Decentration and the Telepathic Faculty

Huxley shows signs of being persuaded by telepathy before his career as a writer begins. In a 1915 letter written while a student at Balliol College, Oxford, he describes having seen a thought-reading performance by 'one of the best telepathists going', Gilbert Murray. For Huxley, Murray is 'astonishing' – and not merely as an illusionist (Grover Smith 86). Particularly impressive is his apparent ability to perceive his daughter's thoughts when she is thinking of passages from books that she has read: Huxley records that 'he got almost word for word' an episode from Joseph Conrad's new book (87). At one point, Huxley himself is invited to imagine a scene. He thinks of the Master of Balliol, J. L. Strachan-Davidson, listening to an essay on George Meredith's *The Egoist*. Murray, after holding Huxley's hand for half a minute, declares that 'it's the old Master of Balliol being embarrassed', by, he suggests, 'a conversation about a new poet'. This, for Huxley, is sufficiently close to be compelling: he declares that Murray possesses 'a wonderful gift'. With time, however, Huxley becomes more cautious about trusting his own experience, developing greater consciousness of the range of factors which might colour his understanding. While he remains curious towards the paranormal, writing by 1934 that he has 'attended a certain number of séances' (*Supernatural* 171), he is, at this point, no longer ready to offer his own experience as evidence for psychic phenomena. As Huxley puts it, 'after sitting for half an hour in a dark and very stuffy room, listening to a gramophone playing the same tune over and over again, I am not prepared to accept even my own testimony of what occurs' (*Supernatural* 171). Huxley, though, stops at suggesting that circumstances like these lead to poor observation and recollection; he does not raise the possibility of bad faith on the part of self-declared psychics and mediums.

This distrust of himself, married to implicit trust in others, is characteristic of Huxley's developing thought. Becoming less trusting of his own perception and recollection is double-edged. There is scepticism: Huxley realises that he cannot assert he has participated in the paranormal if other reasonable explanations remain. But there is also a growing sense that his thoughts are not his alone: that the immaterial world he locates them in is one where personal boundaries cannot be assumed to be firm. In September 1931 he recommends Gerald Heard's *The Social Substance of Religion* to literary critic G. Wilson Knight. Describing Heard's work as 'curious and interesting', Huxley suggests that 'perhaps the solitary life of individuals is impracticable, psychologically speaking', and that there might be a need for humanity to return 'to the snugness of contact and co-consciousness' (Grover Smith 353).

Huxley's acclamation of Heard's work stems in part from his personal connection with the author. Huxley had met Heard for the first time in January 1929, when both were guests of the editor Raymond Mortimer. Their rapport with one another was instant. They 'stayed talking till past 1 a.m.' and then walked more than three miles together to Heard's home, in spite of this being a significant diversion for Huxley, making plans for 'another session the following week' as they went (Heard, 'Poignant' 50). Among the consequences of Huxley's resulting friendship with Gerald Heard was increased involvement in occult circles. With Heard, he attended lectures by P. D. Ouspensky and paid a number of visits to the country house which acted as Ouspenksy's headquarters (Heard, 'Poignant' 56). Such experiences seem to have primed Huxley to take a more credulous attitude towards the apparent advances in telepathic research made by Rhine. Their research allows a dissonance to dissolve. It lets Huxley wed his curiosity towards the occult and paranormal and his sense that interpersonal communion might be possible to a long-established conviction that a belief should have scientific support to be seriously held.

What follows, though, is that, where telepathy is concerned, reason begins to reason itself out of Huxley's system of thought. In the 1934 essay 'Mind Reading', Huxley contends that 'telepathy and clairvoyance [. . .] are incompatible with intellectual activity of an analytical kind' and suggests that 'if we want to develop our extra-sensory gifts we must discover a technique for ridding ourselves of the analytical habit' (166). The belief is one which remains with Huxley. In a 1946 letter to Rhine, he suggests that 'too much concentration defeats its own end, and that effective concentration has to work by a process of decentration' (*Letters* 551). The telepath, for Huxley, can more reliably transmit or interpret thoughts by limiting attention to the task – presumably allowing the mind to operate in a more automatic, more impersonal condition, in which its boundaries are less apt to be falsely registered as boundaries of thought.

This is reflected in Huxley's novels. In *Time Must Have a Stop* (1944), Huxley suggests a need to wed the products of analysis to the insights gained though decentred, unanalytical concentration. Paul De Vries, a character who describes himself as a *pontifex minimus* – a 'little priest', but, as Jake Poller highlights, more literally a 'little bridge builder' (263) – bemoans the refusal of intellectuals to engage with psychical research. For Paul, 'if you read the Proceedings of the Society for Psychical Research, you couldn't fail to be convinced', which, he suggests, is 'why most philosophers so scrupulously refrained from reading them' (91). The refusal to engage can be seen to have deeper cause than the need to accept a new intellectual orthodoxy. Instead, psychical research supports a mode of thinking – and, indeed, an understanding of what thought itself is – which is antithetical to that of philosophy. On accepting telepathy, clairvoyance and other faculties as real, not only would ontological philosophy and the nomology of mind be upended, but the practice of philosophy would need to be broadened to address products of both reason and decentred apprehension.

For the bridge-builder Paul, what is needed to span 'the gap between the phenomena of spiritualism and the phenomena of psychology and physics' is 'a thought-bridge that would permit the mind to march discursively and logically from telepathy to the four-dimensional continuum, from poltergeists and departed spirits to the physiology of the nervous system' (92). As such, for Paul, ostensibly incompatible systems of understanding can be united by the logical faculty. However, when, later in the novel, young poet Sebastian Barnack decides he shall write an analytical synthesis of religious and philosophical accounts of transcendence, he is cautioned by his mentor, Bruno, that as he writes he will 'know progressively less instead of more', writing being 'an all-absorbing labor' and an 'obstacle in the way of further knowledge' (251). For the spiritually pure Bruno, whom Sebastian describes as 'a kind of thin transparent shell, enclosing something incommensurably other than himself – an unearthly beauty of peace and power and knowledge' (310), true knowledge consists in the immediate apprehension of impersonal reality and human analysis and discourse cannot help but be dim, distorted reflections. That analysis must, moreover, be produced at a distance from transcendent experience, insomuch as, for Huxley, the analytical faculty must be disengaged for transcendence to occur, meaning, at best, a memory of it is addressed.

Given that Huxley published his own synthetic religious analysis, *The Perennial Philosophy*, in 1945, and given that large portions of Huxley's own essays are interpolated by *Time Must Have a Stop* and attributed to Sebastian, as a novel it represents a self-conscious reflection on the potentially self-defeating aspects of attempting to analyse – and, indeed, evangelise – an unanalytical mode of being in novels and essays. The implication is that spiritual writers like Huxley and Sebastian perform a form of self-sacrifice, diminishing their personal mental openness in order to disseminate wisdom. However, the project is not, as Huxley sees it, innately futile. While accepting a claim he attributes to later Buddhist philosophy that 'language is the main source of the sense of separateness and the blasphemous idea of individual self-sufficiency' (*Perennial* 134), for Huxley, there is a moral imperative for writers to produce literature which not only evokes beauty, or rouses emotion, but also induces in the reader a state of mind in which something of reality can be apprehended. He contends that 'the use and purpose of reason is to create the internal and external conditions favourable to its own transfiguration by and into spirit' (141). The novel of ideas, juxtaposing rational and irrational thought systems, philosophical and mystical knowledge, might be the best existent tool for the writer to effect that leap between mindsets. As Paul De Vries asserts, without an established synthesis of philosophical and mystical knowledge, 'for the present, the best one could do was just to skip from one world to the other', in the hope of receiving 'a hunch, an illuminating intuition of the greater synthesis' (92). In the clashing of thought systems in the novel of ideas, the hope is that interfaces and affinities might be accidentally discovered. For writer and reader alike, the novel of ideas might inspire the thought-bridge between rational and irrational knowledge.

In the novels of ideas of other writers, there is also the sense that analytical activity might be supressing other faculties. Murdoch, in *The Flight from the Enchanter* (1956), has Rosa Keepe torn between acquiescence with wider psychic flows and a compulsion to intellectualise them, even as doing so abates them. As the narrator explains, 'at certain moments she was prepared to let go and allow herself to be carried by a stronger force; and if she later demanded of herself an account of these surrenders there was usually a selection of labels ready made to bring the violence of the spirit under some clinical and domestic heading' (257). That oscillation is suggested to be characteristic of a type of mentality invested in analysing itself, Rosa being 'like all emotional rationalists' in her fluctuation between inviting psychic experience and entering into analysis which removes her from that experience. Like Huxley seeking to delimit and define telepathy, clairvoyance and other forms of extrasensory perception, Rosa realises that description of certain orders of psychic experience is innately translation, that translation being not only the rendering of non-verbal experience linguistically, but also the encapsulation of interpersonal experience from an individuated perspective. *The Flight from the Enchanter* embeds Rosa and its other characters in a complex web of personalities of differing extension. As well as Rosa's own wavering acceptance of psychic forces, it renders 'a personality without frontiers' in Peter Saward (34) and 'the centre of an extra-ordinary solitude' in Annette Cockeyne (267). Rather than the debate between differing schools of thought, as in *Point Counter Point*, it is the direct interfaces between different modes of thought which are central to *The Flight from the Enchanter*.

Byatt's *The Virgin in the Garden*, meanwhile, presents the ascription of higher purpose to decentration as the function of an unrestrained drive to corral all mental activity into systems of meaning. Marcus, the child taken for a psychic by his teacher, Simmonds, develops the practice of decentration as a solitary game. It is explained that on playing fields close to his home, Marcus 'had played a game called spreading himself', which, it is said, 'began with a deliberate extension of his field of vision, until by some sleight of perception he was looking out at once from the four field-corners, the high ends of the goal-posts, the running wire top of the fence' (27). The game decentres his perception and in this condition his mind appears to transcend his body, such that, 'sometimes, for immeasurable instants he lost any sense of where he really was, of where the spread mind had its origin'. In this state, however, Marcus does not gain the revelations of a Huxleyan mystic – nor, in spite of Simmonds's projections, does this aptitude for decentration prime him to transmit or receive specific, articulatable thoughts. When he protests to Simmonds that 'I don't know how anyone can see what is anyone else's head. I don't know how or why they should try' (63), the comment is disregarded, Simmonds, informed by the psychical literature persuasive to both Stapledon and Huxley, is dogmatic and doctrinal that Marcus possesses 'special gifts of consciousness – that might extend the limits of human power' (61). What Simmonds fails to appreciate is that in decentring himself Marcus achieves both removal from his human body and from discursive thought, perceiving not ideas but the 'inhuman clarity' beneath them (262).

Marcus, content that 'message or no message, the things received were to him, in their limitations, manageable and pleasant' (262), experiences no desire to freight his decentration with analysis. His acceptance that certain orders of being should fall outside the sphere of human interpretation – and are the more clear for it – acts a response to the insistence of figures like Huxley that, through the combination and recombination of theory and speculation from philosophical, scientific and mystical domains, a way might be found to verbalise the meaning of raw experience. Simmonds grabs haphazardly at theories of being from different domains and, like Huxley, seeks sparks of inspiration in the friction between them. When Simmonds becomes 'excited by the interrelatedness of volumes grabbed at random from the library shelves' (298), those volumes include favourites of Huxley. Between 'Frazer, Jung, the records of the Society for Psychic Research, Gerard's *Herbal*, J. W. Dunne, [and] Gerald Heard', Simmonds finds equipment to theorise every aspect of Marcus's experience – often before Marcus has been able to express himself in more than the most general terms. When Byatt's narrator cuts in to assert that 'unlike every other person in this story', Marcus has no desire 'to prove his skill at reading people' (145), the mode of reading in question is that of seeing people and their circumstances through textual precedents. Where Simmonds is attracted to quasi-scientific theories of everything, literary works fill a similar role in the minds of other characters, providing each with means to channel any conversation, any moment of tension, any sexual encounter through a textual model: *Hamlet*, *Lady Chatterley's Lover*, Eliot's *Four Quartets* and others are invoked repeatedly, the comparisons often strained, triggered, perhaps, by hearing a superficially similar turn of phrase rather than by any meaningful resemblance. Even when situationally appropriate, they are distancing and practically unhelpful. Thoughts of 'Constance Chatterley's florid spreading circles of satisfaction' fill Frederica's head when she has sex with Wilkie (420), but when he comments that she 'didn't come', 'she did not quite know, despite earlier thoughts about Lady Chatterley, what he meant' (421). Where there is a common complaint that in novels of ideas characterisation is obscured by the focus on ideas, *The Virgin in the Garden* suggests that in life it is often an intentional choice to use ideas to hide from sometimes confusing, sometimes painful, experience.

In his final novel, *Island* (1962), Huxley explores similar territory, offering that even without using pre-existing literature to estrange the self from immediate experience, the insistence that the personal life story be coherently narratable is limiting. It presents a utopia which works in service of a single prevailing idea – that of how a whole society might achieve and maintain awareness of the fluid, present reality of a 'Mind at Large' (138) – but presents it to an outsider protagonist who defines himself by his past history rather than his present experiential state. Set on the fictional South-East Asian island of Pala, in *Island* both physical and spiritual tools are employed to expand consciousness. The Palanese cultivate a drug known as '*moksha*-medicine' and nicknamed 'the reality-revealer' (136) which 'does something to the silent areas of the brain which opens some kind of neurological sluice and so allows a larger volume of

Mind with a large "M" to flow into your mind with a small "m"' (138).¹ Palanese art is also celebrated for facilitating consciousness of the Mind at Large. *Island*'s outsider, the British journalist Will Farnaby, is shown work by the most celebrated Palanese landscape painter, Gobind Singh, whose paintings, he is told, offer 'actual manifestation [. . .] of Mind with a large M in an individual mind in relation to a landscape, to canvas and to the experience of painting' (181). Singh's work is hailed as 'genuinely religious', in contrast to 'pseudo-religious pictures [which] always refer to something else, something beyond the things they represent – some piece of metaphysical nonsense, some absurd dogma' (182). *Moksha*-medicine and art alike, then, are intended to make possible an expansive, encompassing vision of present reality, one shorn of the limiting categorisations of language and ordinary discourse.

As a novel, *Island* injects tension by employing a protagonist burdened with a level of backstory atypical of utopian literature. Rather than a largely blank everyperson representative of the outside world, Will is struggling to come to terms with recent events in his life and, in many senses, is more concerned with understanding them than with understanding Palanese society. He arrives on the island cynical, guilty and despondent, trying to process why he was the kind of person to embark on a lustful but shallow extramarital affair and is still shaken by what resulted from its discovery: that being his wife driving away angrily in heavy rain, losing control of the car, resulting in her death. Will obsessively replays events to himself, apparently attempting to fit these pieces into a narratable personal history which does not render his present self useless with self-loathing. What Pala gives him is an unconsidered option: to decentralise his individual story in his account of himself, to approach it as an interposition impairing appreciation of present experience. When he ultimately takes the *moksha*-medicine, there is revelation in perceiving 'the gifts of immediate experience' for once 'uncorrupted by the personal history, the secondhand notions' which typically overlay them (266). In this condition, in which the narrated self ceases to interpose itself, Will not only finds joy in a heightened awareness of immediate stimuli, but he also finds himself aware that eternity is 'as real as shit' (267). In effect, Will achieves a decentration, recognising that a more developed individual self represents an enclosure. While Will may have justifiable guilt over his wife's death, renouncing the expectation that his present condition be narratively readable from past events is, for Huxley, the most healthy course of action. In one regard, this makes *Island* a novel which rejects narrative, but, in another, the development in Will's thinking is more considerable – and more coherent to the reader – than practically any other of Huxley's protagonists.

Ultimately, Pala, like Will, faces an existential crisis. Pacifistic, it is ill-adapted to withstand the expansionist ambitions of its militaristic neighbour, Rendang, and is invaded at the conclusion of the novel. Ending in this way is partly a concession from Huxley that the material conditions to make his utopia possible do not exist. However, if for Huxley much of reality consists in immaterial consciousness, then physical existence is an incomplete metric to evaluate a society's viability. The idea of Pala exists – and this, for Huxley, is enough to give *Island* value. Where June Deery claims that an author writing utopian fiction hopes 'that some ideas will be enacted in reality – that is, defictionalized – as is the case in Huxley's *Island*' (34), this is only partly true of Huxley's project in imagining utopia. While it can be assumed that Huxley would wish for the real-world application of ideas from *Island*, on local if not national scales, the worth of the project does not have to be linked to this kind of enactment. Pala exists as an idea – as does Will's revelation – and there is impact to them without programmatic recreation of *Island*'s society.

The Atomic Character

Underlying the possibility of decentration for Huxley is an understanding of character as atomic, such that elements of personality are not bound to one another, with no given facets constituting a necessary core. In 1926 he writes to the poet Robert Nichols, explaining that in *Point Counter Point* he wants 'to make a picture of life in different aspects, the synchronous portrait of the different things an individual simultaneously is – atoms, physiology, mystic, cog in the economic machine, lover, etc' (276). Immediately after discussing his novel, in the same paragraph of the letter, Huxley reports that he has been reading William McDougall's *Outline of Abnormal Psychology* (1926). The association by juxtaposition speaks to a common concern for the creation of character and a common sense of its atomic nature. McDougall correlates healthy psychological development with the formation of a personality in which one element prevails, proposing that a 'well-knit character, one that can resist all disintegrating influences' is one which 'depends upon the organisation of the sentiments in an ordered system dominated by a master sentiment; and of all possible master sentiments the most effective is a sentiment for an ideal of character, an autonomous self' (538). In effect, the healthiest character, for McDougall, is one unflinchingly convinced that a single aspect is superior and one certain of its own boundaries.

However, McDougall admits, at least indirectly, that such confidence can only be false. When dreaming, McDougall suggests, 'the normal personality reveals his composite nature' (551). In a dream, McDougall offers, the dominant element of personality – which he terms the 'chief monad' – experiences 'the telepathic reflection' of 'bits of the mental life of many subordinate members of the hierarchy of monads'. The evocation of telepathy is not metaphorical: McDougall finds evidence for telepathy between distinct organisms 'very extensive', and suggests that 'much of it is of high quality' (551). In a single being, for McDougall, aspects of personality are conceptualised as communicating but not connecting: stability comes, then, through silencing disruptive voices, rather than through synthesis. Quarles's inability to settle in his personality comes not with a rejection of the basis McDougall's claims, but with a self-consciousness that the autonomous self it imagines is a matter of self-delusion, requiring the conviction that bonds exist where there are none.

In his own essays of this time, Huxley expands upon his doubts concerning the reality of the integral individual. In 'Personality and the Discontinuity of the Mind', from 1927, Huxley contends that 'most of us go through life incompletely unified – part person, the rest a mere collection of discontinuous psychological elements' (266) – a conception similar to McDougall's. In 'The Idea of Equality', from the same year, a slightly different picture emerges. In it, Huxley reflects upon the way in which a child learns, building upon a conviction that as a child's character is formed, there is no distinction between established truths and a society's emergent ideas. Thus Huxley proposes that 'notions which for one generation are dubious novelties become for the next absolute truths, which it is criminal to deny and a duty to uphold' (162). For Huxley, the child becomes inseparable from the ideas she or he absorbs: Huxley now does not conceptualise ideas as occupying space in the child's mind; instead, he regards ideas as forming the fabric of the mind itself. He writes that in a child a philosophy 'becomes, by familiarity not a reasonable hypothesis but actually a part of the mind, conditioning and, so to speak, canalizing all rational thought' (162). The upshot, for Huxley, is that 'for most people, nothing which is contrary to any system of ideas with which they have been brought up since childhood can possibly be reasonable'. Huxley, then, recognises that time before a child enters the world is flattened. An idea a child grows up with, however recently emerged, is not marked as provisionally or contingently true. The proposal that these ideas directly constitute elements of the mind has significant implications with respect to the understanding of character. If ideas form the mind, rather than fill it, then Quarles's insecurity in his own identity is especially justified. Not only are beliefs and values contingent, by this view, but so too are ways of thinking, to the extent that the mind's structure determines its operation.

It is in light of this uncertainty as to the possibility of authentic character that *Brave New World*'s exploration of conditioning is best read. Huxley does not start from the point of view that intensive conditioning is immoral as an effacement of the true self, insomuch that the idea of a true self is one Huxley rejects. While much that the Director of Hatcheries and Conditioning says is distasteful, there is little that would be out of place in an essay like 'The Idea of Equality'. The Director justifies his work through reasoning that it does not alter or displace any authentic self. As he puts it, 'the child's mind *is* these suggestions, and the sum of the suggestions *is* the child's mind. And not the child's mind only. The adult's mind too – all his life long' (32, emphases from source). For Huxley, it would seem, the reason the Director's work feels objectionable is not because a person's true self is lost, but because it exposes that there is no true self to lose. To say that something is in one's nature or not becomes absurd when received ideas are understood as being the mind and not merely its contents.

For Theodor W. Adorno, the result is that *Brave New World* imagines 'children of society in the literal sense', such that 'conceptions of a merely external influence of society upon individuals, through agencies like psychology or the family, are recognised to be obsolete' (100). Adorno recognises that Huxley's interest is in the identity between thinker and idea, such that, for Adorno, in *Brave New World* 'men no longer exist in dialectical opposition to society but rather are identical with it in their substance' (100). For Adorno, however, 'people completely collectivized [. . .] might as well abandon all communication at once' (102). The World State, however, nullifies through constant communication. It trains its inhabitants that ideas should simply be received, absorbed wholly, then potentially passed on, unaltered by individual invention. That many World State inhabitants always have on the radio, the television, or both, exemplifies the sense that participation in society is equated with acting as a receiver of information, with no productive contribution impelled. The major tool of conditioning, hypnopaedia, inculcates this. The deployment of continual 'words without reason' develops the sense in its subjects that constant receipt of information is a human imperative (31), but that no personal development should be expected from it.

Relatedly, the society of *Brave New World* flattens in its disavowal of time. There has been 'a campaign against the Past', which includes the closure of museums, the destruction of monuments and the suppression of historical books (60), and the future is also fought against to the extent change is minimised and innovation stifled. Neglecting, wilfully, the dimension of time, the World State of *Brave New World* frustrates the creation of a personality. If time is reduced to a repetition of alike days, there is reduced possibility to be anxious through fearing the future, reduced possibility to be excited and so on. Only to the extent that the World State is incompletely realised do these qualities persist.

The World State might be taken as denying natural fact in its response to time: even if certain emotional states can be stifled, the body ages and that change will precipitate mental responses that develop over a period. However in 'Personality and the Discontinuity of the Mind', Huxley suggests that time, as it is usually experienced, is a human fabrication. In it, he asserts that 'the psychological materials out of which the individual must construct his personality are discontinuous in time', such that 'in order to create a personality one must discover some principle of continuity, one must devise an ideal framework in which the naturally discontinuous materials can be harmoniously fitted' (262). The impression is of past, present and potentially future states simultaneously observed, their chronological arrangement deduced rather than innately understood and with it a narrative of development realised. It may be that Huxley had in mind the experience of memories becoming confused, the confusion evidence in itself that memory of what happened when it is not formed once and fixed, but is instead iteratively amended – and distorted – over time. However, Huxley may also be imagining more concrete access to temporally remote experiences, of the kind suggested by Dunne in *An Experiment with Time*. Dunne's picture of drawing meaning out of the confusion of past and future experiences in dreams resembles the work of self-interpretation Huxley suggests is required to fit together the elements of the personality. The proximity in time could mean Dunne was on Huxley's mind at the time of writing: *An Experiment with Time* was published in March 1927, Huxley's 'Personality and the Discontinuity of the Mind' in November of that year. Huxley had certainly read Dunne by 1929 at the latest: in that year he cites *An Experiment with Time* as 'that very interesting book' ('Pascal' 385) – a formulation with resonance of established familiarity. Indeed, in the 1929 essay 'Pascal', Huxley is confident enough to suggest that 'there is tolerably good evidence to show that the future is in certain circumstances foreseeable', it being 'quite conceivable' that prophetic powers are 'latent in the vast majority of individuals' (385). By the time of *The Perennial Philosophy*, Huxley has become convinced of the possibility of premonition, though at this point it is not Dunne alone who inspires this belief. In it, Huxley asserts confidently that 'the anecdotal evidence collected by the Society for Psychical Research and the statistical evidence accumulated during many thousands of laboratory tests for extra-sensory perception point inescapably to the conclusion that even human minds are capable of foreknowledge' (186).

When, then, the chronologically smashed up *Eyeless in Gaza* enacts the process of drawing meaning from temporally discontinuous elements, it is, for Huxley, a reflection of a genuine process which occurs in the depths of the mind. Chapter by chapter the novel jumps between different periods in the life of its protagonist, Anthony Beavis: the earliest chapters chronologically are dated 1902, during Beavis's boyhood, the latest dated 1935. The reader, then, is given discrete elements from which she or he can compose a narrative of Beavis's development. However, extended periods of Beavis's life are unavailable – there are no chapters covering events between 1905 and 1911 inclusive and between 1915 and 1925 inclusive, in addition to the years before 1902. Thus, a filtering has already occurred before the material reaches the reader: as *Eyeless in Gaza* is presented, a decision has already been made as to which periods are significant in the make-up of the present Beavis. The reader has little power to dispute whether the included periods do indeed comprise key years for Beavis – whatever that is taken to mean. The fact that events such as the death of Beavis's mother and the marriage of Helen to Hugo Ledwidge occur in the excluded periods marks the fact that selection against certain episodes contributes to the making of self-concept as much as selection towards certain others. Ultimately, though, there is no single answer as to who Beavis is. *Eyeless in Gaza* offers not so much the making of a person, per the bildungsroman, but his continual, contingent remaking. Jumping from one period to another colours the reading of following chapters, just as a painful memory, unexpectedly arising, might intrude to sour what should be a happy moment. Conversely, knowing something of the 1920s or 1930s Beavis informs the reading of chronologically earlier chapters – like the premonitions Huxley takes to be possible.

In one episode, the 1926 Beavis is seen working on a chapter of his book, *Elements of Sociology*, to be dedicated to the individual and personality. In writing the passage, the Huxley of the mid-1930s returns to the mindset of the Huxley of the mid-1920s who produced essays like 'Personality and the Discontinuity of the Mind' – the act of composition in itself, therefore, a splicing of one decade's mindset into another. To an extent, Beavis produces an analogue of Huxley's compositions of the 1920s, recapturing Huxley's sense, as then expressed, that the integral personality is illusory. Beavis suggests in his chapter that we only 'imagine that we have coherent experiences and personality' (112). He proposes that instead the human personality consists of 'psychological atoms' – discrete, individually fixed entities which in themselves are 'unlike normal experience and still more unlike personality.' Only because the units are too small and too numerous to perceive individually do we imagine connections between them. Beavis's work, though, has the quality of an ironic gloss on that of the younger Huxley. His conclusion that we fail to appreciate the illusion of personality because 'our minds work slowly and have very feeble powers of analysis' does not in substance contradict the argument of the 1920s Huxley (112–13), but offers implicit self-criticism to the extent that the author's own analytical limitations can be assumed to be the basis for this claim. Moreover, after he finishes writing, Beavis is pleased in general with what he has written, but is already conscious that 'unjustifiable generalizations' have entered his work, stemming, he feels, from approaching 'the world in general as though the world in general were like himself' (119). There is a tacit *mea culpa* from Huxley in this. It admits that in his search for universal truths, he has given too little thought to the position from which he writes. While a writer does nothing wrong in drawing upon her or his own experience, Huxley belies the fear that he has insisted that the universe cohere with his needs, instead of seeking to cohere in himself with the needs of the universe.

Eyeless in Gaza is written at the point when Huxley commits to voicing belief in telepathy. Two essays from 1934, 'Mind Reading' and 'Science Turns to the Supernatural', advocate telepathy as real. In 'Mind Reading', Huxley contends that 'the reality of telepathic communication was definitely established in the eighties of the last century', while in 'Science Turns to the Supernatural', he writes that 'at least one class of supernormal phenomena has been demonstrated, it seems to me, beyond all reasonable doubt', that class being the class of cryptaesthesia, including, Huxley lists, 'telepathy, or thought transference, clairvoyance, psychometry, water divining, and all other forms of abnormal perception, not passing through the ordinary channels of the senses' (168). However, in terms of the implications of telepathy, Huxley is, at this point, less ready to commit. While he suggests questions which research into ESP can help illuminate, including 'the nature of mind and its limitations; [. . .] the relations between individual minds and their bodies, the material world and other minds, [and . . .] the nature of time and our knowledge of it' ('Supernatural' 177), he does not venture answers. Huxley is only confident that telepathy is more successful when analytical activity is reduced – when the telepathist 'learn[s] to "decentrate"' and to 'face the world in a state of integrated quiescence' ('Mind Reading' 166–7). To the extent that Huxley associates holding together a self with analytical effort, decentration implies letting go of the self and being receptive to new thoughts in a particularly literal sense.

In *Eyeless in Gaza*, mental openness is associated with goodness. In reflections which close the novel, and which appear at its latest chronological point, Beavis asserts to himself that 'the good man is merely a less completely closed universe than the bad' (499–500) – a line of reasoning which makes a virtue of the previously troubling sense of instability in identity. For Beavis, 'minds are [. . .] unique, but unique above a substratum of mental identity' (498). Rather than defining himself by that which is separate and distinct, Beavis refocuses upon the connected aspects of his being and so doing experiences 'peace as a dark void beyond all personal life' (503). As such, when Imogen Woodberry suggests that Huxley 'eschewed a conception of human consciousness as adrift in unconscious waters', 'not from a Hulmean denial that those depths existed, but rather from a concern with how they could be constructively orientated towards the good' (1458), this partially captures the association Huxley makes between goodness and engagement with the impersonal. However, it is fundamental to Huxley's worldview from the 1930s onwards that the waters are not unconscious at all and that human minds are part of the water itself, rather than floating upon it. As Beavis finds, there are 'at the surface, the separate waves, the whirlpools, the spray; but below them the continuous and undifferentiated expanse of sea, becoming calmer as it deepens, till at last there is an absolute stillness' (502). Achieving awareness of the impersonal is, however, the product of attention to the self. For Beavis, 'we can adjust our instrument deliberately, by an act of the will', the result being 'modifications in the personal experiences which underlie our philosophy, the data from which we argue' (416). A person does not start to see connections by changing something in the outside world; a person does so by changing something in herself or himself – distributing attention differently between the senses, or interpreting inputs differently. It is reasoning on the pattern of Huxley's suggestion that the telepathist aiming for decentration must work on herself or himself – an idea which reinforces the individual perspective as significant at the same time as the limits of the individual are contested.

Eyeless in Gaza suggests literature has played a role in perpetuating an incomplete understanding of human nature. In a 1934 diary entry, Anthony Beavis suggests that imaginative literature has lied 'by omission' (423). He observes that 'the implications of literature are that human beings are controlled, if not by reason, at least by comprehensible, well-organized, avowable sentiments', but that, instead 'the facts are quite different'. What is more, literature has promulgated an image of human beings as well-organised in themselves and not only in the sentiments which shape them. In *Literature and Science*, Huxley suggests that the writer of literature has 'the paradoxical task of rendering the randomness and shapelessness of individual existence in highly organized and meaningful works of art' (10). *Eyeless in Gaza*, through tempting critics and readers to identify reason in its ordering of chapters, demonstrates that, even when the writer endeavours to signal shapelessness, readers will infer patterns and assume symbolic significance. For example, Daniel Aureliano Newman suggests in his consideration of *Eyeless in Gaza* that Huxley is 'more schematic than James Joyce, T. S. Eliot, or Virginia Woolf in the pursuit of the world's complex fullness' (406), proposing that the novel's anachrony 'mimics a model of development Huxley adapted from contemporary biological research, much of it by his brother Julian, on frogs and salamanders' (403). Pierre Vitoux, by contrast, emphasises a two-stage model of spiritual development 'from self-awareness to transcendence', finding that 'here, given the peculiar structure of the book, the two phases are made to overlap' (50). While each interpretation is justifiable, grounded in Huxley's life and interests, Huxley is capable of signalling, more explicitly or less, a structuring logic. The omission of such signs suggests the most significant representational manoeuvre is the deformation in itself.

In novels of ideas after Huxley, the sense that personality is a fragile epiphenomenon of 'atomic' forces remains in evidence. Murdoch, in *Henry and Cato* (1976), explores this through attention to the acquisition and loss of religious faith, suggesting that neither is necessarily explicable in terms of personality or life experience. In it, Cato Forbes, raised irreligious, finds the faith which subsequently compels him to become a priest after a moment of revelation without discernible cause. Instead, as he experiences it, he undergoes 'an invasion of spirit which seemed totally alien to his "personality" as he had known it before, but which became the very selfness of his self' (30) Cato, in retrospect, finds it 'difficult to connect these revelations with the ordinary history of times and places', his conversion not having arisen 'out of spiritual anguish, misery, extremity or any pressing need for transcendent consolation'. The unnarratability of this decisive moment in his personal history provokes insecurity: it is a pure conversion in the sense that it cannot be reduced to the product of circumstantial need, but with no personal agency involved, it defies explanation as a function of character. Indeed, so at odds is Cato's conversion with how he has understood himself that the legitimacy of personality as a concept is thrown into doubt.

As time passes, Cato comes to feel himself 'a priest, he felt, with all the atoms of his being' (99), but loses faith in comparably abrupt fashion. It is on seeing a sign that Cato rejects God, but, pathetically, the sign in question is the neon-lit 'TROUSERAMA' in the window of a clothes shop. Seeing it triggers in him 'a piercing desire to laugh and cry', and begets the conviction that 'there was no God and the world was damned' (99). Rather than render conversion as the finding of self, for Murdoch it is a bewildering loss of personal certainty. The 'TROUSERAMA' sign triggers an opening in Cato's mind like that trigged in Will Farnaby by the *moksha*-medicine, with 'gate after gate in his mind seem[ing] quietly to open, until there was no person there any more' (99). However, unlike for Will, in Cato's case that opening is so unexpected, the cause so unlikely, that it induces in him the sense that the underpinnings of his personal identity are too uncontrollable for him to know himself on an individual level. When Martha C. Nussbaum contends that 'for Murdoch [. . .] hell is being walled up inside one's own fat cosy ego without means of egress to the other or to the Good; heaven is the place of true and selfless vision' (37), there could be more nuance to the binding of good and ill. Cato's loss of faith is experienced as an opening up. For Murdoch, apprehension of the porousness of the self is apt to be frightening and bewildering.

John Brunner's *Stand on Zanzibar* (1968) experiments with structure to address to atomisation and synthesis. Set in 2010, *Stand on Zanzibar* acts as a global novel of ideas, rendering the spread and interaction of thoughts on a worldwide scale, with information technology obviating the need for psychic faculties to underpin interpersonal flow of ideas. In it, surveillance technology and artificial and human intelligence combine to map the diffuse, often spatially distant extrinsic agencies which sculpt patterns of thought and behaviour across the globe. Its supercomputers are effectively telepathic: as a commercial proudly announces, the Shalmaneser supercomputer 'sees all, hears all, knows all' (2). Shalmaneser and other supercomputers, as well as human synthesists, aim to extract usable data from their observations, raising consciousness of otherwise unseen interrelationships, such that, for example, 'an entomologist [might] be informed about a new air-pollution problem' (41). Brunner, like Huxley, finds that literature misrepresents by exclusion when it does not speak to far-reaching interconnections, recognising that for the novel to present the individual as autonomous agent means a range of external influences are either excluded or interpreted as internal impulses. However, when the connections are so remote as to be indiscernible without immensely powerful technology or full-time study by people of particular aptitude, there is anxiety of constitution of the self. Protagonist Donald Hogan, a synthesist, comes to doubt his own integrity, experiencing 'the sense that there was no such person as Donald Hogan but only one among millions of manikins, all of whom were versions of a Self without beginning or end' (43). Saturation in data baffles the ascription of significance. The novel formally reproduces the experience of drowning in information. Chapters covering the main story are interspersed with single-chapter vignettes of life around the world, as well as chapters which collate short snatches of verbal information in a manner reminiscent of a Twitter feed – newspaper headlines, advertising jingles, database entries and other texts follow one another without hierarchy and without explanation for their selection. Anticipating the over-connection of the networked world of the twenty-first century, *Stand on Zanzibar* suggests that the construction of identity from a surplus of systems of understanding is as provocative of anxiety as attempting to read the self without apprehension of the wider forces shaping it. Like the Huxley of *Point Counter Point*, Brunner sees lived experience as best represented as a clash of systems of thought, *Stand on Zanzibar* illustrating that a comprehensible story is not built up from nothing, but instead hewed down from an excess of connections.

The Writer's Own Projection of Personality

When, in *After Many a Summer*, Propter claims that good 'exists as the experience of eternity, as the transcendence of personality, the extension of consciousness beyond the limits imposed by the ego' (146), he articulates an understanding of transcendence to which Huxley would largely subscribe. The chief ill is to take the human level as complete: an ill Propter sees as pervasive among those with power. Politicians, he pronounces, are 'all humanists', and, as such, 'live in a world of illusion, a world that's a mere projection of their own human personalities' (146), which, for him, results in a world unsafe 'for ourselves as animals and as spirits' (147). For Huxley, the challenge which confronts a writer is to show the incompleteness of the world as ordinarily understood while using the same lexical resources which limit full appreciation of reality in the first place. As he writes in *The Devils of Loudun*, what we refer to as 'the world' (in quotation marks) is in actuality 'a system of verbal categories taking the place of the fathomlessly beautiful and mysterious particulars which constitute reality' (75).

The notion of language as a barrier between the individual and a wider consciousness can help to delineate Huxley's understanding of the writer's work from that of modernist peers. Where, for Stephen Kern, modernism is to be associated with a 'shift in the spatiality of the novel as it relocated toward the interior consciousness of characters' (91), for Huxley, that spatial shift is conceptually flawed, to the extent that consciousness is not purely individual. Huxley, along with Lawrence, shares the modernist investment in consciousness, but not the certainty that consciousness is interior, and thus neither of them would accept that a turn towards the representation of consciousness has to be understood as an inward, introspective turn. Similarly, Pericles Lewis's suggestion that the modernist novel 'concerns itself with the relationship between the individual consciousness and the external reality that it confronts' speaks to a terrain which Huxley very much inhabits, but with an implicit assumption Huxley would not accept (4) – there does not have to be a point of confrontation between the individual and external reality if consciousness surpasses the individual. While a person might experience a sense of incompatibility with the world, this may be dissolved by recognising this frontier as illusory.

In his final years Huxley continued to publicly extol telepathy. In a 1954 article for the magazine *Life*, entitled 'A Case for ESP, PK and Psi', Huxley offers the hypothesis that a 'World Mind' exists, with psi 'represent[ing] a leakage into personal consciousness of some of the mental material which the brain normally either excludes or directs into utilitarian channels' (102). The stance follows from his first experience taking mescaline in 1953, which he credits with showing him that the brain's primary function is to filter an undiluted impersonal consciousness and not to generate individual thoughts. He writes in *The Doors of Perception* that

> I find myself agreeing with the eminent Cambridge philosopher, Dr. C. D. Broad, 'that we should do well to consider much more seriously than we have hitherto been inclined to do the type of theory which Bergson put forward in connection with memory and sense perception' whereby 'the function of the brain and nervous system and sense organs is in the main *eliminative* and not productive.' (10, emphasis from source)

For Huxley, 'the function of the brain and nervous system is to protect us from being overwhelmed and confused by this mass of largely useless and irrelevant knowledge, by shutting out most of what we should otherwise perceive or remember at any moment' (10–11). At this point, then, Huxley sees telepathic events as momentary lapses in systems which have evolved to prevent mental contact. Not only does telepathy expend energy in a way likely to be redundant for a person's individual survival, but there is a danger that a person awoken to this World Mind ceases to conceptualise herself or himself as an individual and therefore no longer sees personal survival as imperative.

This occurs in *Island*. Will's transcendence through decentration leaves him unconcerned with personal preservation when the Rendang military arrives in Pala. For Gerald Heard, Huxley himself enjoys a similar, albeit more gradual dissociation. Suggesting that Huxley 'grew relatively free of his ego' ('Poignant' 69), the result, Heard offers, is a personal freedom at odds with the forces pushing the maintenance of a persona as a writer and a public intellectual. As William Tindall diagnoses as early as 1942 in 'The Trouble with Aldous Huxley', 'the romantic movement, which affects readers as much as writers, has encouraged an interest in personality as well as in its expansion' (464). That interest in personality, for Tindall, manifests as engagement with the character of the writer as much as with the personalities of the writer's creations. Thus, he offers, 'despite the desire of Propter, Heard and Huxley to transcend their personalities, readers are interested in the personality of Huxley' (464). This attitude can be identified in the critic as much as in any other reader. The very goal of better understanding the writer as an individual presents a tension, albeit not irreconcilable, when the writer's work interrogates the very value and legitimacy of individuality as a concept.

Even if a critic does not share Huxley's views of telepathy or the impersonal mind, the assumption that literature should concern itself with the individual character underlies the recurring criticism of him as unable to create distinct, distinctive individuals, and the wider criticism of the novel of ideas. If it is granted that Huxley may have been unwilling, rather than unable, to produce literature invested in coherent individuals, then his career as a writer of fiction may be reappraised as an exercise in decentration of personality – an exercise like that of the telepathist or mystic unfocusing to see beyond herself or himself. In *Point Counter Point* and *Eyeless in Gaza*, the long shadow of the bildungsroman is visible, as the respective protagonists struggle with the impossibility of taking control of their own stories and thereby making something of themselves. By *Island*, the coherent personal story and coherent personality are seen as limiting and artificial: a healthy society, Huxley offers, is one which facilitates the loss of self, rather than self-discovery. Along the way, Huxley sets in motion an idea, in the novel of ideas, which, as ideas are wont, transcends his individual control. Fitted to speak to an age of information saturation, the novel of ideas evolves, through Murdoch and Byatt, through Brunner's *Stand on Zanzibar*, into the decentred network novel, and with it becomes central to the novel's vitality in the twenty-first century.

Chapter 4

Doris Lessing, Deindividuated Characters and Hybrid Identity

The Collectivist Self and Character as Role

In her final novel, 2007's *The Cleft*, Doris Lessing problematises the identification of character with physically individual being. The novel imagines an exclusively female society thousands of years in the past as it is disturbed by the birth of its first male children. Among the features the society has developed is a binding of names to roles. For instance, whoever acts as recordkeeper has the name Maire. As the reader encounters Maire, she resists being perceived as a physical individual rather than the embodiment of a role. Pondering, in a record, that the reader might want to know more about her, she elects not to provide information about her appearance or personality, offering only that 'my name is Maire' and that 'there is always someone called Maire' (9). Though Maire suggests that it does not matter if multiple people have the same name because 'you can always tell by looking at someone' (11), this, of course, is not possible for the reader. As years pass, one embodiment of Maire can be assumed to replace another, though *The Cleft* does not mark these transitions. Presented as the reconstruction by Transit, a Roman historian, of a time patchily recorded, the novel provides absence of evidence as justification for its omissions. The historian admits to having 'no means of knowing how long the Cleft's story took to evolve' and also to having 'no idea' how long it took for Maire and other characters 'to become more than themselves' (102). As the historian smooths over gaps in the historical record, the reader has no choice but to accept Maire and other figures in *The Cleft* as characters whose extension is not delimited by a given physical body.

What *The Cleft* refuses is access to the particular: Maire, as a role, as a category, is a generalised entity. Denied witness to the specifics of particular Maires (and likewise of other roles), the reader is unable to invest in the development and well-being of the individual embodying Maire at any given time. Because of this, the way Maire can be read is not analogous to the way an individuated character is read. To be Maire means being the maker of records: that definitional fixity precludes the narrative of finding oneself or of making something of oneself. To the extent we do not see how individuals become or cease to be Maire, or anything of their personal comfort or discomfort in the role, we see only shifts in how the role is performed, and how it fits into society at large. As such, focus is pushed to the development and well-being of the society as a whole: the reader can perceive changes in social structure as the appearance of male children is addressed, but with scant sense of the thoughts and emotions of particular individuals. Development on that collective level is the only development which can be spoken to with any confidence. In this much, *The Cleft* contests claims about the working of the novel which insist one of its defining qualities is to conceive of the world through the interaction of bodily individuals. When Marta Figlerowicz asserts that 'to represent the social world through characters, as novels do, is to insist on the primacy of the particular' (123), it fails to apply to *The Cleft*. It and others among Lessing's more speculative novels, including *The Marriages Between Zones Three, Four, and Five* (1980) and *The Making of the Representative for Planet 8* (1982), go to exceptional lengths in probing the ability of the novel to represent existence as predominantly collective and give primacy to the type over the physical individuals embodying those types. Obscuring the individual behind given roles, and empowering the group to think and feel with a single mind, these novels probe the limits of the novel's ability to represent psychic connection, suggesting that society might be constituted and comprehended through the prism of the health and motivations of the collective.

In this much, Lessing's work represents an apogee in twentieth-century experimentation in representing psychic connection in the novel. Across her whole career, in both realist and speculative fiction, Lessing senses and suggests that investment in physical individuals misrepresents the breadth and persistence of character. She draws on parapsychological and panpsychic accounts to underpin a sense that participation in a culture meaningfully amounts to participation in a common mind. In seeking to represent collectivity, Lessing tests whether the novel can dispense with the story form of an individual's quest for self-transcendence found in much prior literature of psychic connection. *The Cleft*, *The Making of the Representative* and *The Marriages* each imagine societies in which selfhood has long – if not always – been experienced collectivistically.

Doing so, she goes beyond the likes of D. H. Lawrence and Olaf Stapledon before her, generating collectivist representational strategies for novels in her wake. When, in *The Rainbow* (1915), Lawrence has Ursula experience the epiphanic realisation that 'she was Woman, she was the whole of Woman in the human order. All-containing, universal' (412), it is a revelation which arrives at the culmination of a long, novelistic journey of individual self-discovery. Growing up in a small mining town, Ursula feels herself unlike those around her, and strives through education and accomplishment to mark herself out from others. The encompassing sense of self she finds, its discovery precipitated in large part by her university education, is experienced as additional to a narrower one, rather than an effacement of it: Ursula's feeling is that, while she has 'another, stronger self that knew the darkness', 'her everyday self was just the same' (418). That wider self being an addition, Ursula's psychic development constitutes a personal growth comparable to that of the classical novel. Improvement as distinction is invalidated, but betterment remains equated to personal growth.

Comparably, in *Star Maker* (1937), when Stapledon imagines a universe-spanning 'communal mind' (139) which belongs to a 'communal "I"' (136) underlying individuality is still not effaced. As the narrator experiences connection to ever more consciousnesses across the cosmos, he asserts that 'it would be untrue to say that we had lost our individuality, or were dissolved in a communal individuality, as to say that we were all the while distinct individuals' (134). The scale of *Star Maker* tips the balance towards the communal, such that the narrator finds recall of events and experience as his previous, purely terrestrial self difficult, but ultimately Stapledon's use of an additive model stretches the novelistic arc of the individual's growth rather than contesting it on a foundational level. *Star Maker* gives the individual much, much more room to grow, and that growth entails sharing space with others, but the sense that elevation is occurring depends on continual reference to the expanded reach of the narrator as an individual.

Lessing acknowledges debt to Lawrence and Stapledon in precipitating her engagement with literature's ability to reflect psychic connection. In her 1988 afterword to Tarcher's edition of *Last and First Men*, she describes having read Stapledon during her childhood, and asserts that to read his work 'means taking a leap out from our provisional and temporary sets of mind' (307). She identifies Lawrence, whose work she also read during her youth in Southern Rhodesia, as 'reaching out to other dimensions' and as possessing 'supranormal sensitivity' ('The Fox'). However, Lessing demonstrates that, while the addition of psychic connection stretches the novel, a qualitatively greater challenge to its limits occurs when it dispenses with elements previously assumed necessary, including that of the individuated self as a starting point for later psychic connection. Even in her more realist fiction, Lessing offers collectivist conceptions of the self as valid to the exclusion of individuated conceptions. *Briefing for a Descent into Hell* (1971), for instance, imagines its mental patient protagonist as experiencing affinity with a universal mindedness which sees him reject his name and the constriction of identity associated with it.

For Lessing, the centrality of psychic connection in her work is wed to a sustained belief in telepathy and group minds as real. On a number of occasions across the second half of her life Lessing voices the conviction that telepathy exists and, indeed, claims that she herself has 'experienced telepathy' (Bigsby 84). It first enters her novels as an irruption in her realist fiction – overturning established understandings of self rather than adding to them. *The Four-Gated City* (1969), the final novel in her five-novel *Children of Violence* series, has series protagonist Martha come to understand that she is telepathic, a realisation which precedes a dramatic shift as the novel moves from the present time into the future, imagining the foundation of an island community built around psychic development (though on one of Scotland's Western Isles, rather than the subtropical paradise of Aldous Huxley's Pala). By dint of that irruption, *The Four-Gated City* suggests the present understanding of reality to be a contingent one, puncturing, specifically, an increasingly individualist Britain she sees emerging. It is a moment which confounded critics at the time, dismayed at an apparent abandonment of social realism, but it anticipates the kind of role telepathy would play in other literary fiction in the latter half of the twentieth century. When Salman Rushdie and David Mitchell use it in *Midnight's Children* (1981) and *Ghostwritten* (1999), respectively, it offers means to speak to the provisionality of present structures for interpreting society and to the abundance of connections identity is formed from, including those invisible in ordinary accounts of personal development.

Where science appears to align with her experiential sense of psychic connection, Lessing draws on it for support. For example, in a 1969 radio interview she comments that 'the atmosphere's changed about something like telepathy' in the past ten years, with 'different forms of extrasensory perception [. . .] being seriously researched and accepted' (Terkel 25–6). As illustration, she mentions an announcement from the Soviet Union 'that they were experimenting into the use of telepathy for space travel' (26). What, specifically, Lessing is referring to is unclear, in part because there was a considerable amount of research into telepathy and related phenomena in the Soviet Union across the 1960s, continuing into the early 1970s (albeit few findings were publicly announced). A declassified US Defense Intelligence Agency file suggests that in 1967 the USSR had an annual budget of over thirteen million dollars for research into parapsychological phenomena, conducted at twenty or more centres (LaMothe 24). With respect to space, the report claims that 'the Soviets are training their cosmonauts in telepathy to back-up their electronic equipment while in outer space' and quotes rocket scientist Konstantin Tsiolkovsky as saying that 'in the coming era of space flights, telepathic abilities are necessary' (25). Lessing's conviction that telepathy is on the way to being proven invests too much in governmental attention as validation, but it is symptomatic of a moment, like that of the mid- to late 1930s, in which the media excites itself over the very fact of paranormal enquiry being conducted, even while demonstrable results are completely absent.

However, as time passes and as less credence is given to the prospect that telepathy might be the secret weapon to swing the Cold War, such rumours diminish (which coincides with a declining presence for telepathy – psychotronically bolstered or not – in science fiction literature). Lessing, however, trusts experience ahead of science and continues to assert that telepathy is real. In a 1974 interview, she states that 'my view now is that we all of us all the time use capacities which science says don't exist' and that 'we couldn't exist for five minutes without them' (qtd in Whittaker 77). She continues, claiming that 'we communicate with [these capacities] all the time' and that 'we're just on the verge of a complete revolution in how we make sense of things'. Unlike Rhine's understanding of the telepathic process, which expects intentional action on the part of the transmitter (willing, for example, particular images to be projected in the Zener card experiments), for Lessing telepathy does not refer to willed transmission or reception of specific items of data. Describing how her experience of telepathy has been, she claims that 'we are probably at it all the time without knowing it' and that 'ideas flows through our minds like water' (Bigsby 84). This description of the telepathic experience is one which gives no role to human agency. It is also one Lessing reiterates in the introduction to *The Sirian Experiments* (1980), in which she writes that 'it seems to me that ideas must flow through humanity like tides' (ix). For Lessing, like Huxley, the unbidden appearance of ideas in the mind is indicative that thoughts frequently lead thinker, rather than the reverse.

As agency is attributed to the idea itself, what Lessing evokes comes to resemble Richard Dawkins's meme: the sense that ideas might, in and of themselves, possess varying strengths, varying abilities, to be disseminated with speed and across cultural conditions.[1] In 1976's *The*

Selfish Gene, Dawkins writes that 'memes propagate themselves in the meme pool by leaping from brain to brain via a process which, in the broad sense, can be called imitation' (206) – implying, semantically at least, that the idea acts, with the mind the setting of that action more than a participant in it. However, while Lessing's image of ideas flowing through minds also implies the mind to be fundamentally passive in this process, in her essay 'Group Minds' she suggests that the role of the thinker in this process should be addressed. For Lessing, while 'one may watch how an idea or an opinion, even a phrase, springs up and is repeated in a hundred reviews, criticisms, conversations – and then vanishes', it is the case that 'each individual who has bravely repeated this opinion or phrase has been the victim of a compulsion to be like everyone else, and that has never been analyzed' (51). Lessing undersells her own contribution with this claim: much of her fiction examines how powerful ideas interact with the minds they pass through and how, in her view, they create webs of connection.

Lessing and We-Narration

To narrate novels in which character is above all collectivist requires reconfiguration of the narrative underpinnings of the novel. In the fragment of *The Cleft* Maire herself narrates, a wider perspective informs her story through verification by consensus. Her faith in what she recounts, and the concept of self resident in it, rests on collective endorsement. She explains that when the story of her people

> is told to the young ones [. . .] it is told first among ourselves, and one will say, 'No, it was not like that,' or another, 'Yes, it was like that,' and by the time everyone is agreed we can be sure there is nothing in the story that is untrue.' (8–9)

Indeed, so fundamental is this communal verification that it is rendered as collective thought, Maire stating that 'we thought we' (7). Maire, as a representative of a group, narrates more authoritatively than she could as an individual, because the group has been able to collectively reconstruct the flow of ideas. Save identifying herself by name, she tells a history of her people collectively, naming no other individuals. Maire's communally verified narrative is a function of her awareness of her individual limitation and her faith in the wider group – as well as the group's faith in her. It also approaches individual selfhood as contingent. While Maire speaks of a 'new talk', in which 'I say I, and again I, I do this and

I think that' (7), the collective sense of a less individuated self-concept persists, with numerous thoughts, feelings and actions attributed to the collective Cleft society rather than any given member.

In Lessing's work more widely, acceptance and recuperation of we-thought is seen to be essential to restoring humanity to lost health. In 1979's *Shikasta* it is offered that 'to identify with ourselves as individuals is [. . .] the very essence of the Degenerative Disease' (55). Further, *Shikasta* presents a lack of a material known as 'the substance-of-we-feeling' as a root cause of the ill-health of the Earth at large (96).[2] *The Sentimental Agents in the Volyen Empire* (1983) similarly positions the group as essential to a human being, with the claim made that 'the human animal, so recently evolved from a condition of living in groups, groups within herds, packs, flocks, troops, and clans, cannot exist now without them' (132). The absorption of ideas of the group is understood as inevitable: to be without a group is 'denying millions of [. . .] years of evolution', and the young group member is 'unarmoured, without protection against being swallowed whole by some set of ideas that need have no relevance to any real information that moves or drives the society' (132–3). Admittance that the human retains a compulsion to belong to a group and will absorb its ideas is suggested to be essential in understanding of the nature of the self.

In placing we before I, Lessing follows a lineage of quasi-evolutionary accounts in which collective identification and collective thought are seen as evolutionary states preceding primarily individual identification and individual thought, among them Gerald Heard's *The Ascent of Humanity* (1929) and H. G. Wells's *A Short History of the World* (1922). What she challenges is the suggestion that individuation is necessarily an advancement. Lessing, emphasising consensus, approaches language as a societally tuned tool, wherein meaning is established collectively and, by extension, the attribution of thoughts and feelings to a collective fits the communal generation of the means of their expression. When considered against Lessing's work, Brian Richardson's proposal that '"we" narration easily slides into distortions of ordinary usage and readily becomes nonrealistic or [. . .] "unnatural"' feels invested in a narrow understanding of what qualifies as realistic ('Representing' 200). For Richardson, the bounds of the realistic, when it comes to narration, can be inferred to be mapped to the bounds of individual perception. Addressing the intervals of we-narration in Joseph Conrad's *Narcissus* (1897), for instance, Richardson suggests that they contribute to 'a transcendence of the strictures of realism' insomuch as 'the "we" voice cannot know the private thoughts of many of the seamen' which it seems to encompass (*Unnatural* 41). In taking this position,

Richardson disregards many means by which the group's thoughts might come to be apprehended. Even without invoking any paranormal possibilities, those thoughts might have been reckoned by inference or known through discussion prior to the unspecified time when the narrative is recounted. Per Lessing's recordkeepers, a given mouth can be the authoritative articulator of the group's sentiment, aggregation producing an account not subject to the distortions of individual moments of confusion, and not forced into ellipses when a given individual was absent at given moments.

Richardson's suggestion that there is an intrinsic opposition to realism depends on conflation of the immediately knowable with the real. While assertions about the nature of prehistoric thought are inevitably speculative, as are, by extension, claims for its persistence in quiescent form, the endeavour behind Lessing's deployment of it in *The Cleft* is to encompass more of the real in her understanding of the world and to produce literature which encompasses more of the self. Richardson's suggestion that it is most useful to see the we-narrator in literature 'like a postmodern first person narrator who is not bound by the epistemological rules of realism' (*Unnatural* 58) also feels ill-suited to what Lessing does with the device. Maire does not use 'we' unilaterally: a group has approved the narrative offered and the immediate narrator is their authorised representative. *The Cleft* demonstrates that it may be most useful to see any given I-narrator as containing an implicit we-narrator, rather than the reverse, insomuch as a story necessarily and continually refers to perspectives beyond the individual when it articulates the passage of thoughts and feelings and, moreover, uses language generated collectively.

For the reader, we-narration does often entail doubt and misapprehension, but this can equally be true of I-narration. When, in the case of the crew of the *Narcissus*, we-narration is often imprecise with respect to the extension of the group it encompasses, and with respect to changes in the composition of the group in question, it is reflective of the experience of being in an environment of shifting, unspoken alliances. The reader may find their imagination of a scene has been mistaken if an individual assumed to be encompassed by 'we' transpires to be the object of the group's feelings or the antagonist to its actions at a given moment. However, the reader's uncertainty as to the group's constitution is often mirrored by group members. In *Narcissus*, a sense that an unexpressed bond unites the crew gives way to uncertainty as to the status of a bond which is never articulated, crew members becoming prone to fear others are not pulling their weight and are not to be trusted in a crisis. That no individual is identified in *Narcissus* as the narrator behind the 'we' is fitting – no individual could be sufficiently assured of their inclusion in the group to serve as its mouthpiece. In this much, *Narcissus*'s we-narration enables an internal perspective to be voiced without affording any individual an artificially assured status within the group. Distinction between 'I' and 'we', between exclusive and inclusive subjectivity, may best be seen as one of emphasis, rather than nature: there is no voicing 'I' without drawing upon collectively obtained knowledge and collectively developed conceptual and discursive products. *The Cleft*, in kind with other works by Lessing, demonstrates that given a broad enough perspective, especially one extended in time, any given individual is largely – if not entirely – reducible to a manifestation of a position within a group, to an embodiment of a role, rather than a fundamentally individuated entity.

Identity is also dissociated from bodily individuality in Adrian Tchaikovsky's *Children of Time* (2015), in which, like in *The Cleft*, names cohere with roles. However, in this case, biological inscription renders recordkeeping redundant. It imagines a situation in which the use of a nanovirus to render a planet a fit new home for humanity unintentionally leads to a species of jumping spider, *Portia labiata*, evolving rapidly, developing a sophisticated society. When the development of this society is narrated, 'Portia' is used as a name for whichever of a long lineage of spiders is the leader of the society is at a given time. A character is attributed to Portia: she – whoever embodies her at a given time – is a warrior, but also a born mystic, possessing 'the fearful and the wonderful understanding that there is more in the world than her eyes can see, more than her feet can feel' (206). Similarly, the name Bianca is applied to the members of a line of great scholars. The repeated use of these names might be taken as reductivist, the product of an outsider narrator unable to perceive the spiders as individuals, unattuned to their vibrational communication, but the emphasis on continuity is reflective of the spiders' relationship with their ancestors. Born with what are termed 'Understandings', the spiders have 'evolved the ability to pass on learning and experience genetically, direct to their offspring' (575). They are, in effect, natural recordkeepers, these inborn Understandings a communally generated wisdom, albeit refined through generational iteration rather than discussion as a society. Where the narrator sees a 'problem with human records' in that 'so much is lost forever as the grinding wheel of the years groans on', this biological inscription is seen to preserve awarenesses unmediated by language, preventing loss or distortion through shifts in context. Ultimately, the dominant element of the spiders' identity is in the continuous rather than the momentary, such that, for Bianca, 'the core of what she considers herself to be is simply her capacity and desire to learn, not any individual facility she might briefly take with her' (426). Building on epigenetic research which suggests acquired characteristics might be heritable,[3] Tchaikovsky presents the intergenerational transmission of concepts as acting like a temporally removed telepathy; like in Lessing's work, what results is that the collectively verified is seen as more dependable than the products of individual apprehension or reason.

The Making of the Representative for Planet 8 is also heavily invested in the balance between individual and collective selfhood, tracing changes in that balance as a cataclysmic cooling in the climate of Planet 8 necessitates dramatic changes in how life is lived. In it, there is a degeneration into individualism and competition as a function of increasingly harsh conditions, though Lessing points to a way forwards in which microscopic physical bonds are invested in as a basis for experiencing the self as connected. In contrast with *The Cleft*'s fading sense of 'we' as a dominant mode of selfhood, *The Making of the Representative* opens with group identity still predominant for its people. Narrator Doeg (like Maire a recordkeeper), reports that 'the clan was our basic unit, and we felt it as our strength, our foundation as a people' (42). Identity is bound to function within the clan, such that multiple people might bear the same name if they perform the same function and such that appellations change with a change in function. The name 'Doeg' is used by multiple people. On their return from another planet, Planet 10, a group is 'all Doeg, for then we travelled everywhere over our planet and told what we had seen' (54). In accordance with the primacy of collective identity, we-narration is dominant, at least in the opening stages of the novel. Assertions such as 'we all knew, we all understood' (42) and 'we voiced what we were thinking' (44) are regularly made, with implicit confidence that the bonds of the clan are tight enough for it to represent a single actor. In *The Making of the Representative*, common purpose leads to coordination and coordination impels a holistic view of identity. As Doeg reflects, to an external observer the occupants of Planet 8 are not 'swarming myriads, but sets of wholes' (82) They are, Doeg continues, like 'shoals and flocks' which constitute to 'superior supervising eyes, a whole, an entity, moving as one, living as one, behaving as one – thinking as one' (82–3). The we-narration of *The Making of the Representative* is not offered as generalisation, but as reflective of a reality in which a group mind exists. For Lessing, this is not a fantastic possibility. In the introduction to *Shikasta*, she explains that she 'believe[s] that it is possible [. . .] to "plug in" to an overmind, or Ur-mind, or unconscious, or what you will, and this accounts for a great many improbabilities and "coincidences"' (9). *The Making of the Representative* suggests that, with favourable conditions, connection to this 'overmind' could be persisting, rather than temporary, and in this case, the collective mind would predominate in the formulation of selfhood.

However, as the climate cools on Planet 8 and changes in social roles are impelled, the facility with which all-encompassing 'we' statements are made decreases. The harmony which comes with knowing one's place in society wanes as old ways of living and working become climatically impossible and new practices prove only temporarily effective. The shift away from a primarily collective selfhood is not immediately apprehended, nor its consequences understood. When, at an early stage of the upheaval, previously unknown crimes begin occurring, Doeg's response is that it is 'not reasonable' that 'the individual victims of a murder or a casual looting made us more uneasy and angry than when twenty people died because of a sudden snowstorm' (38). There is a failure to comprehend that, while these crimes cause less immediate loss, they are indicative of a social sickness and a diminution in the group's ability to act with one purpose and one mind. Comparably, an increase in 'I' language in Doeg's narration, like 'I felt' (49) and 'I knew' (49), betrays the fact that a change in primary selfhood from collective to individual has occurred, some time before Doeg shows self-awareness that a shift has taken place.

Ultimately, Planet 8's increasingly disparate and increasingly desperate inhabitants look to a more fundamental level to reassert that they share bonds. A group of Planet 8's inhabitants, newly unsure of their roles and so unsure of their identities, reason that they have 'lost what we had been' and are now 'a group of individuals, yet a unity' because they are bound together as parts of 'webs of matter or substance or something tangible, [. . .] sliding and intermingling' (118). The material kinship means, for these people, more than a broadly defined sense of being of one flesh, or breathing the same air – as the same forces shape them, including shaping their mental processes, they determine that 'we were feelings, and thought, and will' (118). An apparently natural sense of collective selfhood has, with effort, to be replaced by a notion of interconnection invested in the most basic of units, particles, producing a unity reasoned more than it is felt. For Claire Sprague, this revised understanding of connection sees *The Making of the Representative* 'press its transcendent point too much', as, she argues, 'Lessing openly abandons the body and the environment' (9). However, while the new vision of connectedness invests in the most fundamental of matter – and thereby does not speak to environmental particularity – it is a vision which emerges in response to environmental change.

Interviewing Lessing in 1983, Stephen Gray puts to her that in *The Making of the Representative for Planet 8* she has 'the provocative idea that character and role are not always related, that the role can be passed on and people are really interchangeable', and that she has 'detached the individual from a personal destiny' (338). Lessing's response contests the understanding that a person's self-realisation should coincide with individuation: she suggests that 'you start off with your life and the need to define yourself and this frightful struggle to make this statement of what you are, to find out what it is. Then you do sort of float away from that – instead of being embedded in it, you see yourself from a distance' (339). In effect, gaining a particular role entails identity with others performing the same role. The quest to make something of oneself as individual leads, for Lessing, away from individuation: for the something one becomes to be recognised means acting according to certain role-defined conventions, as well as presenting certain qualities, such that the role constricts possible directions for development. In Lessing's own case, she explains that 'for a long time I've seen "the writer" as a kind of function of humanity; I feel connected with other writers because I feel that in a sense we are one, doing perhaps slightly different things' (338). This understanding is in evidence in the second *Canopus in Argos* novel, *The Marriages Between Zones Three, Four, and Five*. It offers another recordkeeper as narrator, this time Lusik, a chronicler in the collectivist Zone Three. Lusik sees the recordkeeper in the way Lessing sees the writer – not as an individual trying to understand a whole they are remote from, but as a function of society. When 'any of us [. . .] call ourselves Chronicler or song-maker', he offers, 'we are the visible and evident aspects of a whole we all share, that we all go to form' (197). The chronicler or song-maker is, for Lusik, not the generator of this identity; it is applied based on an individual's position in a social fabric: a relational descriptor. In this much, for Lusik 'these guises, aspects, presentations' are 'only manifestations of *what we all are* at different times, according to how these needs are pulled out of us' (197, emphasis from source). Society requires storytellers (and the societies of *The Cleft*, *The Marriages* and *The Making of the Representative* see this as a fundamental need and venerate their storytellers and historians accordingly), and as a result of an aptitude to fill that need Lusik is incarnated into the role. It may have been experienced as a choice, but its availability as an option is a function of Lusik's society, and it is a choice Lusik's character disposed him to make.

Lessing's understanding of the role of the writer is a view that privileges society's effect on the individual above the individual's effect on society: social forces will impel a certain number of people (within a range) to be writers, or, say, builders or politicians, and those who fill these roles are subject to sufficiently similar pressures that like patterns of thought and behaviour will manifest in them. Responding to Lessing, Gray suggests that, in 'talking of people in terms of function instead of in terms of the previous individual psyche', she has moved 'very far from [her] social realist mode of thinking' (338), a remark which appears to take investment in the individual as essential to realism – even socialist realism. However, literature which treats social constructs as products of the individuated mind is no more obviously realist than the reverse, whereby the individual nature is approached as a by-product of social forces. Lessing challenges the preconceptions of a reading public, critics included, invested in the individual as literature's basic unit. In her work, she casts doubt on the ostensibly inevitable identity between bodily individual and individuated character, suggesting both that other models of selfhood are theoretically possible and also that they might, unrecognised, operate underneath presently predominant models for understanding the self. Outside the text, she also reacts against the veneration of the writer as an individual, possessed of unique talents. Her claimed kinship with other writers and presentation of herself as fulfilling a function of humanity seek to minimise the degree to which her creations are considered the products of individual, irreplicable talent.

Hybrid Subjectivity and the Doubling of Self

For Nancy Armstrong, novels, having developed 'to distinguish the modern middle class from a people of different ethnic practices, especially different literacies', will unavoidably 'think like individuals about the difficulty of fulfilling oneself as an individual under specific cultural historical conditions' (10). New generations of novels, she contends, whether they 'involve[] resistance, complicity, mimicry, or hybridity do[] not alter the basic fact' that form is bound to the individual subject (10). Lessing, however, finds the hybrid subject, be that a migrant or other figure belonging to multiple groups, innately exposes the individuated self as a fiction. The coexistence of multiple mentalities in a single bodily individual exposes, for Lessing, the arbitrariness of social inscription which, in certain cultures, takes thinking as an individual to be natural and necessary. Novelistically representing hybridity, Lessing resists rendering these overlaps and intersections as sources of tension, approaching hybridity as inclusion in multiple collective selves and as a fact to be accepted. Fulfilment, in her work, does not come from finding means to define oneself as an individual from disparate material, but from recognising the impossibility of doing so. For Lessing, inclusion in multiple cultures is substantially equivalent to inclusion in multiple minds, psychic connections within a group having meaningful existence. However, Lessing is not alone in finding telepathy a valuable device to impel reappraisal of the meaning of group-belonging. In Rushdie's *Midnight's Children*, Muslim Indian protagonist Saleem has the telepathic ability to listen to any of India's inhabitants. The result is that the group is situated inside the individual rather than the individual in the group, exposing individualistic conceptions of freedom and independence as artifices which misrepresent how much the supposedly individual will is socially formed.

In its consideration of the relationship between individual and society, *Re: Colonised Planet 5, Shikasta* (1979), the first *Canopus in Argos* novel, employs the established science fiction device of alien visitors to Earth adopting human form to observe our behaviour. In it, multiple representatives of the galactic empire Canopus are seen to live on Earth (known by them as Shikasta), using their great longevity to live out full human lifespans embodied in human form, before returning home to report on their experiences. Such is the nature of the embodiment, encompassing development from childhood into adulthood, that these emissaries largely or completely lose track of their Canopean identities while in human form, often remembering aspects of their preceding lives only in poorly understood dreams or hallucinations. As such, these visitors frequently regard themselves – or are regarded by others – as insane. One such figure is Lynda Coldridge – a character previously encountered in *The Four-Gated City* – now revealed to be the human embodiment of a Canopean. In notes written as part of psychiatric treatment, she grasps that her human form does not constitute the entirety of her self, suggesting that 'we are several people fitted inside each other. Chinese boxes' (*Shikasta* 233). In the layered selfhood Lynda experiences, the levels align, but do not connect to one another: she describes feeling the boxes separate from one another, such that one self can 'look[] down at the others, or other' (234). While the presence of an alien being within Lynda marks her out as particular (at least to the extent that the alien within is literal in her case), her understanding reaches through to what Lessing would see as a wider truth. Different aspects of the self – perhaps better understood as different selves – coexist in any given person.

The Sirian Experiments (1980) develops related ideas. It focuses on Ambien II, a diplomatic representative of Canopus's rival galactic empire, Sirius. Ambien II finds herself increasingly estranged from other Sirians after spending large amounts of time on Earth in the company of Canopean emissaries. Ambien feels the pressure of cultural context in moulding her, becoming adapted to a new environment and companions with previously unfamiliar cultural values. More than this, however, she feels so little control over her character that she is uncomfortable defining it as hers. Ambien asserts that 'it is not possible for an individual to think differently from the whole he or she is part of' (272) and that 'each event, or person, or even an overheard remark becom[es] an aspect of a whole – a confluence whose sources go back into the past, reach forward into the future' (65). She concludes that, while 'each person everywhere sees itself, thinks of itself, as a unique and extraordinary individual', they are instead 'a tiny unit that can exist only as part of a whole' (272). In asserting a disparity between what individualistic culture accepts as selfhood and the understanding which comes from considering a fuller context, Ambien gives explicit voice to a tension which formal experimentation in Lessing's work consistently strives to encapsulate.

In this light, the treatment of roles as characters in *The Cleft* and *The Making of the Representative* indicates societies which refuse exceptionalism: independent thought and nonconformism dissolve as possibilities if the primary self is a collective one and if thought is seen to flow between entities – that is, put another way, if psychic connection is real. As such, they reject central assumptions of the traditional novel, wherein the individual defines themselves in opposition to wider society, their identity chiefly invested in those features which are distinct from assumed norms. Like Huxley, Lessing does not accept the conflation of development and differentiation. Each sees the novel in which this conflation exists as perpetuating limited and limiting understandings of personality and human potential. Lessing sees the illusion László Földényi points to in the traditional novel, whereby it depends upon 'the myth of the private person, contrasting the individual with society, with its institutions' ('Novel' 7). For Földényi, as for Lessing, the precept on which the contrast depends is faulty, to the extent that 'the public is present in every gesture of the private individual' (7). This is an attitude Ambien II explicitly shares and a foundational assumption for much of Lessing's work, which rejects the striving for distinction as a misdirection of effort.

Shikasta brings into conversation differing timeframes. Its first half covers tens of thousands of years of imagined prehistory to human society, replacing a narrative of evolutionary growth towards humankind with one of decline from lost races of noble giants. The second is dedicated to snapshots of human life across the globe in the twentieth century. Shifting from one to the other, *Shikasta* communicates a sense that flows of wider culture unavoidably underscore what an individual experiences as a personal response to a situation. For the Canopeans observing Earth (and intervening in it), the particularities of human behaviour only make sense as the product of the long-term degeneration which led to the present species. It is a perspective of a kind sought by Ursula K. Heise, Dipesh Chakrabarty and Charles M. Tung, who respectively consider that chronological expansion of the frame in which humankind is understood is necessary to more fully appreciate what it is to be a species with planet-altering power. As Tung puts it, 'we arrive at our contingency and global responsibility by enfolding a decentred humanity in ever-larger totalizing frames' (516). *Shikasta*'s imaginary history makes no pretence of offering a definitive account of human origins: it self-consciously inverts scientific and scriptural accounts which treat humankind as a pinnacle (also a facet of Stapledon's *Last and First Men*), serving as a corrective to the implications of established narratives. In this regard, it is effective in illustrating that, just as individuation does not equate to development, evolution (itself characterised by diversification) does not equate to progress.[4] By extension, Lessing implies that being part of something larger is not ennobling or enriching in itself.

Interplay between levels of self is not only central to Lessing's speculative fiction. In 1962's *The Golden Notebook*, protagonist Anna Wulf records different sides of her character in four differently coloured notebooks, to then construct – or reconstruct – a whole in the fifth, golden, notebook. That fragmentation of identity has drawn comparison with the techniques of modernism and postmodernism, notwithstanding the fact that it is the golden notebook's synthesis which constitutes the novel's most striking element. Tonya Krouse, for one, suggests that *The Golden Notebook* might be located 'betwixt and between modernist and postmodernist conceptions of the subject' (40), while Suzette Henke characterises it as 'a paradox of postmodern play' (159). For Krouse, the fractured nature of *The Golden Notebook* can be considered a function of its 'obsessive consideration of freedom' (40). Krouse suggests that through creating her notebooks Anna explores whether freedom should be associated with separateness, achieved through an 'integrated subject's refusal to live according to social conventions', or, alternatively, whether freedom might better be understood in terms of 'the disintegration of individual subjectivities' (which Krouse characterises as a 'cracking up') (40). With respect to this tension, between freedom as individual independence and freedom as a dissolution of boundaries, including those between individuals, Lessing increasingly leans towards the second. In her 1971 introduction to *The Golden Notebook*, she characterises the writing of the final, golden notebook as the 'triumph [. . .] of unity' over Anna's 'fear of chaos, of formlessness' (vii). Anna's apprehension that she will lose distinction if she lets the aspects of her self merge is overridden by a realisation like Quarles's in *Point Counter Point* that atomised elements of a personality do not retain marks of connection to one another, their presence in the given individual a contingent fact rather than a necessity.

Lessing, across her work, speaks to what Homi K. Bhabha sees as a humanity's '*repetitious* desire to recognize ourselves doubly, as, at once, decentred in the solidary processes of the political group, and yet, ourself as a consciously committed, even individuated, agent of change – the bearer of belief' (93, emphasis from source). As early as the 1957 essay 'The Small Personal Voice', Lessing describes her work as 'a study of the individual conscience in its relations with the collective' (14), something she bemoans that 'not one critic has understood', although she 'should have thought [it] would be obvious from the very first chapter' of 1952's *Martha Quest*. It may, though, have been more obvious to critics than Lessing realised – too obvious, indeed, to mention. In the first chapter of *Martha Quest*, as in the novel at large, the fifteen-year-old Martha prods at the attitudes of her family and wider society, testing limits and seeking hypocrisies to expose. She reads, for example, Havelock Ellis in front of her mother, apparently hoping for censure and later quarrels with her about attitudes to marriage. In this much, Martha does what innumerable adolescents have done before her, in literature and in life. These tensions between the individual and society – and especially between individual and family – are at the core of so much fiction that it is likely critics saw no cause to give special mention to their presence in *Martha Quest*. It takes time for Lessing's investment in connectedness to develop into a more distinct literary contribution. It is by the time of *The Golden Notebook* that the question of what it is to be connected turns inward, breaking down the previously assumed integrity of the individual as a connecting subject.

An experience of hybrid identity informs Lessing's exploration. Born in Persia to English parents, but raised from the age of five in Southern Rhodesia, Lessing felt the sensation of both belonging to the place she lived in and not, and of home being both here and a distant, dimly understood there. In *African Laughter* (1992), she terms her move from Southern Rhodesia to Britain in 1949 as the time 'when I left home to come home' (12). With respect to the composition of identity, this leads Lessing to suggest that 'to most people at some point comes home that inside our skins we are not made of a uniform and evenly distributed substance, like a cake-mix, or mashed potato, or even sadza,[5] but rather accommodate several mutually unfriendly entities' (12–13). The modes of thought and personality traits a person acquires are, for Lessing, shaped by environments more than by accordance and harmony with that person's existing qualities. The group is the instiller of behaviours which enter a person from outside. Rather than forming internally in logical or emotional response to outside stimuli, a person acquires a collage of behaviours generated by the various groups in which she or he participates. While sometimes Lessing's fiction addresses this hybridity in terms of migrant experience, as in the case of Ambien II of *The Sirian Experiments*, her work suggests that disparity between behaviours is not only experienced when caught between geographically separate cultures. Migrants may be more apt to experience tension, in that the groups in which they participate may intersect little and have inharmonious expectations, but Lessing, not minded to take the personal as exceptional, suggests that the migrant experience simply makes more recognisable processes which sculpt human experience at large.

Lessing is not alone in refusing to treat hybridity as a challenge to overcome in the self-definition of the novelistic subject. In Rushdie's *Midnight's Children*, forming an identity from hybridity is the task both of its protagonist, Saleem, and of India as a nation. Speaking to the birth of India as an independent nation – a country which is itself a composite, containing multiple faiths, home to speakers of dozens of languages, with uncountable cultural identities – Rushdie deploys the device of telepathy. Saleem, the first of 1,001 children born in India within an hour of its independence from Britain, possesses telepathic power, 'the greatest talent of all' (196), while the other children born that hour possess various other abilities, including conjuration, transmutation and flight. Able to tune into any inner voice in India – with those using languages he does not speak 'replaced by universally intelligible thought-forms' (166) – he, in miniature, reproduces the conditions in which India must define itself, his mind open to millions of discrete voices. Attuned, by dint of his telepathic faculty, to the fact that Indians 'as a people [. . .] are obsessed with correspondences', Saleem observes that 'similarities between this and that, between apparently unconnected things, make us clap our hands delightedly when we find them out', which he describes as 'a sort of national longing for form – or perhaps simply an expression of our deep belief that form lies hidden within reality; that meaning reveals itself only in flashes' (291). With so many different elements to form an identity from, resemblance – be it likely coincidental – can provide a focus point for character to consolidate around. Coalescences at certain points ultimately become defining features by which to recognise the whole. In the nation and Saleem alike, that definition occurs in spite of the fact that the atoms, moving independently, could have coalesced in entirely different forms.

For Bhabha, in the encounter with 'an unrepresentable social totality [. . .] there is an underlying, prosthetic injunction' (311), which he articulates by quoting Frederic Jameson's appeal that a new architecture is needed to answer 'an imperative to grow new organs, to expand our sensorium and our body to some new, yet unimaginable, perhaps impossible, dimensions' (qtd in Bhabha 311–12). The telepathic faculty provides that new organ in *Midnight's Children*, making possible the novel's otherwise unrealisable assertion that 'to understand just one life, you have to swallow the world' (108). Rushdie, like Lessing in *The Making of the Representative for Planet 8* or *The Cleft*, enacts an ideal of collective belonging by deploying telepathy to allow the many elements of the hybrid identity to be definitively placed inside a single mind. For Ankhi Mukherjee, 'in his utopian imagination of interiority as a synaesthetic spilling or swarm', Rushdie offers 'a collectivity where [. . .] one does not differ or defer from social, geographical, or psychic others' (74). Telepathy makes visible a reciprocity, where Saleem is not only part of India's plural identity, but India's plural identity is part of him, a sense given extra significance by the fact that Saleem, like Rushdie, is born part of India's Muslim minority. Telepathy provides a vehicle for Rushdie to convey a sense that listening to other parts of the collective culture should coincide with meaningful incorporation of them.

In Lessing's case, the prosthetic injunction is more literal. In the late 1960s Lessing asserts the belief that humankind is literally developing a new sensorium of the kind Jameson would later figuratively suggest it needs, contending that telepathic research is reflective of a burgeoning development whereby, in her words, humankind is 'breeding new kinds of imagination and ways of thinking and experiencing' (Terkel 25). Lessing, like Huxley, has the sense that the East is in closer contact with a form of knowledge, or a way of knowing, which Western culture has all but obscured. In *The Four-Gated City*, the first chapter of part four is preceded by three extracts all connected with a new sensorium: a short passage from Idries Shah's *The Sufis* (1964), a quotation from the thirteenth-century poet and Sufi mystic Rumi and a phrase from a schools television broadcast on biology (which asserts that a cell from a toad's gut could be implanted into its head and would be capable of acting as a brain cell). These passages each speak to a sense that mindedness is not exclusively a property of the brain. While the schools broadcast implies that the toad's gut cells have everything needed to think, given the opportunity, Rumi offers that there are 'a thousand other forms of Mind', with earlier forms of perception and intelligence having been forgotten (qtd in *Four-Gated City* 426). In the extract from *The Sufis*, meanwhile, Shah claims that 'humanity is evolving towards a certain destiny', whereby 'the human being's organism is producing a new complex of organs [. . .] concerned with the transcending of time and space' (qtd in *Four-Gated City* 426). For Shah, the quoted passage continues, 'what ordinary people regard as sporadic and occasional bursts of telepathic and prophetic power are seen by the Sufi as nothing less than the first stirrings of these same organs.' They point, collectively, to an expansive conception of mind which takes shape in Lessing's work, which not only finds thought transmissible, but also finds potential for thought to emerge in new places and new forms.

The way these passages connect with events in the novel is, itself, more literal than figurative. As it enters the 1970s and moves beyond – that is, as it starts to address the future – it imagines a sea-change in the understanding of consciousness, with scientific standards of verification being seen to have obscured simple truths. What had been regarded as evidence of schizophrenia or manic depression in Lynda, and other mental patients, comes to be recognised as psychic ability: her visions of nuclear catastrophe prove prophetic and she demonstrates ability to communicate telepathically. Protagonist Martha also develops psychic powers after 'a decade of private experimenting without anything to guide her but hunches and a naturally tough constitution' (587). From this future perspective, it is 'extraordinary now that they couldn't see what was staring them in the face' (584). Doctors in the past are seen to have been 'on the edge of the truth', but 'were badly handicapped by their "scientific method"' (584). This shift entails the world waking up to a way of thinking close to Lessing's, or Shah's, the change being that the material verifiability required by science comes to be seen as an obstacle to the acceptance of experiential truth, as well as an inappropriate requirement for phenomena whose existence is outside the material domain.

Addressing those passages in which Martha and Lynda exhibit psychic power, Molly Hite suggests these are 'passages that must [. . .] be read allegorically or typologically' (24), an injunction which rejects Lessing's repeated assertions that telepathy is real and that she has experienced it: the manoeuvre has the feel of a critic minimising an awkward aspect of an author they address, even as doing so nullifies much of their contribution. Nevertheless, Hite's further claim that Lessing 'proposes vaguely allegorical or typological models of reading' by bringing psychic connection into the novel speaks to the bigger value of *The Four-Gated City*'s climax (24): that making sense of society's contradictions requires reading it differently, rather than reading it more carefully. For Hite, by raising the possibility of psychic contact and collective consciousness Lessing 'destroys the coherence traditionally associated with individuality, and thus with realist notions of character' (25). Instead of viewing Lessing's approach as destructive, the refusal to establish boundaries around the individual can be seen as generative, enabling new constructions of character. The individuated self by its nature consists in discontinuity, every individual isolated from every other, each thinking slightly differently (and doing so independently). The referent of 'I' or of a given name may be stable, but that it is a preferable means to represent character is not self-evident, even if extrasensory phenomena are rejected. As Hite writes, 'some violation of coherence seems to be necessary to leave room for representation – which is to say, for possibility' (27). That Lessing's driver to represent differently has flawed scientific foundation does not automatically undermine the literary exploration which results.

Clare Hanson reads the climax of *The Four-Gated City* as unsuccessful. In her view, because 'the social and political contradictions explored in this long and complex novel are [. . .] resolved by means of a eugenic fantasy in which a "superior" species with "a comprehension we can't begin to imagine" takes control' (86), the novel's turn to the fantastic represents a refusal to proffer realistic responses to society's contradictions. However, Lessing's conviction is that those contradictions are a contingent function of perspective and can be dissolved rather than resolved. There is, for Lessing, the possibility of humanity developing new modes of perception; the novel can prepare for that development through reconfiguration of its representational apparatus, and thereby heighten consciousness of the provisionality of present understandings. Where Rushdie deploys telepathy it may not be in service of the same apprehension of humankind's future, but the sense is equally there that, as Bhabha exhorts, rendering an interconnected society of immense complexity requires empowering the reader with apparatus to perceive connections indiscernible to ordinary human subjectivity.

Briefing for a Descent into Hell, The Unconsoled and Panpsychism

Possible understandings of the universe as panpsychic have long been mooted in novels of psychic connection: in 1911 Algernon Blackwood's *The Centaur* offers that 'the entire blessed universe was conscious' (43), while in May Sinclair's *Mary Olivier: A Life* from 1919, there is the suggestion that 'Space and Time were forms of thought' (208). However, for as long as it is structured around bodily individuals as characters (porous and unpredictable as they may be), the novel tends to treat a minded cosmos as a betweenness. It is rendered as the material through which thoughts pass from one mind to another; it is a territory which, in fleeting, transcendent moments, the individual mind apprehends itself as interpermeating – otherwise it is largely background. In making role the nexus of character in many of her works, Lessing engenders conditions for her novels to make a minded cosmos a more active presence. The mind of the bodily individual loses privilege as container of a particular selfhood and the reappearance or transfer of given selfhood entails attendance to psychic conditions of an extended environment. In *Shikasta*, a psychic 'Lock' the Canopeans establish with Earth is dynamic, subject to 'ebbs and flows and oscillations' and is also vulnerable, whole cities needing to be 'watched, adapted' in order to maintain it (49). Monitoring both built and natural environment, the Canopeans approach mind as function of and resident in a wider environment, its health intertwined with that of the bodily individuals inhabiting it. For the Canopeans, the architecture of the geometrically arranged cities gives meaning in a substantive sense, artistry imbuing the world with positive or negative energies and potentially other, more nuanced psychic content. In this, there is reflection of a sense that the promise of art, not least literature, is elevated by panpsychism, equipped to confer meaning not just on the experience of living, but also on the very fabric of the universe. It is a sensibility with sufficient reach for Kazuo Ishiguro to react against it in *The Unconsoled* (1995), a novel which has its dreamlike world waiting pregnantly, liminally, for the artist protagonist to imbue meaning.

Briefing for a Descent into Hell (1971) provides Lessing's most explicit intimation of a panpsychic universe. Its protagonist, a man hospitalised with complete memory loss (eventually identified as Cambridge Classics professor Charles Watkins) experiences a number of intense visions, including being adrift on a raft in the Atlantic Ocean and walking through the ruins of a stone city. The visions are sufficiently lucid that he takes them for reality, while he refuses to accept the hospital or doctors as real. As in *The Four-Gated City*, the refusal to be held to a singular identity mappable to a single body is diagnosed as insanity. There is similarity, also, with Propter's suggestion in Huxley's *After Many a Summer* (1939) that 'if we were consistently human, the percentage of mental cases would rise from twenty to a hundred', whereby what are identified as mental illness are 'little flashes of illumination – momentary glimpses into the nature of the world as it is for a consciousness liberated from appetite and time' (121). *Briefing*'s patient – freed, in part, by being a patient, provided with nourishment and time to reflect – is given an environment which empowers that wider awareness, rejecting Charles Watkins even after family are traced and visit him.

During one vision *Briefing*'s protagonist (it feels wrong to identify him by a name he rejects) experiences a Stapledonian sensation of cosmic perspective, able to watch the Earth remotely. From this vantage point, he identifies humanity with microbes, finding that collectively it 'transcends itself' when 'it begins to slowly sense itself as one, a function, a note in the harmony' (109). The protagonist regrets that 'some sort of a divorce there has been somewhere along the path of this race of man between the "I" and the "We," some sort of a terrible failing away' (109). Offering 'we' as a more healthy subject for selfhood, the protagonist supports this with a suggestion that consciousness is all-pervasive, contending that 'there is nothing on Earth, or near it, that does not have its own consciousness, Stone, or Tree, or Dog or Man' (57). This sense is accounted for by proposing that the consciousnesses in apparently inert beings are 'not inside the same scale of time' as that of humanity – an idea resonant of Stapledon and indeed J. W. Dunne, both of whom find the supposedly impossible possible when scales are transformed, timescales especially. Attributing consciousness to the stone, as the protagonist of *Briefing* does, the implication is that its response to physical forces is incomprehensibly slow from a human perspective and, as such its consciousness runs in geological time, similarly inscrutable to human perception. The man's cosmic experience has shown him his inclusion in greater subjectivities than the human, grounding what is by nature an unjustifiable claim for a human to make (speaking as it does to perception the human cannot experience).

In contradistinction to telepathy, panpsychism does not require that verbal thought be able to exist outside of minds, nor that transmission of any kind might occur. Instead, it holds that a more nebulous field of consciousness exists – like that advanced by Bergson. Unlike telepathy, it has retained support within the academy, seen by some philosophers of mind as the most elegant, economical means to account for consciousness in individuals: if a form of psychism is pervasive, each new individual does not have to be associated with the emergence of psyche from nothing. Writing in the twenty-first century, Philip Goff suggests, for instance, that 'the brains of organisms are coloured in with experience' and that 'the most elegant, simple, sensible option is to colour in the rest of the world with the same pen' ('Panpsychism'). What *Briefing* implies is that, if there is a diffuse consciousness, then reflection upon experience need not yield purely personal insight, but might provide insight into the constitution of the universe. What the artist draws from inside speaks, by this view, to the outside not by mere analogy, but by substantial commonality and interfusion between the locally experienced psyche and an extended one.

In the introduction to *Shikasta*, Lessing not only postulates the existence of an overmind, but also offers writers as particularly suited to interfacing with it, suggesting that it is 'not only for novelists' to 'plug in' to the overmind (9). That Lessing feels it necessary to say that it is not novelists alone who may connect to the overmind implies that she feels novelists are particularly capable of making such a connection, or are particularly likely to do so. Put another way, the connection between being a writer and having capacity to apprehend the overmind is sufficiently obvious to Lessing that she assumes that without qualification her remark might be taken as applying to writers only. Similarly, Lessing's experience with mescaline engenders connection with another layer of being in a way that she also links to writing. She, like Huxley, tried mescaline – taking 'one dose out of curiosity' in the early 1960s – and describes having had 'the most extraordinary experience', feeling there to have been 'several different people, or "I's" taking part' (Newquist 58). Suggesting that 'it wasn't me, the normal "I" who conducts her life' who was the subject of the visions and experiences of her trip, Lessing continues to reflect that 'the question of I, who am I, what different levels there are inside of us, is very relevant to writing' because 'every writer *feels* when he, she, hits a different level' (58, 60, emphasis from source). Lessing also explains that she 'deliberately evoked the different levels' to write the different parts of *The Golden Notebook*, birthing a creature who was 'immensely ancient', and 'neither male nor female' with 'no race or nationality' (60). Breaking down the self, Lessing's experience is not of finding a personal, unique core, but instead of recognising that the elements of her self link to more than just other people, other women, or other writers, but to a much more universal selfhood.

What Lessing finds in her reflections might be no more than the imaginative application of experiential flavour to her existing beliefs about interpersonal connection. However, it speaks to an abundance of connection that the individualistic novel seeks to break up and canalise. For Pierre Macherey, 'literary writings exude thought in the same way that the liver produces bile; it is like an oozing secretion, a flow, or an emanation' (232). Idealistically, Macherey offers that literature introduces into systems of thought 'a collective and shared polyphonic reflection stemming from the free circulation of images and schemas of narration and enunciation' (233). That flow can only be so free, albeit the novel of psychic connection affords more freedom than the conventional individualistic novel. The individualistic novel binds characteristics and binds significations to given individuated characters (imperfectly, inevitably). The success of the art is largely in the arrestation of ideas, in the impression that an author – and, by extension, any other person – might enjoy a semblance of control over the irruption and flow of ideas and emotions. Giving primacy to the flow of ideas, the novel of psychic connection comes closer to Macherey's ideal, though at a cost to readability for a reader trained on individualistic novels.

The presumption that the artist is specially equipped to give shape and meaning to others is played with in Ishiguro's *The Unconsoled*, which imagines an unspecified European town and its townspeople convinced that a visit by the celebrated concert pianist, Ryder, will be a defining event, both for the town collectively and in the personal lives of many inhabitants. Reinforcing this sense, Ryder is invited to participate in a question-and-answer session prior to his performance, speaking not about himself or his work, but about 'gravely important' issues facing the town (381) – a subject he shows no qualification to address. Written in a dreamlike mode, *The Unconsoled* makes of Ryder the emitter of meaning the townspeople assume him to be, with the novel's story continually creating itself around him. When Ryder's status as a great artist sees townspeople approach trivial conversations with him as greatly significant, *The Unconsoled* supports that investment of meaning, the world reinventing itself such that Ryder is central to the life of the town and its inhabitants. For instance, a conversation with the concierge of his hotel sees Ryder invited to meet the concierge's daughter, Sophie, to help with an unspecified personal difficulty. Meeting Sophie, a sense that she is familiar drifts into a dreamlike apprehension of having had a long and intimate relationship with her, including having discussed buying a house together. The world remakes itself such that Ryder is qualified to help Sophie with her personal life – and such that he might fitly speak to the wider situation of the town. However, at the centre of this creation and recreation, Ryder shows deep confusion: if the flow of meaning becomes so one-directional, the artist imparts meaning without being able to draw on understanding.

As a narrator, Ryder is preternaturally able to fix the meaning of inconsequential acts and to define the precise thoughts of counterparties. A single, small cough, in Ryder's narration, can be recognised as containing in it, all of the cougher, Mrs Collins's, 'perfectionism, her high-mindedness, that part of her that would always ask of herself if she was applying her energies in the most useful way possible' (360). Similarly, when Ryder is with an aspiring pianist, Stephan, he is able, merely from catching 'sight of his profile in the changing light' to understand very concretely that Stephan 'was turning over in his mind a particular incident from several years ago' (65). Moreover, Ryder is able to narrate that incident in great detail: an unsuccessful performance by Stephan on his mother's birthday. The nature of the trauma – hinging on a failed piano performance – is such that it invites a central role for Ryder in Stephan's recovery: Ryder is able to guide Stephan to choose a piece, as well as an approach to playing it, that allows him to impress his parents and thereby gain their support for his choice of career. As such, although Ryder solves Stephan's problem, it is only after determining its existence in the first place. When a local musician, Christoff, claims his protégés have 'always found their meanings through me' (191), it succinctly captures the pretensions *The Unconsoled* rejects. The artist can give aesthetic pleasure and potentially philosophical stimulation, but lives are not lived waiting for art and artists to bestow meaning upon them, nor is the meaning of a life made and remade continually with each new artistic encounter. An artist, like Lessing, might feel that in their work they connect with a wider consciousness, but the practice of writing or performing art can only narrowly be creative of meaning. When Jonathan Kramnick suggests in response to Philip Goff's panpsychism that 'you should turn to literary art' in order to 'color in the rest' of the experiencing universe (159), it calls for a writer where a reader is required – if the universe is an experiencing one, its experiences may await the interpretation of a reader, but not a writerly ascription of meaning.

The Incorporation of Others as Extensions of Self

In a panpsychic universe, there are no *terrae nullius* for the benign expansion of consciousness. Where Lessing sees the writer as equipped to map the networks of thoughts, she is conscious that interest in that domain might not be motivated by a wish to understand, but to control. In *Shikasta*, Canopus's colonial project is driven by the compulsion to spread their ideas. The colonisation of Earth by the Canopean empire is a vehicle to disseminate values: the territory is neither used for physical habitation by the Canopeans, nor are the planet's resources exploited (including the labour of its existing inhabitants). When the Canopeans introduce species to the Earth from other planets they have colonised, it also is in the service of the spread of artistic and scientific ideas. Canopus, it is explained, has 'decided to subject Rohanda [the name by which the Canopeans initially know the Earth] to an all-out booster, Top-Level Priority, Forced-Growth Plan' (28), setting the conditions for the establishment of their so-called psychic Lock with the planet. This Lock, the Canopeans claim, will enable the 'free flow of thought, ideas, information, *growth* between planet and planet across our galaxy' (33, emphasis from source). As such, the colonisation can be associated with mimetic rather than genetic imperialism: the spread of their ideas matters more to Canopus than the spread of their species. That a 'Lock' is associated with freedom belies the hypocrisy at the centre of the project: it is wholly intended that Canopean ideas promulgate on Earth and other colonised worlds and is not expected that ideas from Earth might spread and revise Canopean thought. It is a function of empire familiar to Lessing. In Southern Rhodesia, she saw the disparity between the coloniser's rhetoric of liberty and opportunity and the limitation of the colonised, including in their cultural self-expression and self-determination. While acknowledging in the first volume of her autobiography, *Under My Skin* (1994), that in her youth she and other white inhabitants of the country took the native population 'for granted' and talked little about them, she could see the difference between the 'warm-hearted, generous, open sharing of the benefits of "white" civilization' the British purportedly offered and the 'doors shut in their faces, coldness, stinginess of the heart' which manifested in reality (113).

In her understanding of the mechanisms of interface between cultures, Lessing shows considerable sympathy with the ideas of anthropologist Edward T. Hall. Her debt to his work is one she makes explicit. Speaking in 1993 to Ivan Tyrrell, Doris Lessing describes her frustration with most interviews. She contends that 'an interview is usually a map of the mind of the interviewer', and that she 'can go through the whole interview replying to questions that totally bore me' ('Cultural Insanity'). As for subjects she would be keen to speak about, Lessing offers that 'I might like to talk, for example, about the discoveries of Edward T. Hall which he wrote up in books like *The Silent Language*, and *The Dance of Life*', but finds that when she does so 'the interviewers' faces fall and they quickly steer me back to my childhood, feminism or how many words a minute I write'. Tyrell's response is unfortunate, immediately supporting Lessing's claim. He does not invite her to speak more about Hall, in spite of her express wish to do so. Instead, Tyrell, a follower of Idries Shah, steers the conversation towards Shah and his understanding of human behaviour. Even though there is kinship between interviewer and interviewee in their positive attitudes to Shah, and Lessing appears to enjoy their discussion, the sensation is of another interview steered in the direction of the interviewer's predetermined topics.

Tyrrell is not alone in his inattention to Lessing's engagement with Hall's ideas. Lessing criticism has not explored this connection, in spite of Lessing's professed enthusiasm for his work and in spite of the concordance between Lessing's ideas concerning shared consciousness and those of Hall. In the interview with Tyrell, Lessing offers that Hall's 'books are full of revolutionary observations about what we are like', as he articulates 'the unspoken ideas behind cultures and the rhythms of time and life'. Hall seems, in particular, to have been on Lessing's mind in the first half of the 1990s. *The Dance of Life* provides a lengthy epigraph for *Under My Skin*. In full, Lessing quotes:

> No matter where one looks on the face of the earth, wherever there are people, they can be observed syncing when music is played. There is popular misconception about music. Because there is a beat to music, the generally accepted belief is that the rhythm originates in the music, not that music is a highly specialized release of rhythms already in the individual. Otherwise, how can one explain the close fit between ethnicity and music?
>
> Rhythm patterns may turn out to be one of the most basic personality traits that differentiates one individual from another.
>
> . . . when people converse . . . their brain waves even lock into a single unified sequence. When we talk to each other our central nervous systems mesh like two gears in a transmission.
>
> The power of rhythmic message within the group is as strong as anything I know. It is . . . a hidden force, like gravity, that holds groups together.
>
> I can remember being quite overwhelmed when I first made cinematographic recordings of groups of people in public. Not only were small groups in sync, but there were times when it seemed that all were part of a larger rhythm. (*The Dance of Life*, qtd in *Under My Skin*, n.p.)

In Hall's claim, Lessing finds spiritual support; art, he claims, has a substantive role in harmonising the members of a group. It is not a by-product of culture; it produces culture – without it, there would be no consolidation of disparate people into recognisable cultural groups. Albeit it is music Hall addresses and not literature, the sense that the artist's work can have a binding force seems to be an affirmation for Lessing. Moreover, Hall provides a scientifically expressed model into which Lessing's long-developing sense of interpersonal connection can be fitted. The transmission of brain waves invoked is reminiscent of the ether model of telepathy, albeit in *The Dance of Life* Hall offers more contemporary sources of support for these ideas. He draws heavily upon the work of philosopher of consciousness William Condon and in particular his concept of entrainment, which Hall defines as 'the process that occurs when two or more people become engaged in each other's rhythms, when they synchronise' (177). This synchronisation, for Condon, manifests in a harmonisation of brain waves. This inspires Hall to speculate that 'it is possible that Condon's work may ultimately explain some of what is now seen as psychic', because 'some form of "entrainment" is taking place whenever two central nervous systems become engaged', and, for Hall, 'it is not too farfetched [. . .] to think that some form of entrainment can occur at a distance' (182). Hall's speculation is a leap from Condon's focus on the response to sound, recasting the measurable activity of an individual brain as the vaguely defined brain wave of historic psychical speculation.

That Hall describes brain waves as locking together, forming a single pattern, resembles the psychic Lock Canopus establishes with its colonies in *Shikasta*. Moreover, the Lock is referred to as a mesh, another of the descriptors Hall uses for the psychic interface he describes. As such, Lessing's advocacy of Hall, and her use of this specific passage, can be seen to stem from a sense of validation, that research is backing up her understanding of interpersonal connection.[6] In *Shikasta*, the Canopean emissary Johor speaks of a '"mind" shared between Rohanda and Canopus', which does not mean that 'every thought in every head instantly became the property of everyone at once', but instead entails the sharing of 'a disposition, a ground, a necessary mesh, net, or grid, a pattern which was common property, and was not itself static, since it would grow and change with the strengthenings and fallings off of emanations' (52). It is a confusing, dense explanation: Johor offers six consecutive suggestions for what this collective 'mind' shares, all of which are broad terms. On top of this, there is the fact that what is being explained is, itself, in quotation marks, making it questionable whether Johor considers the item being defined a form of mind, or merely akin to one. The passage is one which brings extra depth to Katherine Fishburn's claim regarding the *Canopus in Argos* series that Lessing's 'purpose in these five novels [. . .] is to question the fabric of reality itself' (198). There is a very strict sense in which this is true: Lessing is interested in the woven connections that underlie everything – the literal fabric of things. That fabric is composed of experience, as per panpsychism.

The unclarity in Lessing's explanation of the Lock is to some extent a signal that *Shikasta* is not invested in precise explanations for the speculative possibilities it depicts. Lessing herself distinguishes *Canopus in Argos* from science fiction, terming it instead space fiction (*Sirian* viii). While *Shikasta* does sometimes echo science fiction in using pseudoscientific phrases, it undercuts associated expectations. For instance, a substance – possibly a visible gas or light liquid – is introduced by Johor, named Effluon 3. This substance is explained to have 'the property of drawing in and sending out qualities as needed' (89), suggesting it is valuable, and possibly essential, to the Canopean project on Earth. It is distinguished from Effluon 1 and Effluon 2 as 'the most sensitive and yet the strongest of conductors, needing no machinery to set it up, for it came into existence through the skilled use of concentrations of the mind' (making it pivotal in the connection between mind and matter). Finding a quantity of Effluon 3 in an unexpected location, Johor concludes that a rival empire – either Puttoria or Shammat – must have stolen it and must also be interfering in affairs on Earth. As such, the ground is set, in principle, for a science fiction quest in which the theft of the Effluon is investigated, with its misuse by one of these rival empires examined and exposed. Along the way, the unusual characteristics of Effluon 3 might be explained through a filter of scientific possibility, including how it can be that mind generates matter. Instead, Effluon is never mentioned again, either in *Shikasta* or in the rest of the *Canopus in Argos* series, its entire inclusion limited to a span of four paragraphs. It may be that the passage was initially written with the intention that Effluon 3 would take a substantial role in the novel – if it was intended as misdirection, there is no knowing wink, no sign to the reader rereading *Shikasta* that a trick is being played. Nevertheless, the fact that there is no pay-off works neatly – that the imaginary substance amounts to nothing is apt. The prevalence of fictional materials in science fiction – the dilithium of *Star Trek*, or the dalekanium of *Doctor Who* – is one of the genre's most unscientific features. By threatening to lean into this trope, only to defy that expectation, Lessing provides illustration that the more concrete the material of science fiction is, the more unscientific it is apt to be.

The Lock can be read as a cultural connection, to the extent it is an exchange of thought along shared patterns. It is not, however, set up to be an equal exchange. The imbalance of power between coloniser and colonised allows for asymmetry in what is shared, such that the inhabitants of Rohanda 'would not know anything that Canopus did not want them to know' (52). Canopus, the coloniser, imagines it can control the image it projects of itself – that its colony can be made to see Canopus as a centre of moral right, at the same time as the colonial project stifles free thought and prevents self-determination. The constrictive conditions generated by the Lock are reflected in the experience of Canopean emissaries embodied in human form on Earth. One, identified only as Individual One, is said to have been 'afflicted, and from her earliest years, with feelings of being confined' (148). The language she attaches to this feeling overlaps with that used to define the Lock. Individual One 'understood she was in, or on, some invisible mesh or template, envisioned by her in bad black moods as a vast spider web, where all the people and events were interconnected, and nothing she could do, ever, would free her' (149). Only aware of the Lock through its effects while she is in her human form, Individual One nonetheless apprehends the superstructure which encompasses her and apprehends it as inflexible. The Lock, then, emerges from an awareness that a person does not think in isolation and thus the wider network of ideas is fundamental to personal health. However, it also shows a failure to see that ideas cannot be arrested in their development – and refuses to countenance that what appears favourable from one perspective may be detrimental from others. Like the British casting their colonial project as civilising the uncivilised, the need to pin down the object of the project can only, ultimately, entail suppression. For Lessing, ideas have their own agency and those who would hold thought back instead hold themselves back, given that thought will inevitably run on, irrespective of their wishes.

While Lessing's space fiction gives her space to explore entrainment between radically different cultures, a similar understanding of the mechanisms of interpersonal connection informs her realist work. In 1984's *If the Old Could. . .*, published under the pseudonym Jane Somers, narrator Janna moots shared ideas as literally shared, suggesting that 'our thoughts fly back and forth between us, so fast; we think the same thoughts' (392). While it might be read as an expression of her like-mindedness with lover Richard, it is not offered as metaphor, there is no dilution of the sentiment through, for example, expression of romantic compatibility or similarity of opinion. They are entrained per Hall's understanding of the term, brain waves locked into a unity. Similarly, in the short story 'The Temptation of Jack Orkney' from 1972, when the death of Jack's father induces radical change in Jack's personality, it is presented as the product of the irresistible agency of intruding thoughts. As Jack finds that 'thoughts he would never have believed he was capable of accommodating were taking root in him', it is 'as if armies of others waited to invade' (604). The day of his father's death follows the first night Jack has dreamed after an extended period not dreaming (or, at least, not remembering any dreams on waking). For Jack, dreaming is experienced as an irruption from another world 'behind the face of the sceptical world', one which 'no conscious decision of his could stop him exploring' (626). In effect, the time of his father's death, a period of personal weakness, provides a moment for Jack's constructed, stable personality to be disrupted, and the result is an awareness of the interpersonal flows of thought which lie behind the facade of the stable, individuated self.

Across her work, Lessing develops a redefinition of mind which does not invest in individual brains so much as in analogous cultural configurations which precipitate like thoughts and like actions in group members. That is to say a group whose common experiences and common behaviours generate common beliefs can, for Lessing, be said to share not only a mindset, but a mind. That sense that a common culture substantively begets a common mind is similarly observable in Hall's work. In *Beyond Culture*, from 1976, he offers that 'culture is [. . .] very closely related to if not synonymous with what has been defined as "mind"' (166) – his 'mind', like that Johor defines in *Shikasta*, in citation marks. Hall's mind (or 'mind') then, like Lessing's, is not confined to individual subjects – and indeed is composed of an ever-changing cohort of constituent entities (also a facet of the narrating mind of Conrad's *Narcissus*). Further, for Hall, there can be no clear demarcation between humankind and its cultural products. He contends that 'not only is culture imposed upon man but it *is* man in a greatly expanded sense' (*Silent* 213, emphasis from source). So intrinsic are cultural formations to humankind's understanding of itself, and a given human being's understanding of self, that they are to be viewed as part of human nature. This, combined with Hall's mind-culture identity, contributes to a picture whereby the supposed individual inevitably reaches beyond themselves to the collective in formulating a self-concept.

For Hall, the culture-mind is associated with unconscious communication. Writing about his focus as a writer, he explains in 1966's *The Hidden Dimension* that 'all of my books deal with the *structure of experience as it is molded by culture*' (x, emphasis from source). That structure is, for Hall, constituted by 'those deep, common, unstated experiences which members of a given culture share, which they communicate without knowing' (x). By way of example, Hall's work highlights the cultural construction of ostensibly fundamental realities, such as a view of time as monochronic (that is linear, divisible into segments) which, while pervasive in certain cultures, can be contrasted with a polychronic view (wherein time is cyclical) pervasive in others. For Hall, exposure to other cultures, with other concepts, may not necessarily lead to learning, but to confusion and communication at cross-purposes. For Hall, a cross-cultural dispute over, say, punctuality might be seen as a disagreement about how important that quality is, but a fuller understanding would recognise that in the very concept of punctuality inheres a presumption of time as a limited commodity – an understanding the two sides might not share. More broadly, the colonialist who sees a colonised people as uncultured can be understood to do so because of a failure to understand the cultural universe of that people on a fundamental level. In respect of these baseline misunderstandings, in Hall's view '*one of the principal functions of the artist is to help the layman order his cultural universe*' (81, emphasis from source), a perspective close to Lessing's view of her function as a writer. In the terminology of Hall, in the *Canopus in Argos* series Lessing can be seen to imagine how a consciously ordered cultural universe might look. Both the Canopeans and Sirians are largely self-aware of their cultural and mental structures – that is, they are cognisant of mimetic reproduction and seek control of it – and extract power from this knowledge. However, order implies rigidity, and this results in abrasion and eventual fracture at the point where their empires meet: Earth. Where, then, Phyllis Sternberg Perrakis suggests that *Shikasta* shows an 'intuitive awareness of the interrelationship among all peoples' (235), the focus on interrelationship ought to be considered significantly more calculated and more calculating than this allows – *Shikasta*, in kind with Lessing's fiction at large, builds upon a sophisticated and systematic, albeit contentious, analysis of the human mind within both the individual and the group, as well as the cultural formations which might be considered functions or extensions of it. It and *Canopus in Argos* at large address the mechanisms by which ideas spread, offering the kind of study Lessing insists should be undertaken in her afterword to *The Making of the Representative for Planet 8* (129). Albeit there Lessing speaks to 'controlling' ideas as goal of such study, *Canopus in Argos* implies that the drive for intellectual control is a vain ambition, built on assumptions of superiority.

Whereas *Shikasta* focuses on Canopus's cultural colonialism, *The Sirian Experiments* focuses on the movement between cultures of roughly equal power. The larger part of the novel follows Ambien II, acting as a Sirian representative, spending extended periods in the Canopean-controlled part of Earth, often in the company of a Canopean emissary, Klorathy. At first, adjusting to this environment causes her to experience 'ideas and limitations beyond her role as Sirius' (ostensibly meaning its representative on Earth, although the turn of phrase is suggestive of a deeper identification of Ambien II with her home culture) and, as such, she feels she is 'beginning to separate off in myself these two entities, or ways of experiencing living' (156). If the mind is a matrix of cultural connections, then an individual being inhabiting two environments with few connections between them can be felt a component of two distinct minds. This split identity coheres with the understanding of hybridity advanced by Marwan M. Kraidy, wherein hybridity 'unhing[es] the identities of its ingredients without congealing into a stable third term', resulting in 'a vicious circle where its condition of existence is at the same time its kiss of death' (66). By nature, hybridity speaks to a condition in which component elements remain recognisable and distinct to some degree. *The Sirian Experiments* recognises that, by Hall's understanding of mind, a condition of hybridity in identity implies the coexistence of multiple minds in a single person. Following *The Four-Gated City* and *Briefing for a Descent into Hell*, which each contest the necessity of conflating multiple identity with mental illness, *The Sirian Experiments* offers a multiply minded hybrid identity as a tenable (if tiring) subject-position – and, indeed, one which grants insight into the very nature of mindedness.

In their determination of the health of the Earth, it is humankind specifically whom the Canopeans focus on. That Canopeans conflate the health of humankind with the health of the planet is justified in that humanity is uniquely positioned to alter its environment. For Hall, the human being can be 'distinguished from the other animals by virtue of the fact that he has elaborated what I have termed *extensions* of his organism' (*Hidden* 3, emphasis from source). By extensions, Hall means technologies which stretch organic capability – so the computer is, for Hall, an extension of the brain and the telephone an extension of the voice – and also cultural products such as language, which, Hall writes 'extends experience in time and space' (3). Such is the entanglement with these extensions, that, for Hall

> the relationship between man and his cultural dimension is one in which both man *and his environment participate in molding each other*. Man is now in the position of actually creating the total world in which he lives, what the ethologists refer to as his biotope. In creating this world he is actually determining *what kind of an organism* he will be. (4, emphasis from source)

As such, the Canopean ability to adopt human form can be seen as a furtherance of an ability humanity itself possesses, rather than a categorically distinct, fundamentally fantastic power.

If Hall's ideas are combined with a cosmic perspective, then Earth as a planet has been cultivated into an extension of humankind, as have other species inhabiting the planet. The charge that Canopeans are anthropocentric in focusing on humanity dissolves from a disinterested cosmic perspective: viewing the Earth as a total system, it is more human extension than independent, organic entity, such is humankind's spread and its transformative impact on its environment (that human-induced environmental change causes increasing harm to humanity speaks to incomplete understanding of the extension). In Hall's words, 'man and his extensions constitute one interrelated system', such that 'it is a mistake of the greatest magnitude to act as though man were one thing and his house or his cities, his technology or his language were something else' (188). To stop at humankind's formal constructions and to not to consider their wider environment misrepresents the scope of human effect and is also a denial of responsibility: even that environment humanity supposedly elects not to disturb though formations such as the national park or nature reserve are tended, with human selection determining which favoured species are preserved. As Salim Kemal and Ivan Gaskell write: 'human creation and nature so interpenetrate [. . .] that they apparently preclude the likelihood of producing clear conceptual distinctions. Human beings are a fragment of nature and nature is a figment of humanity' (3).[7] From this perspective, Ambien II's identification with Sirius is not only an ambassadorial presumption, but also a recognition of the reach of her extensions. Scaled up, Hall finds 'all nature (life) paradoxically is both discrete and continuous – simultaneously and without contradiction' (179). Individual selves can be recognised, but they overlap, sharing extensions and, as Lessing's novels of psychic connection suggest, acting as extension of one another. Background and foreground, setting and character, interpenetrate. Canopus adjusts physical geography to maintain its psychic lock, because that geography is part of the mind/'mind' of earth.

What Lessing finds is that a novel speaking to psychic connection should reconfigure not only its representation of relationship between people, but also their relationship to setting. The impermeability the traditional novel brings to character is wed to a solidification of setting. Ian Watt finds Daniel Defoe 'the first of our writers who visualised the whole of his narrative as though it occurred in an actual physical environment', there being, Watt offers, a 'solidity of setting' to his work unfound in the vaguely defined spaces of the Elizabethan stage or the picaresque (26). Where that firm, defined environment is taken as a representational accomplishment by Watt, for Lessing, the solid setting, like the solid character, only appears so by dint of limited perceptual apparatus. Active and reactive in ways not wholly understood, Lessing's unpredictable planets and spaces illustrate that an Anthropocene fiction needs not only to find means to speak to human smallness, but also planetary greatness, empowering the Earth to answer back. When the expression of the non-human is confusing and incoherent in human narrative terms, that should be accepted as an admission of the limits of human comprehension, rather than taken as artistic failing.

When the novel's interest is more local – be it a single human's life or short series of events – it may nonetheless speak to a dynamic world by empowering what would normally be background to express itself. Saleem in *Midnight's Children*, emotional upon re-entering India from Bangladesh, declares himself to be 'everyone everything whose being-in-the-world affected was affected by mine', and declares that he is 'begin[ning] to grow thinner, translucent almost' (370–1). Albeit Saleem has lost his telepathic faculty by this time – the literal way in which background spoke to him – he has come to recognise that the interpermeation of himself and those around nonetheless continues: Saleem is the extension of those he encounters, and, by dint of repercussion, of those they have encountered, and so on. His telepathy, exceptional as it was, masked the universality of this order of interfusion, such that, he realises, 'each "I," every one of the now-six-hundred-million-plus of us, contains a similar multitude' (370).

Mitchell's *Ghostwritten*, meanwhile, composed as it is of a succession of tangentially connected local dramas across the world, refuses easy distinction of background and foreground, of significant characters and minor presences. When the protagonists of previous chapters make fleeting appearances in succeeding ones, it speaks to the fact that the web of connections which generates any given event is incalculably complex: any given figure's reasons for being in a certain place at a certain time might be as storied as that of the hero's. Pulling out a few strands for focus, Mitchell suggests that the representational compromises the novel typically makes in delimiting important and unimportant presences not only simplify but distort. This is spoken to pointedly when the protagonist of one chapter, Marco, reflects on chance and the novel's usual erasure of it. Marco, a ghostwriter, reasons that when a rugby match is watched on video 'every tiniest action already exists', but 'when the players are out there the game is a sealed arena of interbombarding chance' (292). As such, he formulates, 'viewed from the outside, like a book you're reading, it's fate all the way'. Closure, both chronological and in a medium like a book or video cassette, implies order, and implies that emphasis can be assigned with confidence to the most important players. *Ghostwritten*, spanning the globe, suggests that Marco stops short of full realisation: the arena is not sealed, there is no clear outside. The repercussions of chance are not confined to a clearly delimited area of play. No character, no item, is categorically reducible to background, yet the novel routinely makes distinction between its principals and a background cast.

Daniel D. Hutto, challenging views like Hall's, whereby the mind extends beyond the individual body, argues that, in cases where proponents of such philosophies wish to demonstrate that the mind includes external resources, a problem emerges in respect to the interaction between people and between peoples. Hutto asks, 'what should we say about cases in which the external resources include other minds?' (276). Lessing, across her work, answers this question: she suggests that one mind, or one group mind, can colonise another, while two or more minds might coexist in a single person. The blurred boundaries of this conception of mind present issues for comprehension and literary representation, but those challenges have no bearing on the validity of Lessing's understanding. A representationally difficult truth is still a truth. While Lessing's expressed belief in telepathy draws upon dubious supporting evidence – much of it Cold War rumour and misinformation – philosophically, questions of the limits of mind are still live. Lessing's literary exploration of group minds and deindividuated characters could be taken as preparation for a scientific paradigm shift which has yet to happen and might never, but this neglects the degree to which she exposes how many assumptions are resident in current understandings of self and current approaches to its representation, especially in taking individuated selfhood as the only viable, conceivable configuration.

Conclusion: The Network Novel, Inclusion and Infusion

Psychic Entanglement and the Twenty-First-Century Network Novel

The representational tools developed in twentieth-century novels of psychic connection can also speak to the sense of phantasmic connection underscoring the present moment of online community, contactless technology and virtual assets. How to conceptualise the extension and boundaries of the self, a primary issue in the twentieth-century novel of psychic connection, has become a more central question than ever in the novel and criticism of it. For Peter Boxall, it is the 'sense of a profound disjunction between our real, material environments and the new technological, political and aesthetic forms in which our global relations are being conducted that lies at the heart of the developments in the twenty-first-century novel' (9). As Boxall characterises it, twenty-first-century fiction enacts the 'construction of a new and delicate narrative identity, a new mind with which we might think a contemporary global condition' (141). That mind is, however, not as new to the novel as Boxall's account suggests: the interconnected thinking needed to wrestle with global interconnections is already enacted by twentieth-century novels of psychic connection.

In the twenty-first century many novels reject investment in the development of individual characters, instead emphasising how networks of connection come into being and grow. The network novel, in which multiple protagonists succeed one another, tangentially or profoundly influencing the course of each other's lives – exemplified by the likes of Zadie Smith's *NW* (2012), Bernardine Evaristo's *Girl, Woman, Other* (2019) and David Mitchell's *Ghostwritten* (1999) – has become a prominent, celebrated subgenre, credited by Patrick Jagoda with demonstrating that the novel as a literary form 'continues to affect the present' (46). Such novels, invested in intersection and interfusion, do what Berthold

Schoene suggests is needed from the novel today. Drawing on sociologist Ulrich Beck, Schoene asserts that in the twenty-first century the novel 'must do its best to demonstrate that "in a world of global crises and dangers produced by civilization, the old differentiation between internal and external, national and international, us and them, lose their validity and a new cosmopolitan realism becomes essential to survival"' (45).[1] The twenty-first-century novel must, for Schoene, reject the notion of a discrete, impermeable subjectivity, considering 'the domestic and the global as weaving one mutually pervasive pattern of contemporary human circumstance and experience' (46). That refusal of the distinction between internal and external, intended by Schoene to speak to a refusal of national boundaries to culture and identity, does not require completely new representational strategies, given those developed by twentieth-century novels of psychic connection. Much that the twentieth-century novel of psychic connection does, the network novel also does. The productive ambiguity Lawrence employs with respect to who is experiencing sensations and having thoughts is also employed by Smith in *NW* – in which extended passages are narrated with speech indicated only by an introductory dash, the speaker identifiable from context only, if identifiable at all. The centring of the development of ideas over people which characterises Huxley's novels is often magnified by the network novel. In it, the recurrence of ideas across distance and time, in like or mutated form, frequently provides the trajectory of development the reader follows through the text in the absence of consistently present human characters.

What claims for the significance of the network novel often miss is that it does not only speak to connectedness in respect of the forces of globalisation and mass communication; more immediate psychic connection is consistently central, be it interface through telepathy or other psychic powers, or mental convergence in physical proximity. When, in Mitchell's *The Bone Clocks* (2014), Hugo Lamb avers that 'telepathy is as real as telephones' (200), the definitiveness of the assertion speaks to the fact that it is present in the novel as more than a plot device, informing how it thinks of character. The visitations and psychic communications which fill the novel support a sense that viewing the body and the self as coextensive is a failure of understanding. Initially associating the limits of herself with her body, Holly Sykes experiences the psychic inflow of thought as violation, explaining that 'if you've heard voices in your head once, you're never sure again if a random thought *is* just a random thought, or something more' (539, emphasis from source). Accepting this psychic openness as empowering is her epiphany. When her mind is inhabited by the immortal being Marinus, following the death of the body

Marinus had occupied, the two are able to collaborate in the destruction of the Anchorites (a group who derive power by draining the souls of the young), working together to navigate a labyrinth. Holly's realisation that we 'live on, as long as there are people to live on in' is informed by this collaboration (542), it having shown her that accommodating the ideas of others is a matter of addition rather than displacement.

Forms of psychic harmonisation are also central to less fantastically rendered network novels. In Smith's *NW*, which Nick Bentley finds to 'only have faith in localised and subcultural groups' (740), it is offered that if 'you live in the same place long enough, you get memory overlap' (135). The personal and familial histories of the inhabitants of north-west London vary considerably, but shared space induces a common mental geography. Natalie Blake, at the funeral of the father of her childhood friend Leah, reflects on the fact that 'not only was Colin Hanwell dead but a hundred people who had shared the same square mile of streets with the man now recognized that relation, which was both intimate and accidental, close and distant' (341). The relationship in question is not so much that with Colin himself, but the common presence of Colin in their minds. As Natalie appreciates, she 'had not really known Colin' but knew what it was 'to have Colin be an object presented to her consciousness' (341). The emergence of the network novel coincides with the growth of the internet and the mobile phone, which, together, bind the user into a global network of contact on an effectively constant basis, but, for Smith it is shared space which most induces shared ideas.

The persistent presence of telepathy and other forms of paranormal psychic connection in literature speaks, in part, to a sense that it is expedient to think of ourselves as connected to others, whatever the underlying truth. When Smith explains that the 'true reason I read is to feel less alone, to make a connection with a consciousness other than my own' ('Rereading' 57), it implicitly speaks to her understanding of what she is offering as a writer. In *NW*, a brief bus stop encounter between Natalie and an older passenger reflects the desire for the feeling of connection, even if its foundations are questionable. The elderly passenger, discussing her bond with her dog, explains to Natalie that 'when I realized Mindy-Lou could actually speak to me through my mind, well, then I really had a moment, like in a story-book or a film, and I knew I would always be watched over and loved by everybody I met forever the end' (397) . The appended, lowercase 'the end', coming without preceding punctuation, rushed in before any challenge can occur, suggests an awareness that the claim might not stand up to questioning. However, the presentation of the comment on the page backs up the passenger. It appears without quotation marks, at the centre of a paragraph which begins with

Natalie mentally indexing passing streets and shops, such that Natalie's thoughts and the elderly passenger's are, in that sense, blended. The ejaculation 'Clarity!' which immediately precedes the elderly passenger's claimed psychic bond could be Natalie's, could be the woman's, or could be shared between them. Natalie's openness to a person who could easily be dismissed as deluded is backed up by narration which – here and throughout the novel – blurs thoughts together.

Beyond seeing psychic connection as a suggestively possible desire, the network novel often has the distanced, phantasmic connections precipitated by contemporary society and technology interplay with a more ineffable extension of the self. *Ghostwritten*'s physicist Mo Muntervary outlines the ground upon which Mitchell works – in this novel and others – with her gloss on quantum entanglement, when she explains that 'phenomena are interconnected regardless of distance in a holistic ocean more voodoo than Newton' (375), a comment which speaks not only to an understanding of the universe on a material level, but also to the human experience of living in it. In Mo's case, her present self is unable to escape immaterial bonds formed in the past. Her previous employment at the CERN laboratory in Switzerland, conducting research she believed was funded by space agencies, has given the US military supposed ownership of 'whatever comes out of Dr Muntervary's head' (378), impelling them to pursue her to Ireland's remote Clear Island to seize data she is withholding. Mitchell's world is one of psychic entanglements, a fact the character Immaculée Constantin perceives in *The Bone Clocks*, when she suggests of her and Holly Sykes that it is 'as if the universe long ago decided we're connected' (216). In Mitchell's work, immaterial links may be revealed by psychic faculties, but, equally, those self-same connections may be exposed by technology. In *The Bone Clocks*, Marinus observes that technology's capacity to make visible the unseen links between people diminishes the particularity of possessing psychic powers, explaining that 'social media flag up active chakras before we can inoculate them. Horology's drifting towards irrelevance' (412).[2] When Susan Onega offers that in *Ghostwritten* Mitchell 'conveys a transpersonal conception of self and world: that is, one that extends the sense of identity beyond the personal to encompass wider aspects of humankind, life, psyche, and cosmos' (51), the extension is not only one enabled by technology. There has always been an extended, interpenetrating self for Mitchell. By duplicating its mechanisms, technology heightens consciousness of an extended being, but also positions itself to take credit for creating that extension rather than unveiling it.

Evaristo's *Girl, Woman, Other* does similar in its climactic episode, in which familial links are exposed by a DNA testing service. Having purchased a testing kit, Penelope Halifax learns that 'not only did the website show her ethnic breakdown, it connected her with relatives who'd also done the test' (449), precipitating an unexpected meeting with her birth mother, Hattie – who having given birth at fourteen, had been forced to give up her child days after the birth. Thus, the test is able to make known familial relations which neither memory nor bureaucracy records; in presenting a connection outside all social and mental recollection, it generates that connection as much as it discovers it. More than this, though, by showing Penelope that she has one-eighth African ancestry, the test casts her into a new relationship with race; she is pressed to process an association with Blackness, even this part of her heredity had previously been unknown and remains unpronounced in her appearance. Identifying genetics as 'the science that was the deepest, most secret part of herself', she sees 'a collision between who she thought she might be and who she apparently was' (446). What is more, the claim she makes for the relationship between genetic science and identity, could, word-for-word, have been made with respect to Freudian psychology a century earlier. The sense Evaristo challenges is the same one that Lawrence rails against in works like *Fantasia of the Unconscious* and in his novels, that a science which claims access to a true identity even the possessor can be unaware of is committing to a constrictive understanding of what identity is – one which disregards the lived understanding of self and which limits fluidity by positing an immutable baseline.

For Mitchell, dismissal of the possibility of psychic connection is associated with the reach for a certainty about the physical universe which humankind does not have. Just as Mitchell suggests quantum entanglement to be closer to magic than Newton in *Ghostwritten*, in *The Bone Clocks* a similar rhetorical device is employed by Marinus to describe psychic abilities to Holly. When she questions if they are magic, Marinus suggests that if Newton were given 'an hour's access to the Hubble telescope' he would claim its operation to be magic, as 'some magic is normality you're not yet used to' (506). Concretely, Mitchell's work appears to point to panpsychism as a physical possibility apt to be perceived as magic. In *Ghostwritten*, Mo muses to herself that 'matter is thought, and thought is matter' (344), the identity she asserts between the two, far from a truism of contemporary physics, manifests a profoundly panpsychic understanding of the world – all matter being thought means thought is everywhere. For *Ghostwritten* at large, the implication is that what are initially read as the delusions of cultist Keisuke Tanaka in the novel's opening chapter should be reconsidered. Keisuke, who credits himself with possessing telepathic power on account of his 'enhanced alpha quotient' (7), approaches his thought like matter, holding that his 'role was to pulse at the edge of the universe of the faithful, alone in the darkness' (5). That his cult is right about the approach of an Earthbound comet, undetected by observatories, provides further exhortation not to dismiss unconventional beliefs summarily – an attitude reflected elsewhere in Mitchell's work. As Holly Sykes warns in *The Bone Clocks*, 'beware of asking people to question what's real and what isn't. They may reach conclusions you didn't see coming' (378–9). There is the sense in Mitchell's work that the implications of physics which defy conventional thought might induce a mental liberation, promising to revolutionise understanding of the very mechanisms of thinking. While outsiders like Keisuke grasp at faulty and unhealthy schemes to conceptualise the disparity between their experience of thought and the established understanding of it, they are justified in recognising a disparity exists. Like D. H. Lawrence, for whom Einstein shows that 'the multiple universe flies its own complicated course quite free, and hasn't got any hub', meaning that 'we can hope also to escape' (72), Mitchell sees a need for humanity to think differently – in the fullest sense – in order to avert catastrophe. The unseen comet of *Ghostwritten* is superseded by threats of humanity's own manufacture in later novels: the near-future consumerist dystopia of Nea So Copros in *Cloud Atlas*, or the post-oil future of *The Bone Clocks*. Avoidance of each requires rethinking not just existing relationships, but the systems underlying them.

The structure of the network novel is its greatest inducement to think differently. *Ghostwritten*, which Mitchell describes as 'this interconnected novel about interconnection' (McWeeney), has nine protagonists narrate nine faintly linked episodes. The protagonist of the first chapter, the cultist Keisuke, who has fled from Tokyo to Okinawa after carrying out a gas attack on the subway, accidentally calls the record store in which the protagonist of the second chapter, Satoru, works. His coded message registers with Satoru as a prank call, but by keeping him in the shop he had been closing, it means he is there when an attractive customer, Tomoyo, visits for a second time. In turn, Satoru briefly interacts with the third protagonist, Neal Brose, asking him if there is free space at a table when he and Tomoyo (now in a relationship) are in the same Hong Kong café as Neal. Ostensibly trivial in themselves, the reader approaches these interactions as significant, recognising them as the knots which tie the respective episodes into a single novel. As Gerd Bayer suggests with respect to *The Bone Clocks*, 'this novel (if that is what it is) creates coherence between the individual narratives first and foremost at the moment of reception, inspired by the readerly expectations developed by the novel as a genre' (254). For Bayer, readers conscious of the novel's conventions 'will actively look for and then establish the links within individual textual features' (245). In reading Mitchell's work, or another network novel, the reader is invited to experience greater self-consciousness about the meaning-making they bring to the text. The novel can induce substantive effects, inducing recalibration of the reader's analytical tools. As Bayer offers, 'art, for Mitchell, is essentially a form of engagement with reality' (252). The baseline of that is the substantive reality of changes in thought-processes literature and other art can induce.

There remains disagreement as to whether *Ghostwritten*, *Cloud Atlas* and *The Bone Clocks* are best described as novels or as short-story sequences. For Bayer, the issue is that 'what Mitchell attempts in almost all his books [. . .] is to demonstrate that the outer limits of a text are hardly defined by its physical boundaries' such that 'it is not always easy to define the generic nature of a piece of narrative prose fiction' (247). For Tim Armstrong, what he terms Mitchell's story-sequences 'are *not* novels in any recognisable sense' (88, emphasis from source), inhabiting 'an uncertain zone in which the short story "mends" its own incompletion, as it were, by forms of connectedness'. The inducement for the reader to think differently about the connections between elements, and especially between characters, is taken as defiance of the novel as a medium, if not inimical to it. While Bayer and Armstrong show admiration for Mitchell's fiction, the suggestion that his works should not be called novels means they are faced with an exclusion other challenges to the novel's individualism have faced. Just as Olaf Stapledon's cosmic novels are often offered for exclusion from the medium and just as Aldous Huxley is declared not to have been a novelist, it is all too common that novels and novelists contesting the individuation of character – whatever their approach to that contestation – find themselves marginalised or excluded when the possibilities of the medium are under consideration. Insomuch as *Ghostwritten* is subtitled *A Novel in Nine Parts* and *Cloud Atlas* presented as *Cloud Atlas: A Novel* in its first American edition, the appeal that they should be read as such is explicit. The novel as a form is broad (especially if non-Western iterations are considered); not to take Mitchell's works as novels is to sever the psychic entanglements which mark his major contribution to the medium.

Fusion Fiction and Inclusive Identification

The network novel offers the reader the experience of diffuse being. Switching perspectives from chapter to chapter – in the case of *Girl,*

Woman, Other, from mother to daughter, from daughter to teacher, and so on – is a psychic fantasy. *Girl, Woman, Other* deepens that fantasy by resetting time from chapter to chapter, as each protagonist's life story is retold in the present tense, meaning key moments are lived over and over by the reader, new perspectives experienced as additive to those already embodied. The network novel refuses the telepathic narrator as interpreter and connector, instead generating a panpsychic reader, who not only sees into the minds of characters, but inhabits them. Reading *Girl, Woman, Other* the reader arrives anew at intersectional points – always, as indicated by the tense, present there – sharing in the experience of each agent, instead of accepting the temporally distanced summary of a third-person narrator. As an inhabitant of the respective agents in an encounter, the reader works with the novel in 'fusing the women's stories together' in what Evaristo terms 'fusion fiction' (*Manifesto* 142), a process Evaristo's use of the continuous aspect recognises to be an ongoing process at the time the novel is read. Successive narratives do not provoke wholesale shifts in readerly identification; in moving directly from the story of theatre director Amma to that of her student daughter Yazz, for example, the reader brings residual identification with Amma to their appreciation of Yazz's story. As such, when Yazz counts herself as having 'x-ray vision' with which 'she can see through the parental bullshit' (*Girl* 44), the reader is pushed to recognise they manifest this power much more than Yazz. There is disparity between Amma's public and private personae, as Yazz sees, but unlike the reader she does not perceive her mother's conscious struggles with self-presentation working in an establishment-dominated sphere as a Black lesbian. What Peter Boxall says of Robert Bolaño's *2666* can be applied broadly to the network novel as a form, that 'the focus of the narrative is on embodiment, on the way that waves and networks run through our embodied selves, positioning us, making us readable to ourselves' (196). However, there is also interest in the finitude of connection – in the limitedness of the channels of interface and how this effects readability even to those close physically and emotionally.

Evaristo is aware that the canalisation of the self sees external limitations to being inscribed internally: in other words, the ways of society become the individuated self's ways of thinking. In *Girl, Woman, Other*, banker Carole, passing tourists taking selfies on London's Millennium Bridge, reflects on how the sharing of photos is indicative that 'the borders between public and private are dissolving' (144). Her thoughts about boundaries of the self inspires her to recall reading 'that one day humans will have a network of nano-electronics integrated into their neural pathways, implanted at the cellular level', which will mean that 'we'll all be cyborgs [. . .], primed to behave in socially acceptable ways' (144–5). However, Carole's conduct is already controlled. The daughter of Nigerian immigrants, Carole holds the position of vice president of a bank, but has modified her self-presentation considerably in order to achieve the status she has: among other things, she has altered her accent and vocabulary, the food she eats, and the way she dresses and styles her hair: nano-electronics were not required to constrict her. In this much, the network novel's interest in the map is not to the exclusion of an interest in interiority, to the extent that the map is reflected in internalised form. When Keisuke in *Ghostwritten* asserts that he has 'always preferred maps to books', it might seem a simple nod to the novel's structure, but his reason, that 'they don't answer you back' (15–16), speaks to the subtle internalisation of the network.

Through its title, *Girl, Woman, Other* signals one aspect of its interest in identity: its protagonists are all female or, in one case, non-binary. Additionally, each is either Black or, like Penelope, has Black family connection. By restricting its attention to figures with marginalised traits, *Girl, Woman, Other* demonstrates how identification and solidarity do not automatically follow from common possession of those traits. When, in *Girl, Woman, Other*, teacher Shirley King meets Carole, who had been her pupil and achieved her place at Oxford thanks to her extra tuition, Shirley finds that Carole's 'accent is barely recognizable, practically aristocratic' (420) and the meeting – a reunion both participants had long imagined – is stilted and insincere. So many factors inform what a person says and how they say it that taking their voice as a strict function of their identity is faulty. As such, when Lynn Wells offers that 'sympathetic identification with characters of racialised backgrounds is central to the project of postcolonial literature, which creates imaginary spaces in which voices from outside the mainstream can speak and be heard' (99), the network novel recognises that hearing an unfamiliar perspective has little value without awareness of why the voice speaks as it does. The network novel does that by not only situating that voice within a network, but also situating the network within that voice.

Above and beyond the inscription of the network of social power on individuals, the network novel examines the very inscription as an individual. It recognises, as Homi K. Bhabha does, that 'the exercise of colonialist authority [. . .] requires the production of differentiations, individuations, identity effects through which discriminatory practices can map out subject populations that are tarred with the visible and transparent mark of power' (111). When the network novel challenges the sense that individuated identity is an absolute and necessary truth of being, it foundationally undermines divisive, discriminative identity effects. Mitchell sees science as a source of hope, Mo's intimations of psychic entanglement representative of the possibility that a wider paradigm shift might sweep away a present understanding of human limitation. Smith and Evaristo attend, in contrast, to moments of personal experience in which the individuated perspective is felt inadequate. *Girl, Woman, Other* climaxes on a moment of interpersonal fusion. Penelope and Hattie meet for the first time; together they are aware that 'they are mother and daughter and their whole sense of themselves is recalibrating' (452). Within narration which has been focalised upon Penelope's perspective, the harmonisation is presented without ambiguity – there is no equivocation, no suggestion that Penelope is making assumptions concerning her mother. The cessation of individuated alienation feeds into *Girl, Woman, Other*'s closing lines:

> this is about being
> together. (452)

A complete clause both with and without the line-separated 'together', the implication is that both non-connective and connective modes of being coexist in the fully realised self. Fittingly for a novel dedicated to

> the sisters & the sistas & the sistahs & the sistren & the women & the womxn & the wimmin & the womyn & our brethren & our bredrin & our brothers & our bruvs & our men & our mandem & the LGBTQI+ members of the human family (np)

Girl, Woman, Other imagines a fusion which nevertheless preserves diversity, with individuated and connective selfhood concurrent.

For the novel to present connection between possessors of marginalised traits is a powerful act in itself, to the extent that notions of 'common sense' and 'societal values' endow a culturally dominant perspective with the appearance of universality. For Bhabha, 'the direct access from individual interests to social authority is objectified in the representative structure of a General Will – Law or Culture – where Psyche and Society mirror each other, transparently translating their difference, without loss, into a historical totality' (43). By contrast, marginalisation is associated with discreditation as constituent of the societal body politic, such that 'forms of social and psychic alienation and aggression [. . .] can never be acknowledged as determinate and constitutive conditions of civil authority, or as the ambivalent effects of the social instinct itself', as these, for Bhabha, 'are always explained away as alien presences, occlusions of historical progress, the ultimate misrecognition of Man'. The ostensibly simple action of identification between Penelope and Hattie as mother and daughter is the refusal of a false consciousness which takes them as too alien to connect.

When Smith asks if it is 'possible to be as flexible on the page – as shamelessly self-forgiving and ever changing – as we are in life' ('Peonies' 8), the question speaks to the underlying issue with the comprehensible literary character – when fixity, including fixed boundaries, is taken to confer knowability, it alienates the character from a more fluid reality. The network novel and the twentieth-century novel of psychic connection centre interconnection and extension, signalling that character overflows the individuated being it is typically associated with. In *NW*, Natalie – if it is fair, in this moment to identify her as such – realises other understandings of selfhood are actively possible, albeit socially denied, when holding her new-born daughter. She sees in the yet nameless person 'a being not in any way identical with the entity Natalie Blake, who was, in some sense, proof that no such distinct entity existed. And yet was not this being also an attribute of Natalie Blake? An extension' (323–4). Focusing on a moment in which social inscription is incomplete – when the baby does not yet have an ascribed identity – Smith suggests that authorised understandings of selfhood are contingent and that, to the extent that others can be thought, they are real.

The network novel emerges after a century of reconsideration of the supposed necessity of the individual character. When, in 1894, the narrator of George du Maurier's *Trilby* offers that 'history goes on repeating itself, and so do novels, and this is a platitude' (100), the narrator fails to imagine how dramatically the novel was to change over the coming century. The sense that the individuated self is a fiction – the notion which gives telepathy, panpsychism and other forms of psychic connection their fascination – is a key force in driving that change. When Lessing claims that 'all the books that I have written indicate, sometimes in spite of myself, the existence in us of an inexpressible dimension stronger than the theories through which we may attempt to channel it' (Montremy 198), she speaks to the power of imaginative writing to rupture current paradigms and to expose where our accepted picture of the universe is a provisional fiction. Lessing's account of her work hints at a sense of stories which suffer themselves to be told, irrespective of the writer's intentions. Across the twentieth century, psychical speculation prompts numerous writers to open up their characters, begetting reformulation of narratives of development, with individuated agency rejected as a fallacy. Even with telepathy long marginalised, the network novel speaks to lived truths by centring connection in its modelling of character.

Notes

Introduction

1. As Roger Luckhurst notes, Britain's Society for Psychical Research, founded in 1882, had 'virtually suspended' its Committee on Mesmerism by 1884 (*Invention* 72).
2. As exemplar of Rhine's methodological shortcomings, Jonathan C. Smith claims there were 'slight indentations on the backs of cards', and that 'subjects could see and hear the experimenter, and note subtle but revealing facial expressions or changes in breathing.' He notes that 'the psi effect would mysteriously disappear whenever a magician was present in the Rhine laboratory', implying that Rhine's telepathic participants were likely employing techniques a magician would recognise (250).
3. James C. Crumbaugh records no discernible evidence for ESP in 3,000 Zener card runs at the Southern Methodist University (60). Raymond Royce Willoughby at Brown University records 'unequivocally negative' results from conducting 200 runs with each of eight subjects (6). John L. Kennedy at Stanford University also records negative results in his attempt to replicate Rhine's experiments for telepathy and clairvoyance.
4. In the 'The Appeal of Panpsychism in Victorian Britain' Adela Pinch discusses the role for panpsychism in the Victorian conversation around consciousness, describing it as 'a minority position' but 'a curiously persistent and illuminating one.'

Chapter 1

1. A result is that, as Fiona Becket notes, in Lawrence's writings, 'the words "conscious" and "unconscious" are often interchangeable' ('Psychoanalysis' 221).
2. Telepathy is mentioned in the uncompleted *Mr Noon*, in which the married couple Patty and Lewie Goddard are said to have a 'telepathic connection' (6).

3. The echoes of occultism to this terminology are unlikely to be accidental. Lawrence read P. D. Ouspensky's *Tertium Organum* at roughly the time *The Plumed Serpent* was written and Mabel Dodge Luhan, the founder of the Taos artist colony he lived at, would regularly suggest occultist literature to him, as well as exhorting him to visit George Gurdjieff's Institute for the Harmonious Development of Man (Luhan 294).

Chapter 2

1. Stapledon and Mitchison first met in 1931, shortly after the publication of *Last and First Men*, and, as Robert Crossley records, Stapledon became a member of Mitchison's literary circle which met at the Café Royal in London (*Reader*, 281).
2. *Odd John* explicitly acknowledges its similarity to *The Hampdenshire Wonder*. In the opening chapter, the narrator points readers to 'J. D. Beresford's account of the unhappy Victor Stott' as illustrative of 'how pathetically one-sided the supernormal development may be' (16).
3. Heard's *Ascent of Humanity* was among the books and journals from Stapledon's study donated by Agnes Stapledon to the University of Liverpool. Stapledon also writes in the preface to *Last Men in London* that it 'will be obvious to many readers that I have been influenced by the very suggestive work of Mr Gerald Heard' (333).
4. When declaring the shape (one of five) on a counterparty's card, Rhine records that his 'five major subjects' achieved an average of 8.4 successful calls per 25 cards (162). While considerably above the five that should be achieved by pure chance, it means even his best participants were wrong twice as often as they were right.

Chapter 3

1. These effects very closely resemble those Huxley associates with mescaline, his personal experience with which is described in *The Doors of Perception*.

Chapter 4

1. Introduced in 1976's *The Selfish Gene*, the idea of the meme may have been directly familiar to Lessing by 1980: the book was a bestseller. Alternatively, it might, in the spirit of memetics, have reached Lessing through Dawkins's ripples. For more on Lessing and sociobiology, see the chapter 'Doris Lessing's Evolutionary Epic' in Clare Hanson's *Genetics and the Literary Imagination*.

2. The substance-of-we-feeling is often referred to as 'SOWF', noted by Shadia S. Fahim to resemble the word 'Sufi' (182).
3. Recent findings in epigenetics point to the possibility of transmitting traumas or aversions acquired during life (Curry); Tchaikovsky's extrapolation of the possible implications of the still-provisional science is not unlike that of the address to telepathy in work like Stapledon's.
4. Clare Hanson, in 'Lessing, Posthumanism and Deep History', offers a broader consideration of the challenge to the conflation of evolution and progress in Lessing's work.
5. Sadza is a maize porridge eaten as a staple food in Zimbabwe.
6. *Shikasta*, published in 1979, precedes *The Dance of Life*, published in 1983. However, four of Hall's books had been published by the time *Shikasta* was written, including *The Silent Language*, the other book Lessing refers to by name in her interview with Tyrell.
7. Peter Marren, for one, contends that 'nature reserves are among the most intensively managed parts of the countryside' (xviii).

Conclusion

1. Schoene quotes Beck's *The Cosmopolitan Vision*, p. 14.
2. In *The Bone Clocks*, horology is a term used to encompass a range of psychic powers, among them telepathy, telekinesis and mind-control.

Works Cited

Adorno, Theodor W. 'Aldous Huxley and Utopia.' *Prisms*, translated by Samuel Weber and Shierry Weber. MIT Press, 1997, pp. 95–118.
Armstrong, Nancy. *How Novels Think: The Limits of Individualism from 1719–1900*. Columbia University Press, 2005.
Armstrong, Tim. 'Man in a Sidecar: Madness, Totality and Narrative Drive in the Short Story.' *Modernism, Postmodernism, and the Short Story in English*, edited by Jorge Sacido. Brill, 2012, pp. 79–98.
Asimov, Isaac. *I. Asimov: A Memoir*. Bantam, 1995.
Austen, Jane. *Pride and Prejudice*, edited by James Kinsley. Oxford University Press, 1999.
Badino, Massimiliano and Jaume Navarro. 'Introduction: Ether – The Multiple Lives of a Resilient Concept.' In *Ether and Modernity: The Recalcitrance of an Epistemic Object in the Early Twentieth Century*, edited by Jaume Navarro. Oxford University Press, 2018, pp. 1–13.
Baker, Robert S. Introduction. *Complete Essays* by Aldous Huxley, vol. 5, *1939–1956*, edited by Robert S. Baker and James Sexton. Dee, 2002, pp. xi–xviii.
Balfour, Arthur James. *The Foundations of Belief, Being Notes Introductory to the Study of Theology*. Longmans, Green and Co., 1902.
Baron, Helen. 'Disseminated Consciousness in *Sons and Lovers*.' *Essays in Criticism*, vol. 48, no. 4, 1998, pp. 357–78.
Barrett, W. F. 'Note on Telepathy and Telergy.' *Proceedings of the Society for Psychical Research*, Part 76, 1918, pp. 251–60.
Barr Kirtley, David. 'Episode 175: David Mitchell.' *Geek's Guide to the Galaxy from Wired*, 7 November 2015, www.wired.com/wp-content/uploads/2015/11/geeksguide175final.mp3.
Bayer, Gerd. 'The Short Narrative Form in David Mitchell's *The Bone Clocks*.' *Constructing Coherence in the British Short Story Cycle*, edited by Patrick Gill and Florian Kläger. Routledge, 2018, pp. 245–59.
Beck, Ulrich. *The Cosmopolitan Vision*, translated by Ciaran Cronin. Polity, 2004.
Becket, Fiona. *D. H. Lawrence: The Thinker as Poet*. Macmillan, 1997.
———. 'Lawrence and Psychoanalysis.' *The Cambridge Companion to D. H. Lawrence*, edited by Anne Fernihough. Cambridge University Press, 2001, pp. 217–33.

Bell, Michael. *D. H. Lawrence: Language and Being*. Cambridge University Press, 1992.
Bentley, Joseph. 'Huxley's Ambivalent Responses to the Ideas of D. H. Lawrence.' *Twentieth Century Literature*, vol. 13, no. 3, 1967, pp. 137–53.
Bentley, Nick. 'Trailing Postmodernism: David Mitchell's *Cloud Atlas*, Zadie Smith's *NW*, and the Metamodern.' *English Studies*, vol. 99, no 7, 2018, pp. 723–43.
Beresford, J. D. *The Hampdenshire Wonder*. Sidgwick and Jackson, 1911.
Bergson, Henri. *Creative Evolution*. Macmillan, 1911.
———. 'Philosophical Intuition', translated by Mabelle L. Andison. *Selections from Bergson*, edited by Harold A. Larrabee. Appleton-Century-Crofts, 1949, pp. 106–12.
Besant, Annie. *A Study in Consciousness: A Contribution to the Science of Psychology*. Theosophical Publishing Society, 1904.
Bhabha, Homi K. *The Location of Culture*. Routledge, 2004.
Bigsby, Christopher. 'The Need to Tell Stories.' Interview with Doris Lessing from 23 April 1980. *Doris Lessing: Conversations*, edited by Earl G. Ingersoll. Ontario Review, 1994, pp. 70–85.
Blackwood, Algernon. *The Centaur*. Macmillan, 1911.
———. Introduction to 1938 edition. *Best Ghost Stories*, edited by E. F. Bleiler. Dover, 2013, pp. xii–xviii.
Blondel, Nathalie, ed. *The Journals of Mary Butts*. Yale University Press, 2002.
Bloom, Harold. Introduction to *Bloom's Modern Critical Views: Aldous Huxley*, edited by Harold Bloom, 2nd edn. Infobase, 2010, pp. 1–2.
Boulton, James T., ed. *The Letters of D. H. Lawrence*, vol. 1 (September 1901 – May 1913). Cambridge University Press, 1979.
Boulton, James T. and Lindeth Vasey, eds. *The Letters of D. H. Lawrence*, vol. 5 (March 1924 – March 1927). Cambridge University Press, 1989.
Boulton, James T. and Margaret H. Boulton with Gerald M. Lacy, eds. *The Letters of D. H. Lawrence*, vol. 6 (March 1927 – November 1928). Cambridge University Press, 1991.
Bowering, Peter. *Aldous Huxley: A Study of the Major Novels*. Bloomsbury, 2013.
Boxall, Peter. *Twenty-First-Century Fiction: A Critical Introduction*. Cambridge University Press, 2013.
Branham, Robert. 'Stapledon's "Agnostic Mysticism."' *Science Fiction Studies*, vol. 9, no. 3, 1982, pp. 249–56.
Broderick, Damien. *Psience Fiction: The Paranormal in Science Fiction Literature*, McFarland, 2018.
Brontë, Anne. *The Tenant of Wildfell Hall*, edited by Stevie Davies, Penguin, 1996.
Brontë, Charlotte. *Jane Eyre*. Oxford University Press, 2000.
Brunner, John. *Stand on Zanzibar*. Doubleday, 1968.
———. *Telepathist*. Fontana, 1978.
Brüntrup, Godehard and Ludwig Jaskolla. Introduction. *Panpsychism: Contemporary Perspectives*, edited by Godehard Brüntrup and Ludwig Jaskolla. Oxford University Press, 2017, pp. 1–16.

Bulson, Eric. Introduction. *The Cambridge Companion to the Novel*, edited by Eric Bulson. Cambridge University Press, 2018, pp. 1–20.
Byatt, A. S. *The Virgin in the Garden*. Knopf, 1979.
Campbell, John W. Jr. 'Who Goes There?' *The Best of John W. Campbell*, edited by Lester Del Rey. Ballantine, 1976, pp. 290–353.
Carington, Whately. *Telepathy: An Outline of its Facts, Theory, and Implications*, 2nd edn. Methuen, 1945.
Chevalier, Jean-Louis. 'Closing Debate, *Recontres avec Iris Murdoch*.' In *From a Tiny Corner in the House of Fiction: Conversations with Iris Murdoch*, edited by Gillian Dooley. University of South Carolina Press, 2003, pp. 70–96.
Clarke, Arthur C. *Childhood's End*. Pan Macmillan, 2010.
Cottom, Daniel. *Abyss of Reason: Cultural Movements, Revelations, and Betrayals*. Oxford University Press, 1991.
Crookes, William. 'Recent Advances in Science.' *Popular Astronomy*, vol. 7, 1899, pp. 3–11. [The article is miscredited to 'William Crooks'.]
Crossley, Robert. *Olaf Stapledon: Speaking for the Future*. Syracuse University Press, 1994.
———, ed. *Talking across the World: The Love Letters of Olaf Stapledon and Agnes Miller, 1913–1919*. University Press of New England, 1987.
Crumbaugh, James C. 'A Scientific Critique of Parapsychology.' *Extrasensory Perception*, edited by Gertrude Schmeidler. Transaction, 1969, pp. 58–72.
Cuddon, J. A. , *The Penguin Dictionary of Literary Terms and Literary Theory*, 3rd edn. Penguin, 1992.
Curry, Andrew. 'Parents' emotional trauma may change their children's biology. Studies in mice show how.' *Science*, 18 July 2019, www.science.org/content/article/parents-emotional-trauma-may-change-their-children-s-biology-studies-mice-show-how.
Dawkins, Richard. *The Selfish Gene*. Oxford University Press, 1976.
Deery, June. *Aldous Huxley and the Mysticism of Science*. Macmillan, 1996.
Dickens, Charles. *Great Expectations*. Oxford University Press, 2008.
Doyle, Arthur Conan. *The Parasite: A Story*. Harper, 1895.
Du Maurier, George. *Trilby*, edited by Elaine Showalter. Oxford University Press, 1998.
Dunne, J. W. *An Experiment with Time*, 2nd edn. A & C Black, 1929.
Einstein, Albert. 'Ether and the Theory of Relativity.' *Sidelights on Relativity*, translated by G. B. Jeffery and W. Perrett. Methuen, 1922, pp. 1–24.
———. 'On the Electrodynamics of Moving Bodies.' *The Principle of Relativity*, translated by W. Perrett and G. B. Jeffery. Methuen, 1923, pp. 35–65.
Eliot, George. *Romola*. Oxford University Press, 1994.
Eliot, Valerie and John Haffenden, eds. *The Letters of T. S. Eliot*, vol. 3, *1926–1927*. Faber, 2012.
Elkins, Charles. 'The Worlds of Olaf Stapledon: Myth or Fiction?' *Mosaic: An Interdisciplinary Critical Journal*, vol. 13, no. 3/4, 1980, pp. 145–52.
Evaristo, Bernardine. *Girl, Woman, Other*. Penguin, 2020.
———. *Manifesto: On Never Giving Up*. Penguin, 2021.
Figlerowicz, Marta. 'Novels and Characters.' *The Cambridge Companion to the Novel*, edited by Eric Bulson. Cambridge University Press, 2018, pp. 123–37.

Fishburn, Katherine. 'Wor(l)ds within Words: Doris Lessing as Meta-Fictionist and Meta-Physician.' *Studies in the Novel*, vol. 20, no. 2, 1988, pp. 186–205.

Földényi, László. *Dostoyevsky Reads Hegel in Siberia and Bursts into Tears*, translated by Ottilie Mulzet. Yale University Press, 2020.

———. 'Novel and Individuality.' *Neophilologus*, vol. 73, 1989, pp. 1–13.

Foltz, Jonathan. *The Novel after Film: Modernism and the Decline of Autonomy*. Oxford University Press, 2018.

Forster, E. M. *Aspects of the Novel and Related Writings*. Arnold, 1974.

———. *A Passage to India*. Knopf, 1991.

Frick, Thomas. 'Caged by the Experts.' Interview with Doris Lessing from 1987. *Doris Lessing: Conversations*, edited by Earl G. Ingersoll, Ontario Review, 1994, pp. 155–68.

Fludernik, Monika. 'Let Us Tell You Our Story: We-Narration and Its Pronominal Peculiarities.' *Pronouns in Literature*, edited by Alison Gibbons and Andrea Macrae. Palgrave Macmillan, 2018, pp. 171–92.

———. 'The Many in Action and Thought: Towards a Poetics of the Collective in Narrative.' *Narrative* 25, no. 2, 2017, pp. 139–63.

Galsworthy, John. *The Forsyte Saga*. Oxford University Press, 1999.

Gilbert, Stuart. *James Joyce's Ulysses: A Study*. Vintage, 1955.

Goff, Philip. 'Panpsychism is Crazy, But It's Also Most Probably True', *Aeon*. aeon.co/ideas/panpsychism-is-crazy-but-its-also-most-probably-true.

Goodwin, Jonathan. 'Telepathy and Cosmic Horror in Olaf Stapledon's *The Flames*.' *Journal of the Fantastic in the Arts*, vol. 25, no. 1, 2014, pp. 78–92.

Gray, Stephen. 'An Interview with Doris Lessing.' *Research in African Literatures*, vol. 17, no. 3, 1986, pp. 329–40.

Greene, Graham. *A World of My Own: A Dream Diary*. Viking, 1994.

Hall, Edward T. *Beyond Culture*. Anchor, 1977.

———. *The Dance of Life: The Other Dimension of Time*. Anchor, 1983.

———. *The Hidden Dimension*. Anchor, 1990.

———. *The Silent Language*. Doubleday, 1959.

Hanson, Clare. *Eugenics, Literature and Culture in Post-war Britain*. Routledge, 2013.

Hayles, N. Katherine. *The Cosmic Web: Scientific Field Models and Literary Strategies in the Twentieth Century*. Cornell University Press, 1984.

Heard, Gerald. *The Ascent of Humanity: An Essay on the Evolution of Civilization from Group Consciousness through Individuality to Super-Consciousness*. Cape, 1929.

———. 'The Poignant Prophet.' *The Kenyon Review*, vol. 27, no. 1, 1965, pp. 49–70.

Heise, Ursula. 'Science Fiction and the Time Scales of the Anthropocene.' *ELH*, vol. 86, no. 2, 2019, pp. 275–304.

Henke, Suzette. 'Doris Lessing's *The Golden Notebook*: A Paradox of Postmodern Play.' *Rereading Modernism: New Directions in Feminist Criticism*, edited by Lisa Rado. Routledge, 1994, pp. 159–87.

Hite, Molly. 'Doris Lessing's *The Golden Notebook* and *The Four-Gated City*: Ideology, Coherence, and Possibility.' *Twentieth Century Literature*, vol. 34, no. 1, 1988, pp. 16–29.

Hutto, Daniel D. 'Understanding Fictional Minds without a Theory of Mind!' *Style*, vol. 45, no. 2, 2011, pp. 276–82.
Huxley, Aldous. 'A Case for ESP, PK and Psi.' *Life*, 11 January 1954, pp. 96–108.
———. *After Many a Summer*. Vintage, 2015.
———. *Brave New World*. Harper, 1946.
———. *The Devils of Loudun*. Vintage, 2005.
———. *'The Doors of Perception' and 'Heaven and Hell.'* Vintage, 2004.
———. *Eyeless in Gaza*. Vintage, 2004.
———. *Grey Eminence*. Chatto and Windus, 1941.
———. 'The Idea of Equality.' *Complete Essays*, vol. 2, *1926–1929*, edited by Robert S. Baker and James Sexton. Dee, 2000, pp. 150–65.
———. *Island*. Vintage, 2005.
———. *Literature and Science*. Harper and Row, 1963.
———. 'Mind Reading.' *Complete Essays*, vol. 3, *1930–1935*, edited by Robert S. Baker and James Sexton. Dee, 2001, pp. 165–7.
———. 'Pascal.' *Complete Essays*, vol. 2, *1926–1929*, edited by Robert S. Baker and James Sexton. Dee, 2000, pp. 367–406.
———. *The Perennial Philosophy*. Harper, 1945.
———. 'Personality and the Discontinuity of the Mind.' *Complete Essays*, vol. 2, *1926–1929*, edited by Robert S. Baker and James Sexton. Dee, 2000, pp. 259–73.
———. *Point Counter Point*. Vintage, 2004.
———. Preface. *Collected Essays*, Harper and Brothers, 1958, pp. v–ix.
———. 'Science Turns to the Supernatural.' In *Complete Essays*, vol. 3, *1930–1935*, edited by Robert S. Baker and James Sexton. Dee, 2001, pp. 167–79.
———. *Time Must Have a Stop*. Sun Dial, 1944.
Ingersoll, Earl G. 'Writing for Balance: A Conversation with Doris Lessing.' *Ontario Review*, vol. 40, article 13, 1994, pp. 46-58.
'Interview with David Mitchell.' *GoodReads*, 9 September 2014, www.goodreads.com/interviews/show/975.David_Mitchell.
Ishiguro, Kazuo. *The Unconsoled*. Vintage International, 1996.
Jagoda, Patrick. *Network Aesthetics*. University of Chicago Press, 2016.
Jameson, Frederic. *Archaeologies of the Future: The Desire Called Utopia and Other Science Fiction*. Verso, 2005.
Joshi, S. T. *The Weird Tale*. Wildside, 2013.
Kaempffert, Waldemar. 'The Duke Experiments in Extra-Sensory Perception.' *The New York Times Book Review*, 10 October 1937, p. 2.
Kellogg, Chester E. 'Letters to *The Times*: Dr. Rhine's Experiments.' *The New York Times*, 7 December 1937, p. 24.
———. 'New Evidence (?) for "Extra-Sensory Perception".' *The Scientific Monthly*, vol. 45, no. 4, October 1937, pp. 331–41.
Kemal, Salim and Ivan Gaskell. 'Nature, Fine Arts, and Aesthetics.' *Landscape, Natural Beauty and the Arts*, edited by Salim Kemal and Ivan Gaskell. Cambridge University Press, 1993, pp. 1–42.
Kennedy, John. L. 'Experiments on the Nature of Extra-Sensory Perception: Repetition of the Rhine Experiments.' *The Journal of Parapsychology*, vol. 3, no. 2, 1939, pp. 226–45.

Kern, Stephen. *The Modernist Novel: A Critical Introduction.* Cambridge University Press, 2011.

Ko, Charles. 'Subliminal Consciousness.' *The Review of English Studies,* vol. 59, no. 242, 2008, pp. 740–63.

Kraidy, Marwan M. *Hybridity, or the Cultural Logic of Globalization.* Temple University Press, 2005.

Kramnick, Jonathan. *Paper Minds: Literature and the Ecology of Consciousness.* University of Chicago Press, 2018.

Krouse, Tonya. 'Freedom as Effacement in *The Golden Notebook*: Theorizing Pleasure, Subjectivity, and Authority.' *Journal of Modern Literature,* vol. 29, no. 3, 2006, pp. 39–56.

LaMothe, John D. 'Controlled Offensive Behavior – USSR.' Defense Intelligence Agency, 1972.

Lang, William. *Animal Magnetism, or, Mesmerism; Its History, Phenomena and Present Condition.* Mowatt, 1844.

Lawrence, D. H. *Aaron's Rod,* edited by Mara Kalnins. Cambridge University Press, 1988.

———. *Fantasia and the Unconscious. Psychoanalysis and the Unconscious and Fantasia of the Unconscious,* edited by Bruce Steele. Cambridge University Press, 2004, pp. 45–204.

———. 'The Future of the Novel' ['Surgery for the Novel – Or a Bomb.'] *Study of Thomas Hardy and Other Essays,* edited by Bruce Steele. Cambridge University Press, 1985, pp. 149–56.

———. 'John Galsworthy.' *Study of Thomas Hardy and Other Essays,* edited by Bruce Steele. Cambridge University Press, 1985, pp. 209–20.

———. 'John Galsworthy', fragment of an early draft. *Study of Thomas Hardy and Other Essays,* edited by Bruce Steele. Cambridge University Press, 1985, pp. 247–52.

———. *Kangaroo,* edited by Bruce Steele, Cambridge University Press, 1994.

———. *Lady Chatterley's Lover,* edited by Michael Squires. Cambridge University Press, 1993.

———. 'Morality and the Novel.' *Study of Thomas Hardy and Other Essays,* edited by Bruce Steele. Cambridge University Press, 1985, pp. 169–76.

———. 'Morality and the Novel', first version. *Study of Thomas Hardy and Other Essays,* edited by Bruce Steele. Cambridge University Press, 1985, pp. 239–46.

———. *Movements in European History,* edited by Philip Crumpton. Cambridge University Press, 1989.

———. *Mr Noon,* edited by Lindeth Vasey. Cambridge University Press, 1984.

———. 'The Novel.' *Study of Thomas Hardy and Other Essays,* edited by Bruce Steele. Cambridge University Press, 1985, pp. 177–90.

———. *The Plumed Serpent,* edited by L. D. Clark. Cambridge University Press, 1987.

———. 'Pornography and Obscenity.' *Late Essays and Articles,* edited by James T. Boulton. Cambridge University Press, 2004, pp. 236–53.

———. *Psychoanalysis and the Unconscious. Psychoanalysis and the Unconscious and Fantasia of the Unconscious,* edited by Bruce Steele. Cambridge University Press, 2004, pp. 1–43.

———. *The Rainbow*, edited by Mark Kinkead-Weekes. Cambridge University Press, 1989.

———. Review of *The Social Basis of Consciousness* by Trigant Burrow. *Introductions and Reviews*, edited by N. H. Reeve and John Worthen. Cambridge University Press, 2005, pp. 331–6.

———. *Sons and Lovers*, Part I, edited by Helen Baron and Carl Baron. Cambridge University Press, 1992.

———. 'The State of Funk.' *Late Essays and Articles*, edited by James T. Boulton. Cambridge University Press, 2004, pp. 219–24.

———. *The Trespasser*, edited by Elizabeth Mansfield. Cambridge University Press, 1982.

———. *Women in Love*, edited by David Farmer, Lindeth Vasey and John Worthen. Cambridge University Press, 1987.

Le Bon, Gustave. *The Crowd: A Study of the Popular Mind*. Macmillan, 1896.

Lem, Stanisław. 'On Stapledon's *Last and First Men*.' Translated by Istvan Csicsery-Ronay Jr. *Science Fiction Studies*, vol. 13, no. 3, 1986, pp. 272–91.

———. 'On Stapledon's *Star Maker*.' Translated by Istvan Csicsery-Ronay Jr. *Science Fiction Studies*, vol. 14, no. 1, 1987, pp. 1–8.

———. *Solaris*. Translated by Joanna Kilmartin and Steve Cox. Harvest, 2002.

LeMahieu, Michael. 'The Novel of Ideas.' *The Cambridge Companion to British Fiction since 1945*, edited by David James. Cambridge University Press, 2015.

Lessing, Doris. *African Laughter: Four Visits to Zimbabwe*. HarperCollins, 1992.

———. Afterword. *Last and First Men*, by Olaf Stapledon. Tarcher, 1988, pp. 305–7.

———. *Briefing for a Descent into Hell*. Vintage, 1981.

———. *The Cleft*. HarperCollins, 2007.

———. *Documents Relating to the Sentimental Agents in the Volyen Empire*. Vintage, 1984.

———. *The Four-Gated City*. Knopf, 1969.

———. 'The Fox of D.H. Lawrence.' *The New York Review*, 5 December 2002, www.nybooks.com/articles/2002/12/05/the-fox-of-dh-lawrence/?lp_txn_id=1022130.

———. 'Group Minds.' *Prisons We Choose to Live Inside*. Harper and Row, 1987, pp. 47–62.

———. *If the Old Could... The Diaries of Jane Somers*. Vintage, 1984, pp. 255–502.

———. Introduction to *The Golden Notebook*. Bantam, 1981, pp. vii–xxii.

———. *The Making of the Representative for Planet 8*, Knopf, 1982.

———. *The Marriages Between Zones Three, Four, and Five (as Narrated by the Chroniclers of Zone Three)*. Knopf, 1980.

———. *Re: Colonised Planet 5, Shikasta*. Granada, 1981.

———. *The Sirian Experiments: The Report by Ambien II, of the Five*. Knopf, 1980.

———. 'The Small Personal Voice.' *A Small Personal Voice: Essays, Reviews, Interviews*, edited by Paul Schlueter. Vintage, 1975, pp. 3–21.

———. 'The Temptation of Jack Orkney.' *Stories.* Knopf, 1978, pp. 564–626.
———. *Under My Skin: Volume One of My Autobiography, to 1949.* HarperCollins, 1994.
Levenson, Michael. *Modernism and the Fate of Individuality: Character and Novelistic Form from Conrad to Woolf.* Cambridge University Press, 1991.
Lewis, Pericles. *Modernism, Nationalism, and the Novel.* Cambridge University Press, 2000.
Lodge, David. *Consciousness and the Novel: Connected Essays.* Harvard University Press, 2002.
Luhan, Mabel Dodge. *Lorenzo in Taos.* Knopf, 1932.
Lukács, Georg. *The Meaning of Contemporary Realism*, translated by John and Necke Mander. Merlin, 1969.
Luckhurst, Roger. *The Invention of Telepathy, 1870–1901.* Oxford University Press, 2002.
———. '*The Omega Factor*: The Revival of Telepathy in the 1970s.' *Mind Reading as a Cultural Practice*, edited by Laurens Schlicht, Carla Seemann and Christian Kassung. Palgrave Macmillan, 2020, pp. 43–62.
———. *Science Fiction.* Polity Press, 2005.
Macherey, Pierre. *The Object of Literature*, translated by David Macey. Cambridge University Press, 1995.
Marren, Peter. *England's National Nature Reserves.* Poyser, 1994.
Maynard, John. R. 'The Bildungsroman.' *A Companion to the Victorian Novel*, edited by Patrick Brantlinger and William B. Thesing. Blackwell, 2002, pp. 279–301.
McDougall, William. *An Outline of Abnormal Psychology.* Methuen, 1926.
McGurl, Mark. *Everything and Less: The Novel in the Age of Amazon.* Verso, 2021.
McWeeney, Catherine. 'An Interview with David Mitchell.' *BookBrowse* www.bookbrowse.com/author_interviews/full/index.cfm/author_number/480/david-mitchell. Accessed 22 February 2022.
Meckier, Jerome. *Aldous Huxley, from Poet to Mystic.* Lit Verlag, 2011.
Mensch, Barbara. *D. H. Lawrence and the Authoritarian Personality.* Macmillan, 1991.
Miller, Gavin. 'Animals, Empathy, and Care in Naomi Mitchison's Memoirs of a Spacewoman.' *Science Fiction Studies*, vol. 35, no. 2, 2008, pp. 251–65.
Mitchell, David. *The Bone Clocks.* Sceptre, 2014.
———. *Ghostwritten.* Sceptre, 1999.
Moses, Omri. *Out of Character: Modernism, Vitalism, Psychic Life.* Stanford University Press, 2014.
Mukherjee, Ankhi. 'Fissured Skin, Inner-Ear Radio, and a Telepathic Nose: Senses as Media in Salman Rushdie's *Midnight's Children*. *Paragraph*, vol. 29, no. 3, 2006, pp. 55–76.
Murdoch, Iris. *The Flight from the Enchanter.* Chatto and Windus, 1962.
———. 'Force Fields.' [Review of A. S. Byatt's *The Virgin in the Garden*]. *New Statesman,* 3 November 1978, p. 586.
———. *The Good Apprentice.* Viking, 1986.
———. *Henry and Cato.* Viking, 1976.

———. *The Nice and the Good*. Triad/Panther, 1977.
Myers, Frederic W. H. *Human Personality and Its Survival of Bodily Death*. Longmans, Green, 1903.
Newman, Daniel Aureliano. '"Education of an Amphibian:" Anachrony, Neoteny, and *Bildung* in Huxley's *Eyeless in Gaza*.' *Twentieth Century Literature*, vol. 62, no. 4, 2016, pp. 403–28.
Newman, Jenny and James Friel. 'An Interview with A. S. Byatt.' *Cercles*, www.cercles.com/interviews/byatt.html. Accessed 23 November 2022.
Nixon, Cornelia. *Lawrence's Leadership Politics and the Turn Against Women*. University of California Press, 1986.
Nussbaum, Martha C. 'Love and Vision: Iris Murdoch on Eros and the Individual.' *Iris Murdoch and the Search for Human Goodness*, edited by Maria Antonaccio and William Scheweiker. Chicago University Press, 1996, pp. 29–53.
Onega, Susan. 'Oulipian Games, Transpersonality, and the Logic of Potentiality in David Mitchell's *Ghostwritten*.' *Transmodern Perspectives on Contemporary Literatures in English*, edited by Jessica Aliaga-Lavrijsen and José María Yebra-Pertusa. Routledge, 2019, pp. 50–69.
Osborn, Arthur W. *The Superphysical*. Ivor Nicholson and Watson, 1937.
Palmer, Alan. *Social Minds in the Novel*. Ohio State University Press, 2010.
Pinch, Adela. 'The Appeal of Panpsychism in Victorian Britain.' *Romanticism on the Net*, no. 65, 2014. ronjournal.org/s/3363. Accessed 4 April 2022.
Poller, Jake. 'Beyond the Subliminal Mind: Psychical Research in the Work of Aldous Huxley', *Aries*, vol. 15, no. 2, 2015, pp. 247–66.
Price, H. H. 'Haunting and the "Psychic Ether" Hypothesis – 1.' *Philosophical Interactions with Parapsychology: The Major Writings of H. H. Price on Parapsychology and Survival*, edited by Frank B. Dilley. St. Martin's, 1995, pp. 17–34.
Priestley, J. B. *Midnight on the Desert*. Heinemann, 1937.
Rhine, J. B. *Extra-Sensory Perception*. Boston Society for Psychic Research, 1934.
Rhine, Louisa E. *ESP in Life and Lab: Tracing Hidden Channels*. Macmillan, 1967.
Richardson, Brian. 'Representing Social Minds: "We" and "They" Narratives, Natural and Unnatural.' *Narrative*, vol. 23, no. 2, 2015, pp. 200–12.
———. *Unnatural Voices: Extreme Narration in Modern and Contemporary Fiction*. Ohio State University Press, 2006.
Richardson, Dorothy. *Gleanings from the Works of George Fox*. Headley, 1914.
Roberts, Warren, James T. Boulton and Elizabeth Mansfield. *The Letters of D. H. Lawrence*, vol. 4 (June 1921 – March 1924). Cambridge University Press, 1987.
Rosenthal, Michael. 'Isherwood, Huxley, and the Thirties.' *The Columbia History of the British Novel*, edited by John Richetti. Columbia University Press, 1994, pp. 740–64.
Royle, Nicholas. *E. M. Forster*. Northcote, 1999.
———. *The Uncanny*. Manchester University Press, 2003.
Rushdie, Salman. *Midnight's Children*. Knopf, 1981.

Schoene, Berthold. '"Tour du Monde": David Mitchell's *Ghostwritten* and the Cosmopolitan Imagination. *College Literature*, vol. 37, no. 4, 2010, pp. 42–60.
Semmler, Clement. 'Aldous Huxley Revisited.' *The Australian Quarterly*, vol. 42, no. 4, 1970, pp. 74–82.
Sidgwick, Eleanor [Mrs. Henry Sidgwick]. 'A Contribution to the Study of the Psychology of Mrs. Piper's Trance Phenomena.' *Proceedings of the Society for Psychical Research*, vol. 28, 1915, pp. 1–657.
Sinclair, May. *A Defence of Idealism: Some Questions and Conclusions*. Macmillan, 1917.
———. *The Flaw in the Crystal*. Dutton, 1912.
———. 'The Future of the Novel.' *Pall Mall Gazette*, 10 January 1921, p. 7.
———. *Mary Olivier: A Life*. Macmillan, 1919.
———. 'The Novels of Dorothy Richardson.' *The Egoist*, vol. 5, no. 4, 1918, pp. 57–9.
Skrbina, David. *Panpsychism in the West*, revised edn. MIT Press, 2017.
Smith, Grover, ed. *Letters of Aldous Huxley*. Harper and Row, 1969.
Smith, Jonathan C. *Pseudoscience and Extraordinary Claims of the Paranormal: A Critical Thinker's Toolkit*. Wiley-Blackwell, 2010.
Smith, Zadie. *NW*. Penguin, 2012.
———. 'Peonies.' *Intimations: Six Essays*. Penguin, 2020, pp. 1–10.
———. 'Rereading Barthes and Nabokov.' *Changing My Mind: Occasional Essays*. Penguin, pp. 2009, pp. 42–57.
Spencer, Herbert. *The Principles of Psychology*, vol. 2. Appleton, 1875.
Sprague, Claire. *Rereading Doris Lessing: Narrative Patterns of Doubling and Repetition*. University of North Carolina Press, 1987.
Stapledon, Olaf. *A Man Divided*. Methuen, 1950.
———. *Death into Life*. Methuen, 1946.
———. 'Interplanetary Man?' *Journal of the British Interplanetary Society*, vol. 7, no. 6, 1948, pp. 215–33.
———. *Last and First Men*. Tarcher, 1988.
———. *Last Men in London*. *Last and First Men* and *Last Men in London*. Penguin, 1972, pp. 329–605.
———. *Odd John*. Methuen, 1978.
———. *Philosophy and Living*. Penguin, 1939.
———. *Sirius*. Gollancz, 2000.
———. *Star Maker*. Penguin, 1972.
———. *Waking World*, Methuen, 1934.
———. *Youth and Tomorrow*. St. Botolph, 1946.
Sternberg Perrakis, Phyllis. 'The Marriage of Inner and Outer Space in Doris Lessing's *Shikasta*.' *Science Fiction Studies*, vol. 17, no. 2, 1990, pp. 221–38.
Stone-Blackburn, Susan. 'Consciousness Evolution and Early Telepathic Tales.' *Science Fiction Studies*, vol. 20, no. 2, 1993, pp. 241–50.
Tchaikovsky, Adrian. *Children of Time*. Pan, 2016.
Terkel, Studs. 'Learning to Put the Questions Differently.' Interview with Doris Lessing from 10 June 1969. *Doris Lessing: Conversations*, edited by Earl G. Ingersoll. Ontario Review, 1994, pp. 19–32.

Thomas, Northcote Whitridge. 'Telepathy.' *Encyclopædia Britannica*, edited by Hugh Chisholm, 11th edn, vol. 26, pp. 546–7.
Tindall, W. Y. 'The Trouble with Aldous Huxley.' *The American Scholar*, vol. 11, no. 4, 1942, pp. 452–64.
Tratner, Michael. *Modernism and Mass Politics: Joyce, Woolf, Eliot, Yeats.* Stanford University Press, 1995.
Trigoni, Thalia. *The Intelligent Unconscious in Modernist Literature and Science*, e-book, Routledge, 2020.
Trollope, Anthony. *Lady Anna*. Oxford University Press, 1990.
Trotter, David. *The English Novel in History, 1895–1920*. Routledge, 1993.
Tung, Charles M. 'Baddest Modernism: The Scales and Lines of Inhuman Time.' *Modernism/Modernity*, vol. 23, no. 3, 2016, pp. 515–38.
Tyrell, Ivan. 'Our Collective Cultural Insanity.' *Human Givens Institute*, www.hgi.org.uk/resources/delve-our-extensive-library/interviews/our-collective-cultural-insanity. Accessed 21 March 23.
Underhill, Evelyn. *The Grey World*. Heinemann, 1904.
Van Dyke, P. T. and M. L. Juncosa, 'Paranormal Phenomena – Briefing on a Net Assessment Study.' Working Note for the Advanced Research Projects Agency, January 1973.
Vitoux, Pierre. 'Structure and Meaning in Aldous Huxley's *Eyeless in Gaza*.' *Bloom's Modern Critical Views: Aldous Huxley*, edited by Harold Bloom, 2nd edn. Infobase, 2010, pp. 41–58.
Vopson, Melvin. M. 'Experimental Protocol for Testing the Mass-Energy-Information Equivalence Principle.' *AIP Advances*, vol. 12, no. 3, 2022. doi.org/10.1063/5.0087175. Accessed 2 April 2022.
Wallace, Jeff. *D. H. Lawrence, Science and the Posthuman*. Palgrave Macmillan, 2005.
Watt, Ian. *The Rise of the Novel: Studies in Defoe, Richardson and Fielding.* University of California Press, 1957.
Weinstein, Philip. *Unknowing: The Work of Modernist Fiction*. Cornell University Press, 2005.
Wells, Lynn. 'The Right to a Secret: Zadie Smith's NW.' *Reading Zadie Smith: The First Decade and Beyond*, edited by Philip Tew. Bloomsbury, 2013, pp. 97–110.
Whittaker, Ruth. *Modern Novelists: Doris Lessing*. St Martin's, 1988.
Wientzen, Timothy. 'The Modernist Cosmos: Olaf Stapledon, Pierre Teilhard de Chardin and the Crisis of Species.' *Modernism and the Anthropocene: Material Ecologies of Twentieth Century Literature*, edited by Jon Hegglund and John McIntyre. Lexington, 2021, pp. 79–96.
Willoughby, Raymond Royce. 'Further Card-Guessing Experiments.' *The Journal of General Psychology*, vol. 17, no. 1, 1937, pp. 3–13.
Woodberry, Imogen. 'Aldous Huxley: The Unstable Self, Consciousness, and the "Ground of Being."' *Textual Practice*, vol. 34, no. 9, 1455–71.
Wright, Ernest Hunter. 'The Case for Telepathy: A Record of Some Remarkable Experiments.' *Harper's Magazine*, November 1936, pp. 575–86.
Wyndham, John. *The Chrysalids*. Penguin, 1958.

Zytaruk, George. J. 'The Doctrine of Individuality: D. H. Lawrence's "Metaphysic."' *D. H. Lawrence: A Centenary Consideration*, edited by Peter Balbert and Phillip L. Marcus. Cornell University Press, 1985, pp. 237–53.

Zytaruk, George J. and James T. Boulton, eds. *The Letters of D. H. Lawrence*, vol. 2 (1913–1916). Cambridge University Press, 1981.

Index

Adorno, Theodor W., 110
Austen, Jane, *Pride and Prejudice*, 5

Balfour, Arthur, 26
Beresford, J. D., *The Hampdenshire Wonder*, 40–1
Bergson, Henri, 40–3
Besant, Annie, 26
Bhabha, Homi K., 136, 137–8, 165, 166
bildungsroman, 94–5
Blackwood, Algernon, *The Centaur*, 22–3, 39–40
Brontë, Anne, *The Tenant of Wildfell Hall*, 4–5
Brontë, Charlotte, *Jane Eyre*, 94–5
Brunner, John
   Stand on Zanzibar, 116–17
   Telepathist [*The Whole Man*], 100–1
Byatt, A. S., *The Virgin in the Garden*, 91, 105–6

Carington, Whately, 90
Clarke, Arthur C., *Childhood's End*, 83–4
collective consciousness, 11–12, 26–7, 28–9, 53–4, 74, 82, 118
Condon, William, 147–8
Conrad, Joseph, *Narcissus* [*The Children of the Sea*], 127–8

Dickens, Charles, 94–5
Doyle, Arthur Conan, *The Parasite*, 9
Du Maurier, George, *Trilby*, 8–9
Dunne, J. W., 63–4, 74–7, 111

Evaristo, Bernardine, *Girl, Woman, Other*, 160–1, 163–6

Földényi, László, 44–5, 99, 134
Forster, E. M., *A Passage to India*, 49

Hall, Edward T., 146–8, 151, 153–4
Heard, Gerald, 82, 87, 102
Huxley, Aldous, 2–3, 10–11
   After Many a Summer, 89, 117
   Brave New World, 110–11
   Eyeless in Gaza, 12, 99, 112–15
   Island, 7, 106–8, 118–19
   Point Counter Point, 7–8, 97–8
   Time Must Have a Stop, 103–4

Ishiguro, Kazuo, *The Unconsoled*, 144–5

Jameson, Frederic, 57, 137–8
Joyce, James, *Ulysses*, 48

Lawrence, D. H.
   Aaron's Rod, 35, 42–5
   Kangaroo, 45–7, 49–51, 53

Lady Chatterley's Lover, 17, 37, 54–5
The Plumed Serpent, 51–3
Psychoanalysis and the Unconscious, 27, 34
The Rainbow, 28, 40–1, 122
Sons and Lovers, 30–2
The Trespasser, 29
Women in Love, 6, 27
Le Bon, Gustave, 53–4
Lem, Stanisław, Solaris, 65, 77–9
Lessing, Doris, 15
Briefing for a Descent into Hell, 6, 15, 141–2
The Cleft, 120–1, 125–6, 127
The Four-Gated City, 13, 138–40
The Golden Notebook, 135–6
If the Old Could…, 150
The Making of the Representative for Planet 8, 7, 129–131
The Marriages Between Zones Three, Four, and Five, 131
Martha Quest, 136
Re: Colonised Planet 5, Shikasta, 65, 126, 133, 134–5, 141, 145–6, 148–50, 152
The Sentimental Agents in the Volyen Empire, 126
The Sirian Experiments, 133–4, 152–4
'The Temptation of Jack Orkney', 150
Lukács, Georg, 36–7

McDougall, William, 108–9
Macherey, Pierre, 19, 143
mesmerism, 8–9, 32, 34
mind-reading, 39, 101
Mitchell, David, 15–16
The Bone Clocks, 158–9, 161–3
Ghostwritten, 1, 15, 155, 160, 161–3

Mitchison, Naomi, Memoirs of a Spacewoman, 66
modernist novel, 17, 21–2, 36–7, 58–9, 117–18
Murdoch, Iris, 90–1
The Flight from the Enchanter, 104–5
The Good Apprentice, 90
Henry and Cato, 115–16
The Nice and the Good, 90

Osborn, A. W., 73–4
Ouspensky, P. D., 102

panpsychism, 13–15, 140–2
psychotronics, 13

Rhine, J. B., 10, 69–70, 73, 86
Rushdie, Salman, Midnight's Children, 137–8, 154–5

science fiction, 10, 12–13, 14, 15–16, 64–5, 148–9
Shah, Idries, 138–9
Sinclair, May, 20–1
The Flaw in the Crystal, 21
Smith, Zadie, NW, 159–60, 167
Spencer, Herbert, 4
Stapledon, Olaf, 11
Death in Life, 72–3
The Flames, 85–6
Last and First Men, 60–1, 65, 66–7
Last Men in London, 7, 65, 74, 75–6, 81, 84
A Man Divided, 58–9
Odd John, 68
Sirius, 68
Star Maker, 60–1, 63, 71–2, 73, 76–7, 78, 84–5, 122

Tchaikovsky, Adrian, Children of Time, 128–9

telepathy
  emergence of concept, 9–11
  ether model, 32–3, 63, 81–2, 147
  popular belief in, 1–2

Underhill, Evelyn, *The Grey World*, 29–30, 33

'universal consciousness' *see* collective consciousness

Watt, Ian, 4
we-narration, 72, 125–130
'World Mind' *see* collective consciousness
Wyndham, John, *The Chrysalids*, 100

EU representative:
Easy Access System Europe
Mustamäe tee 50, 10621 Tallinn, Estonia
Gpsr.requests@easproject.com